Charles Pigott

Treachery no Crime or The System of Courts

Exemplified in the Life Character and Late Desertion of General Dumourier

Charles Pigott

Treachery no Crime or The System of Courts
Exemplified in the Life Character and Late Desertion of General Dumourier

ISBN/EAN: 9783743408272

Manufactured in Europe, USA, Canada, Australia, Japa

Cover: Foto ©Suzi / pixelio.de

Manufactured and distributed by brebook publishing software (www.brebook.com)

Charles Pigott

Treachery no Crime or The System of Courts

TREACHERY NO CRIME,

OR THE

SYSTEM OF COURTS,

EXEMPLIFIED IN THE

LIFE, CHARACTER, AND LATE DESERTION

OF

GENERAL DUMOURIER,

IN THE VIRTUE OF

IMPLICIT CONFIDENCE

IN

KINGS AND MINISTERS,

AND IN THE

PRESENT CONCERT OF PRINCES,

AGAINST THE

FRENCH REPUBLIC.

Delirant Reges, plectuntur Achivi.

LONDON:

PRINTED FOR J. RIDGEWAY, YORK STREET,
ST. JAMES'S SQUARE.

MDCCXCIII.

L I F E, &c.

FATAL to freedom are the perfidy and corruption of courts. They who have been once infected by that peſtilential atmoſphere, where all partial and excluſive intereſts are centered, muſt be very ill qualified for any truſt, in which the hoſtile cauſe of liberty, and the rights of man, are at ſtake. It was the opinion of Mirabeau, who perfectly knew the eſprit which animated the whole corps, that the new order of things would be never ſecure, till France was entirely purged of her ariſtocracy; and the reſtleſs, ſeditious, diſcontented ſpirit it has ſince evinced, fully corroborates his opinion. Such ſeparate intereſts cannot be reconciled. It is the ſweat from the people's brow, that pampers the lazy effeminacy and luxury of courts. When great noblemen, proud in their anceſtry and their titles, poſſeſſing vaſt riches, are not ſatisfied with their full and tranquil enjoyment, but are mean enough to ſolicit, and to hold places under the crown, of no labour, or advantage to others, with immenſe ſalaries annexed to them, paid by the nation: ſuch minions cannot be regarded as friends to the people. They are to all intents and purpoſes a general nuiſance: plunderers from the common ſtock, aggravating their burthens, taking their money, without rendering any the leaſt ſervice in return. If ſuch places are to be conſidered as honourable, they ſhould be at leaſt gratuitous; as long as the poor and laborious contribute to provide for them, they are unjuſt, infamous, and oppreſſive. I would as ſoon truſt my purſe to a known thief, as my liberty to an arrant courtier. He receives the *public money*,

not

not to perform *public ſervice*, but to *think*, ſpeak, and act, on all occaſions, conformably with the direction and orders which iſſue from the palace *.

Courtiers are hired, bribed by the civil liſts of princes, extorted from the *national purſe*, to uphold excluſive privileges againſt *national rights*, to ſupport the uſeleſs, ſcandalous prodigality of ſinecures and penſions; draining the ſubſtance, the very vitals of a kingdom borne down by nearly three hundred million of debt. The ſoil on which they fatten, the poor man ſtarves; it engroſſes all the manure, and makes the reſt of the country barren and deſerted; ſharpening the ſting of indigence, robbing induſtry and labour of their dear and juſt reward. Such is their bleſſed ſyſtem, which grants *all to thoſe who do nothing, while it witholds all from thoſe who do every thing.*

* Perſons who entertain the leaſt ſcepticiſm on this point, may have their doubts inſtantly removed, by a reference to the uniform parliamentary conduct of gentlemen falling within the above deſcription.

 It

It is the characteriſtic of a courtier to behold things with a jaundiced eye. He will extol as an act of wiſdom and magnanimity, the moſt conſummate infernal treaſon, if propitious to his views or his intereſt; but he is outrageous againſt ſimilar guilt, if militating againſt them; as if there could be any difference in the crime, except from the magnitude of its operations, the ſuperior villainy of its deſign, or the extent of its conſequences.

Reverſing all the rules of juſtice and humanity, matured in the vile arts of adulation, at the ſame time arrogant and overbearing, he will turn his back on tranſcendant merit in the garb of modeſty and miſfortune; while with fawning ſmiles, he will cringe at the heel of the moſt deſpicable folly, or hideous deſpotiſm, if inveſted with the *ſacred* robes of r-y-l impunity.

The trade of courtiers is flattery. It has paſſed uniform and ſyſtematic in its progreſs through a ſucceſſion of ages, and on

princes

princes the leaſt deſerving, it has generally been laviſhed in moſt copious ſtreams. Mæcenas, the patron of genius, degraded his high character, as the paraſite of Auguſtus; and the muſe of Boileau was proſtituted to ſooth the pride, and to gratify the ſplendid vanity and barbarous ambition of Louis XIV. who, during his reign, was the ſcourge and tormentor of Europe *.

Tyrants, whoſe crimes reflect obloquy on human nature, whoſe cruelties are ſufficient to tinge the feeling heart with the darkeſt ſhade of miſanthropy, have been deified during life, and canonized after death; till flattery having loſt its object, reaſon reſumes her empire, and the once triumphant maſter, buried in the duſt, his infamy revives; truth conquers in her turn, and honeſt hiſtory paints him in faithful colours. The ſceptered mur-

* This ſpecies of flattery is thus pleaſantly hit off by La Fontaine.

" On ne peut trop louer trois ſortes de Perſonnes,
" Les dieux, ſa maitreſſe, & ſon roi.
" Æſope le diſait; J'y ſouſcris quant à moi,
" Ce ſont maximes toujours bonnes.

murderer, whom the Chriſtian Church hailed as the faith's defender, and he alſo was nick-named the Father of his People, who received the proſtituted incenſe of praiſe, even from perſons, who, in that age, were regarded as models of primitive ſimplicity and virtue, now ſtripped of his gorgeous and royal robes, long ſince reduced to the common level of mortality, is ſurveyed in his true native light, in compariſon with whom Claudius and Caligula were gods.

Perſons, debauched by the vile habits of a court, can never be ſincere in attachment to popular ſyſtems of government; and it is truly unfortunate, when an union of ſuperior talents, of inordinate ambition, with moral baſeneſs, acquires an aſcendant over public opinion. It is then that confidence ſerves only to feed the rapacity of private intereſt, and the generous cauſe of humanity is no longer conſulted, than it may be convenient or political to do ſo.

There

There is no crime, however odious, however revolting, that may not be varnished by the subtle definitions of Machiavelian sophistry, or that will not, if necessary, be defended by the brazen unprincipled effrontery of aristocratic insolence; but it defies all the genius of their art and delusion to controvert facts. The character of truth is immutable. What is in nature wrong, no words can palliate, no plea can alter. The man who betrays his trust, is a TRAITOR; and he who, entrusted with arms to fight *for* his country, would turn them *against* it, is the BLACKEST of TRIATORS. Yet even the traitor Dumourier, who, in the month of December, 1792, submitted a plan to the Executive Council of France for the conquest of Holland, which was resisted only from a reluctance to form an open rupture with us, or to destroy that insidious neutrality we affected to observe, and who in April, 1793, only four months afterwards, accused the same council of *rashness and precipitancy* in plunging the country in that additional calamity,

calamity, which he himſelf had previouſly adviſed, when the fatal meaſure was already predetermined in the E—g—ſh C—b—n—t that rendered it inevitable;—the treacherous ſanguinary renegade, he, who, on the 16th, 18th, and 22d of March in the ſame year, the treaſon then rankling in his breaſt, inundated the plains of Belgia with the blood of his braveſt and moſt loyal ſoldiers (whoſe patriotiſm he knew obnoxious to his perfidious view) in a cauſe of which it was erſt his glory to proclaim himſelf the enthuſiaſtic defender, and who a very few days afterwards, unable to debauch the majority of his army that remained, ſaved his own miſerable carcaſs by flight; and, from a victorious leader, under the banners of his country, ſtruggling for its independence and freedom, joined the enemy, and degenerated into the ſcorned apoſtate ſatellite of deſpotiſm, whom treachery itſelf dare not truſt;—even Dumourier, that paragon of traitors, who voluntarily led ſuch numbers of his valiant countrymen to ſlaughter, under pretence of fighting for the liberty

of

of mankind, which at that very inſtant it is evident he had reſolved to betray, is deified in the imagination of courtiers, while men like Condorcet, animated by the pureſt flame of patriotiſm and philoſophy, fixed in their principles, faithful to their truſt, are branded as thieves and murderers, gratefully diſtinguiſhed by one of Dumourier's prototypes, the virtuous, conſiſtent B—ke; * as the moſt humane of murderers.

But whither do theſe crooked diabolical politics tend? The paths of treachery de-

* The labours of this philoſopher, branded as a murderer by Mr. B—ke, have been invariably devoted to the inſtruction, and to promote the happineſs of his fellow-creatures. His life, till the revolution, when he enliſted on the ſide of freedom, was almoſt abſtractedly employed in philoſophical reſearches. He was in his judicial character a moſt zealous advocate for preſerving the life of the late king, bitter enemy to the ſlave trade, and in the project of a conſtitutional code, the article aboliſhing the puniſhment of death for all crimes, except treaſon and murder, originated in this *humane aſſaſſin.*

tected, lead to certain disgrace. An honourable war, (if offensive war could be honourable) employs only honourable means to defend it, and it is a sad prognostic both of its principles, and of an unfortunate issue, when they employed in its service, stoop to the basest, most unwarrantable practices, to cover the atrocious designs of injustice, rapine, and illegitimate conquest.

The corruption and sudden conversion of this man, makes peace appear more distant than ever. It would be madness to consider the acquisition of a person whom the combined armies can never venture to trust with command, and the remnant of one regiment of cavalry, consisting of a few hundred men, equally impossible to be relied upon, as a matter of importance. What advantage then is to be reaped from this deserter? His abortive perfidy only proves, that republican principles are universally diffused, and deeply rooted in the minds of soldiers as well as citizens, and it is an irrefragable axiom in politics, that every vio-

lent

lent effort to ſubvert an exiſting ſyſtem, gives ſtability by its defeat, to that it was intended to deſtroy.

When treachery gains its point, the treaſon is loved, but the traitor deteſted; when it fails, he is deſpiſed. The ſcorn and contempt of the combined forces will avenge on him, the cauſe of his betrayed and injured nation; and he, who ſo lately enjoyed the eſteem, and commanded the admiration of every virtuous mind, every lover of liberty, is now ſunk, like his unhappy predeceſſor la Fayette, into the deepeſt mire of infamy and diſgrace, with no other conſolation, then the very partial and precarious freedom, with which he has been indulged under ſufferance from thoſe, on whoſe protection and encouragement, he vainly depended, but by whom, his object blaſted, he muſt be inwardly ſcorned and rejected, as a corrupt and mercenary traitor.

Let us however ſift into cauſes, and we may perhaps unravel the myſtery which at firſt created univerſal ſurprize, and diffuſed ſuch enthuſiaſtic applauſe amongſt the ariſtocratic corps.

Although of Plebian extraction, our hero aſpired to Patrician diſtinctions, and if ambitious of military renown, he was no wiſe indifferent to civil emoluments. The happy verſatility and duplicity of his talents, led him early in life to Verſailles, where ſimilar accompliſhments never paſſed unrewarded, ſo that his genius for intrigue procured him immediate employment in that particular line, which formed a principal department in the antient ſyſtem of that intriguing and ambitious court. Monſieur Dumourier very ſoon attracted the notice of the ſagacious and diſcerning Maurepas, who was then miniſter, and upon his recommendation, he was at once regiſtered on the liſt of *clair-voyants* (what we call in England ſpies,) a term applied to political agents,

agents, who are bribed by courts to inſpire confidence, and afterwards to betray it. A ſpecious addreſs, a total apathy of principle, unreſtrained by the cumbrous ſhackles of modeſty or diffidence, qualified him to ſhine with refulgent luſtre, in this crowded hemiſphere of brilliant ſatellites. He entered upon immediate pay *, and as the military character was always conſidered a paſſport to this honourable ſervice, in order to facilitate his introduction at the courts to which he mght be ſent, he was preſented with the brevet of a captain of infantry. In the capacity of a ſpy, under a military garb, he has been employed at almoſt every court of Europe ; and he generally executed the virtuous office with conſummate ability, to the entire ſatisfaction of his maſters. A perfect harlequin. He knew how to aſſume the moſt oppoſite ſhapes, as occaſion required. In Poland, du-

* Under the old government in France, above four millions ſterling were annually appropriated to the above honourable ſervice.

ring the arrangement of the partition treaty, a very important and multifarious part was allotted to him, and he performed it with his usual eclat. He appeared at different times in that country, under the different characters of an officer, an abbé, a pilgrim, and a monk, and the disguise sat so naturally on him, that he always escaped detection.

In the year 1777 and 1778, our distinguished spy resided in different courts of Germany, where that his happy talents might not rust from inaction, he kept a jealous watch over the emissaries of his own court, many of whom were disgraced by the reports he transmitted of their remissness and misconduct.

England also is a theatre on which his his active versatile genius has displayed itself. In the year 1780, during the American war, when this country was cursed with a weak, unprincipled, and prodigal administration, and threatened by a combination

of

of foreign powers, which, through her own insolent imperious councils, conspired against her; her finances dilapidated, her antient glory tarnished, her commerce almost annihilated, labouring under a complication of misfortunes; agreeably with the old politics of the court of Versailles, French intrigue was all alive, and French gold was profusely circulated in this capital. Monsieur Dumourier was then in London under the disguise of an abbé, an unfortunate persecuted clergyman, banished from his native land, for having published a book, intitled 'La Folie de la France D'Assister des Rebelles." Here likewise he escaped detection; and what his object then was, is still unknown. We find him afterwards in the years 1785 and 1786, in Holland, fanning the flame of patriotism; ardent in zeal to serve the cause in which he was employed, and being at Amsterdam in the year 1787, he had a very narrow escape, his *friend* the Duke of Brunswick, having given orders for his arrest, but a *clair-voyant* is always on

his

his guard, and thus, he was fortunate enough to elude the order.

When peace was reſtored to Holland, as a reward for paſt ſervices, Monſieur de Vergennes appointed him major de place at Cherbourg, which was the higheſt military rank that he attained under the former government. In this ſituation, the powers of his mind had little ſcope for action, and he there languiſhed for freſh opportunities favourable to his genius for intrigue, or hopeful to his views of ambition. The criſis at length arrived.

Deſtitute of every honourable principle, the only ſentiment which ever actuated him, was that of intereſt, whether as the ſatellite of a deſpot, a dangler in the antichamber of a duke, the furious demagogue of a club, the miniſter of a limited monarchy, or the commander of a republican army, all his labours and ambition tended to one uniform point ;—to aggrandize himſelf;

in-

indifferent as to the means, provided he ſaw a probability of accompliſhing it. Thus, when the firſt revolution took place, the complaiſant obſequious ſpy of a court, was at once metamorphoſed into a raving jacobin, and ſeconded by that ſociety (now the grateful object of his execration) he intrigued himſelf into employment, and in the month of March 1792, he ſucceeded the late Monſieur De Leſſart, as miniſter for foreign affairs. During the ſhort time he remained in office, the ſtrongeſt ſuſpicions of peculation were entertained; our *clair-voyant* perceived there was a ſtorm brewing, and with all the art and prudence peculiar to his former profeſſion, after being ſuppoſed to have well *feathered his neſt*, he gave in his diſmiſſion, and having been ſince the revolution, through the jacobin influence, advanced to the rank of marechal de camp, ſuddenly decamped for the northern army. He was well acquainted with the unpopularity of la Fayette, and by his enmity, oppoſition, and impatience to ſuperſede that degraded and unhappy

D general,

general, he flattered popular opinion, while in so doing, he favoured his own rapacity and ambition, by paving the way to the command of that army, which, like his predecessor, in a still more ungrateful and barbarous manner, he afterwards betrayed. The activity, talents, and patriotic zeal, which he at first displayed, obliterated past transgressions, and all memory of his former servile occupations, incompatible with the dignity and virtue, supposed inherent in the mind of a republican commander in chief, was effaced by the vows of inveterate hatred against traitors and tyrants, and by his boasted promise of future atchievements. But was it to be supposed that he who had long submitted to the degradation, and had distinguished himself in the contemptible odious office of a spy, whose trade was treachery, and who had been early infected by the tainted air of the most vicious court in Europe, could ever be loyal to the glorious cause of freedom and equality? From rooted habits, his heart

could

could never glow with congenial ardour, while fighting for principles that were fatal to the ſplendour of palaces, where his notions had been formed, but whoſe ſucceſs might eſtabliſh a far better ſyſtem, eſtabliſhing the liberty, peace, and happineſs of the world.

That Dumourier, an old hoary ſycophant, grisè in the menial ſervice of a vicious arbitary court, would be ſtaunch to any cauſe, as long as he felt an intereſt in it, there could be no doubt, and that he would abandon it, when that intereſt ceaſed, or on any reverſe of fortune, muſt on reflection be equally obvious, notwithſtanding the wonder that his deſertion at firſt created. In a breaſt deſtitute of all honour and virtue, ſelf is always the predominant principle. As an Eſpion de Police, impelled by the above ſentiment, Dumourier would act with the ſame mechanical addreſs, according to profeſſional rule, as acting officially as miniſter of a great nation; and he would lead his ſoldiers to ſlaughter with equal indifference and inſenſibility, as commander of an army fighting for deſpotiſm, or as a leader of ſquadrons ſtruggling for freedom. Men of this deſcription, conſider every thing as a trade. Principle is wholly out of the queſtion, therefore, when Mr. Dumourier's memorials are read, with reference to his original habits, all wonder muſt ceaſe, that he ſhould one day glory in the principles of republicaniſm, and that on the next, after having ſacrificed thouſands and thouſands of the braveſt lives, he ſhould devote himſelf, and the reſt of his followers, to the re-eſtabliſhment of monarchical government. In the proclamations, which he has lately publiſhed, with a view to juſtify his treaſon, he deals like thoſe who corrupted him, in bold unqualified aſſertions, without a ſhadow of argument or reaſon to ſupport them. When he ſpeaks of the glorious victories he had atchieved for his country, he forgets the baſeneſs with which he afterwards ſold it;

when

when he now ſwears to reſtore *royalty*, he forgets his former oaths, to defend to the laſt the *ſovereignty of the people.*—' I ' have ſent a reinforcement to Bournoville, ' who has more than twenty thouſand ' men; *and who will never quit them* ' *(the Pruſſians) till he has exterminated* ' *them. To give the finiſhing blow to* " *this buſineſs, I ſhall join him in perſon.* ' I have ſent you ſome copies of my nego- ' ciation, which I have cauſed to be print- ' ed, becauſe *the commander of an army of* ' *freemen ought to ſuffer no ſuſpicions to* ' *exiſt reſpecting his conduct, with the* ' *enemy.*' (traitor!) ' The preſent circum- ' ſtance will ſoon deliver us from the ' ſcourge of war, and you may aſſure the ' *Auguſt Aſſembly of the SOVEREIGN* ' *PEOPLE*, that I ſwear never to ' know repoſe, until it ſhall be put ' out of the power of tyrants to do us any ' hurt*."

To

* Vide Monſieur Dumourier's letter to the war miniſter, on the retreat of the Pruſſians from France, dated St.

To paint treaſon in its moſt odious colours, it will be neceſſary to refer to other memorials and proclamations of the traitor, and thence, the dulleſt comprehenſion will not be at a loſs to unravel the motives of his late deſertion.—' Monſter, Out of thy ' own mouth will I convict thee.'

' The French nation has decided its fate, ' and foreign powers cannot refuſe to acknowledge the truth of this aſſertion. ' They no longer ſee the National Aſſembly, whoſe powers were confined, who ' poſſeſſed only a conteſted authority, which ' might have been conſidered as uſurped; ' but they now behold a repreſentation inveſted with the complete ſovereignty of ' the French people, authorized by the Conſtitution itſelf, under the name of the ' National Convention.

St. Menehoult, October 1ſt, 1792. It is ſtrongly ſuſpected, that he could have then cut off the retreat of the Pruſſians, and that it is owing to ſubſequent negotiation, that they were ſuffered to effect it.

' This

'This Convention, on the very firſt day 'of its ſitting, actuated by ſpontaneous 'movement, which is the ſame through 'the whole empire, decreed the abolition 'of royalty. This decree was received 'with impatience and rapture; it every 'where augments the energy of the people, 'and it would be impoſſible to re-eſtabliſh 'a throne, overturned by the crimes which 'ſurrounded it. *France then muſt be ever 'acknowledged a republic*, ſince the whole 'nation has declared the abolition of mo-'narchy. No power has a right to im-'poſe laws on ſo great a nation. The ex-'perience already offered, muſt convince 'the King of Pruſſia, *that the conqueſt of 'France is abſolutely impoſſible.* What-'ever difference of principles may exiſt be-'tween his Pruſſian Majeſty, who has been 'miſled, and the French people, neither he 'nor his generals, can any longer conſider 'that people, or the armies which oppoſe 'him, as rebels. The rebels are thoſe in-'fatuated nobility, who, after having ſo

'long

'long oppressed the people in the name of 'monarchs, have compleated the disgrace 'of Louis XVI. by *taking up arms against 'their own country*, by *filling* Europe 'with their crimes and their calumnies; yet 'these men are suffered to remain in the 'Prussian army, and to form the advanced 'guard of it, with a *small number of Au-'strians as barbarous as themselves.*

'Let us now consider these Austrians. 'Since the fatal treaty of 1756, France, 'after sacrificing her allies, became a prey 'to the ambition of the court of Vienna. 'All our treasures served to satiate her 'avarice. At the beginning of our re-'volution, the intrigues of that court 'were multiplied to deceive the French 'nation, to mislead an unfortunate king, 'and lastly, to render him *perjured.*

'It is the court of Vienna that has oc-'casioned the downfal of Louis XVI. It 'represented the French as monsters, while

that

'that court, and the criminal emigrants, 'now ſeconded by other powers, paid *ſpies* 'and conſpirators, and kept up by every 'poſſible means the moſt frightful diſ-'cord.

'The French have aboliſhed royalty, be-'cauſe, ſince Henry IV. they have always 'had weak, proud, or timid princes, go-'verned by miſtreſſes, confeſſors, inſolent 'or ignorant miniſters, baſe and abject 'courtiers, who have afflicted with every 'calamity, the moſt beautiful empire in the 'univerſe.

'The King of Pruſſia will one day bluſh, 'when he ſees his army and his treaſure 'ſacrificed to a ſyſtem of perfidy and ambi-'tion, in which he has no ſhare, and to 'which he is rendered the dupe. He would 'find his intereſt in now treating with 'France, for if ever there was an epocha, 'when a nation could be depended on, 'it is that when the *general will* forms

'the invariable principles of a govern-
'ment *.

'His majesty has still the noblest part to 'act that ever king performed. *His* operations alone have been attended with success. He took two towns, but this success 'was owing to *treachery* and cowardice. 'The French army is now purged of TRAI- 'TORS and cowards, who might have ex-

* The *general will* is still the same; in all countries there are traitors whom interest and gold will corrupt, but they are not to be weighed in the ballance with the rights and sentiments of a whole people. Monsieur Dumourier kindly informs us, in his late address to the French people, dated St. Amand, April 2, 1793, 'that 'arms are every where taken up; murders every where 'committed, and pecuniary supplies are every where 'intercepted; that the *English* foment these murders, 'and will by their succours, supply fuel to them at plea- 'sure.'

Neverthelefs, it is not all the corruption, perfidy, or sanguinary policy employed by foreign powers, nor all the B--t-sh guineas, that Mr. Dumourier insinuates, the B--t-sh G—v-m-n-t will advance for the purpose, that can affect the *general will* of the French nation, which has been fully expressed by its representatives fairly elected by the people at large. In the Prince de Cobourg's system of philosophy, treachery may be virtue; in morals, it is the ultimatum of infamy.

'cited

‘ cited an idea, that France could be eafily ‘ conquered, but fhe will prove herfelf in- ‘ vincible. We have to avenge the ex- ‘ ceffes committed in our fields, and it may ‘ readily be believed, that a war againft ‘ REPUBLICANS, PROUD OF THEIR ‘ LIBERTY, muft be a bloody war, which ‘ can never end, but with the entire de- ‘ ftruction of the oppreffors, or the op- ‘ preffed *.’

The reft of this memorial, favours ftrongly of the old leaven, confifting in the grofseft, moft difgufting flattery of the King of Pruffia, and as fuch it received ftrong marks of reprobation, when read in the National Convention; but let us purfue this loyal republican in the further progrefs of his military diplomatic correfpondence.

‘ Judge yourfelf fir, with impartiality, ‘ forget for a moment that you are a Pruf- ‘ fian; what would you think of a nation,

* Dumourier's memorial to the King of Pruffia, on the 9th of September, 1792.

'that without being vanquished, should 'humble itself before a manifesto, and 'should treat under conditions of slavery, 'when it had declared itself REPUBLI-'CAN *.

'LIBERTY IS EVERY WHERE 'TRIUMPHANT, it will overspread the 'universe, after having crushed despotism, 'and enlightened the people. This war 'will be the last, and TYRANTS and 'PRIVILEGED ORDERS will be the 'sole victims in this struggle of ARBI-'TRARY POWER against REASON. 'The arms which the confidence of the 'nation entrusted to my care, have deserv-'ed well of their country. Songs of joy 'would have made one mistake our formi-'dable camp for one of those camps of 'pleasure, where the luxury of kings for-'merly collected embodied automata, for 'the amusement of their mistresses and 'children.

* Dumourier's answer to Monsieur Manstein, Aid de Camp General to the King of Prussia, September 29th, 1792. First Year of the Republic.

'I am

'I am come to paſs four days amongſt 'you; I ſhall not take any NEW OATH; 'I ſhall ſhew myſelf worthy of command'ing the children of Liberty *.'

Without referring to his diſpatches from Mons, concerning the battle of Jemmappe, and many ſubſequent papers, ſigned with his name, and publiſhed by his authority, the teſtimonials already quoted, throw all former examples of perfidy, baſeneſs, and apoſtacy, as far as the conſequences might have extended into the back ground.

Till the Order of Jeſuits was deſtroyed, the court of France always ſelected her moſt able ſpies from that body; and as a further proof of Monſieur Dumourier's excellence as a diſciple of St. Ignatius, in addition to the extracts already made, let us take ſome notice of the doctrines he has publiſhed ſince his late *reconverſion*.

'My dear countrymen, it is expedient that 'a TRUE AND BRAVE MAN, remove

* General Dumourier's Speech to the National Convention, October, 1792.

'from

'from you the veil which covers all our crimes 'and misfortunes. In 1789, we made 'great efforts to obtain liberty, equality, 'and the ſovereignty of the people. Our 'principles were conſecrated in the decla- 'ration of the Rights of Man; and from 'the labours of our legiſlators, have re- 'ſulted the declaration, which ſays, that 'France ſhall be a MONARCHY; ſe- 'condly, a Conſtitution, to which we ſwore 'fealty in 1789-90 and 1791.'

It muſt appear ſtrange to our readers, if he were not aware of the true cauſe of this apoſtacy, that the general did not remember this former oath, when from the ſhortneſs of time, it muſt have been more recent in his memory, and if ever there were periods when that oath might be ſuppoſed to have operated with effect, it was immediately after the 10th of Auguſt, after the maſſacres of the 2d and 3d of September, or directly after the execution of Louis XVI. But no, his breaſt then ſeemed fluſhed with an additional glow of republican enthu-

ſiaſm;

ſiaſm; it was then he renewed his oath of fidelity to the new government, and it was long after the dreadful ſcenes of the 2d and 3d of September, as will be perceived from the extracts which we have made from his own printed papers, that he continued to glory in his REPUBLICAN PRINCIPLES, that he acknowledged the *general will* of the people as ſacred and inviolable, and ſwore never to abandon the righteous cauſe, till he had forced the enemy to ſubmit to its juſtice; that it was a war of ARBITRARY POWER AGAINST REASON AND PHILOSOPHY. It was not by the death of Louis that his ſenſibility appeared affected, or that he declared the cauſe to be diſhonoured; no, ſubſequent to that period, he attempted the conqueſt of Holland; nor was it till fruſtrated in his views on that country, as a relief from inſanity, which the diſappointment of his ambition ſeemed to threaten, after having (as has been before remarked) ſacrificed the flower of his army, that he attempted in vain to debauch that part which remained, and that he ſold his country

try and his fame, to gratify a curſed avarice, and to ſcreen himſelf from the juſt vengeance of the people he had betrayed.

Such is our new ally, the gallant faithful General Dumourier; who, by affected enthuſiaſm, for the common cauſe in which his country was embarked, by his avowed enmity againſt traitors, tyrants, and privileged orders, ſtill further recommended by his great military talents, faſcinated confidence, and afterwards betrayed it; yet even this traitor, this convicted traitor, as here he ſtands, finds his advocates in the rotten phalanx of ariſtocracy, and the liberties and very exiſtence of a regenerated nation, which the open force of all the courts in Europe united in vain to conquer, was for a moment endangered, by the ſucceſs with which they practiſed their ſecret arts and corruption, on the breaſt of an avaricious, mercenary, deſerter. Unhappy France, ſurely thy exceſſes are in ſome degree palliated by the eternal and matchleſs perfidy thou haſt experienced from thy

own

own ungrateful children, aiming a poinard at their mother's heart. *Candour* will grant ſome indulgence to the paroxyſms of a people thus annoyed on all ſides, mines of treaſon ſpringing up in every quarter; every day bringing to light freſh inſtances of moſt horrible conſpiracies, ignorant whom to truſt, from having been ſo often betrayed; the enemy not ſatisfied with attacking them *without*, but circulating in profuſion their poiſonous gold, to foment murder and civil war *within*: ſold by their generals in whom they had repoſed unlimited confidence and powers, on the faith of moſt ſacred vows, with a brutiſh inſolence, ingratitude, and cruelty, which defy all the powers of language, or invention to deſcribe.

A *philoſopher* will judge for himſelf, he is not to be led aſtray by ſuperficial appearances, by the artifices of a deſigning intereſted faction, or by the clamorous uproar of a miſguided multitude. He will penetrate into primary cauſes, before he preſumes to pronounce on effects, nor will he ſuffer the phrenzy of paſſion, or the torrent of infatuation in others, to ſtifle the ſentiments of truth in his unclouded mind.

Amidſt all their outrages, he will perceive injured men, for the moſt part incenſed to retaliation; he will regard them as thus moulded, thus goaded to ferocity, by the revolting barbariſm of their antient oppreſſors; he will not have forgot the unprovoked bloody manifeſtos of thoſe ruffian invaders, ſtriking at their regenerated freedom and independence, ſtimulating and provoking their revenge; he will feel for a people driven to madneſs from a dread of relapſing into their former deſpotiſm. It would not therefore appear a phenomenon to him, that they who had ſo long been treated as beaſts, ſhould occaſionally act like ſavages, or, that men ſhould become deſperados who had been driven to deſpair.

Treachery breeds revenge; injury may forgive a TYRANT, but it never pardons a TRAITOR. Hence the royal,

the

the civil blood that has flowed. Let indignation then be directed to the proper channel; let it be pointed againſt the vile authors, not againſt the miſerable exaſperated inſtruments of thoſe heart rending ſcenes; againſt the perfidious monſters, who, after having raiſed the dæmon of deſtruction, make him ſerve as a pretext to deceive and enrage the world againſt the horrors they themſelves excited.

Maſſacre, alas, is the inevitable attendant on all great revolutions in ſtates; and for this reaſon, many reſpectable men are averſe to all innovating experiments; but ſhould we ſhrink from truth, from juſtice, from virtue, and a fair proſpect of future happineſs, through a dread of temporary convulſions, however violent, and which originate in thoſe privileged beings, who have not magnanimity to ſubmit to a more equal diſpenſation of ſublunary enjoyments? Is it poſſible, that a rational liberal mind, however ſenſible to the neceſſary painful alternative, ſhould regard theſe horrors of a day in the ſame mirror as he reflects on that ci-devant despotism, which produced evils equally atrocious in the hour of their commission, and inexpressibly more calamitous from the length of their duration? To form a just judgment, we must contrast a moment of horror with ages of felicity.

It has been hitherto the fatal policy of government in all ages to cherish the salutary insensibility, the tranquillizing spirit, which submits to grovel in utter darkness. Have we slaves, the plan is to subdue their minds, and rivet them in their native ignorance. Have we subjects, it is by their impotence, and by oppression, that we labour to enforce obedience. Plenty would only create insolence and mutiny amongst them *. If, however, this were the true philosophy of social institutions, what a frightful abortion would such a system appear. How degrading, how libellous to the human character, the supposition

* The uniform language of tyrants,

'The resty knaves are over-run with ease,
'As plenty ever is the nurse of faction.'

Rowe's Jane Shore.

that

that every thing tending to the inſtruction of man makes him vicious and profligate. But the fallacy of this doctrine is detected on a moment's conſideration. Truth, juſtice, and equality *. can never be a ſource of injury to mankind. It is natural that the firſt developement and illumination of the mind ſhould be attended with diſorder; but order and happineſs are likely

* No word was ever more barbarouſly abuſed or perverted from its real ſignification, for the baſeſt of purpoſes, than this word has lately been. From the *unequal* manner in which nature has dealt out her diſpenſations, *equality* is phyſically impoſſible in our human career, although it is certain we are all born *equal* as to our rights; that is, a man born to no inheritance of riches, has an equal right to eligibility to ſerve his country in any capacity for which his talents or virtues may qualify him, as an Earl of D-l-ng t-n, born to millions, without any talents or virtues whatever; and it is an irreſiſtible proof of bad government (it wrought the revolution in France), that enormous inequality which prevails in them; and however paſſive, from habitual influence, the human mind may ſeem under oppreſſion, it is ſhocked, on ſober reflection, amidſt the want and miſery every where viſible, when it diſcovers, that the king, even of a limited monarchy, receives, as the wages of his office, an income equivalent to the labour of fifty thouſand men, calculating it on an average of one ſhilling a day to each man.

to

to ſucceed it. If men have hitherto ſtrayed far and wide from their true intereſt and happineſs, there can be no reaſon why they ſhould continue to wander in the ſame wretched obſcurity for ever; that they ſhould carry the ſyſtem of error to eternity. It is time that the madneſs ſhould ceaſe, which delegates to an individual the power of injuring or deſtroying a nation.

If our own domeſtic affairs did not yield ample experience, let us only for an inſtant reflect on the example lately afforded by France, truſting all ſhe held moſt dear, a balance, perhaps, in which the fate of worlds hung ſuſpended, to the direction of one apoſtate venal traitor—him whoſe portrait has been given. Nevertheleſs, we are now ſpite of example at the climax of infatuation, and regardleſs of perſonal danger, it is at ſuch a period a virtuous duty, recommended by Solon, to publiſh truth without diffidence or reſerve. The true philanthropiſt will not be checked in his courſe, he will be active in the ſcene, and by his exertions ſtrive to render the operations of thought at once profound and beneficial. He will be the herald of peace and good will amongſt his fellow creatures. ‘ The ‘ tidings of liberty and equality, duly con‘ ſidered, are tidings of joy to *all* condi‘ tions of life; they free the peaſant from ‘ the iniquity which depreſſes him, and ‘ the privileged from the luxury and deſpo‘ tiſm by which he is corrupted. Let thoſe ‘ who hear theſe tidings not ſtain their ‘ benignity by ſhewing that that benignity ‘ has not yet become the inmate of their ‘ hearts *.’

Truth can never be hurtful to the many, however formidable it may appear to thoſe whoſe vanity and imagined intereſts it may attack; and were not thoſe privileged gentlemen conſcious of its virtue—that the more profound its inveſtigation, the more fatal it would prove to them—they would not, with ſuch paſſion and fury, oppoſe its progreſs. Were ſuch my opinions, why

* Godwin concerning Political Juſtice, vol. ii. p. 880.

ſhould

ſhould I heſitate to declare myſelf a republican? There can exiſt no better cauſe, why being a republican under a monarchy, I ſhould enliſt with a deſperate faction to diſturb the public tranquility; than if I were monarchical under a republic *. The buſineſs of an *honeſt man* is to promulgate truth; to wait patiently the victory of conviction, and the government which cannot bear to hear it, is not the government under which an *honeſt man* would chuſe to live. Unfortunately, a contrary ſyſtem prevails, on the principles of integrity we profeſs, let us proceed to examine it.

Inſtead of eſtabliſhing a legitimate empire over the human mind, on the ſolid baſis of reaſon and political juſtice; governments have hitherto enthralled it by the miſerable devices of craft and impoſition, uniformly rejecting all experiments of inſtruction and felicity, employing only ſuch engines, as they found moſt conducive

* Godwin concerning Political Juſtice, vol. ii. p. 880.

to

to their own purpoſes ; in holding it under its native ignorance, and practiſing every unwarrantable artifice, to inure it to the moſt diſgraceful ſervitude, it would appear from an appeal to their practice, as if it was their policy to hold truth in mortal enmity, and to conſider thoſe who would enforce it, as their mortal foes ; but ideas cannot ſuggeſt ſtronger arguments of ſuſpicion againſt their ſyſtem, than what they themſelves afford by the jealouſy of inveſtigation, and the implacable rancour, with which they purſue all thoſe, who are bold enough to deny their power, and to enter on candid diſcuſſion, the only road to truth. How far this jealouſy is founded in a conſciouſneſs of their own imbecillity and injuſtice ; on a perfect conviction that they cannot bear the light of reaſon and philoſophy, we will proceed to examine.

Nations, like armies, have ever been the wretched dupes of catchwords, thrown out by their leaders, for the purpoſe of the day ; church and ſtate, liberty and property, glory

 of

of our arms, immortal conſtitution, trade, and navigation, have all in their turns done their buſineſs here, without having had any meaning, or at leaſt any underſtood by thoſe, who moſt loudly vociferated them*. It muſt be conſidered a very bad omen of a cauſe, when it flies to ſuch ſtale pitiful reſources for ſupport. All the above hacknied phraſes, *cum multis aliis*, ſtill maintain their influence amongſt us, but of the different terms at preſent in vogue, Confidence, is that which rules with moſt abſolute ſway, and which enſures the moſt complete ſucceſs. IMPLICIT CONFIDENCE is the parole now in uſe, by which a HEAVENBORN MINISTER calls forth his vaſſals to rally round his ſtandard of deluſion. Under the ſanction of this magic auxiliary, all enquiry is cruſhed; the ſpirit of reform is conſtrued into treaſon, or perhaps mildly qualified under the appellation, held almoſt equally criminal, of republicaniſm, and whoever is imprudent or daring enough to oppoſe the torrent,

* Works of Soame Jenyns, vol. ii. p. 230.

even

even by the gentleſt inſinuations of reaſon or argument, raiſes a mountain on his back that threatens to cruſh him. He is ſcouted at once as a leveller and republican (words, the true ſignification of which is Hebrew to the generality of his appellants) and *damned* as a diſloyal and dangerous ſubject.

If a man does not ſympathiſe in the glorious news, if he be only luke-warm in expreſſions of applauſe, when Dumourier's *gallant* treachery is recorded; if he does not actually exult when he hears it joyfully and triumphantly proclaimed, that ten or twenty thouſand Frenchmen, whoſe cruelties are the inexhauſtible theme of Britons indignation, have been cut to pieces by the valiant Auſtrians *; if his heart be a ſtranger

* As the delicate nerves of Engliſh ariſtocracy are not proof againſt French cruelty, they may probably be tortured in peruſing the following genuine account of Auſtrian and Emigrant barbarity:

'The Auſtrians continued to pour into Liege a prodi-

ſtranger to ſuch divine enthuſiaſm, and that his tongue diſdains to belie his heart, he is marked

'prodigious quantity of ſhells and red-hot balls for many 'hours after it was evacuated by the French, whereby 'a number of citizens were killed, and many houſes 'deſtroyed; after which, a part of the troops entered 'the city, and the moſt horrid ſpectacle preſented itſelf, 'that ever eyes beheld. Men, women, and children, 'every human creature that they met was indiſcrimi-'nately, butchered. The houſes were broke open, and 'the ſhops plundered. The women were firſt violated 'and afterwards murdered. Two ſtreets in particular, 'la rue de St. Nicolas & rue St. Anne, experienced all 'the fury of the ſoldiers, nor did the Officers ſhew 'more moderation or humanity then the common men. 'La rue St. Nicolas is a waſte of ruins, and its inhabi-'tants are deſtroyed. Some of thoſe belonging to the 'rue St. Anne, eſcaped with their lives; but the number 'of men, women, and children killed, after the enemy 'had left the city, is eſtimated at ſix or ſeven thouſand.'

The above fact is here literally related as it was communicated to the author by an Engliſh officer of untainted veracity, who was at Liege, when the horrors were perpetrated.

So much for our new Allies!

The ſubſequent account is a literal tranſlation from the addreſs delivered at the bar of the National Convention, on the 29th of September, 1792, by Citizen Robert,

marked as a ſuſpicious character, and his CONFIDENCE impeached; but if he ſhould

Robert, Mayor of Vancq, attended by Benier, Rector of that Community.

'Repreſentatives of the French People; I addreſs 'you in the name of ſeven or eight hundred citizens, to 'whom nothing remains but the aſhes of their habita- 'tions and their fidelity to the Republic, and who for 'their attachment to the Laws of their country, have 'experienced the vengeance of the enemies of liberty.

'On Monday the 24th of this month, (September) 'the municipality of Vancq, in the diſtrict of Vouſiéres, 'and department of Ardennes, received an order in 'the name of the ci-devant Marechal de Broglio, com- 'manding a body of emigrants, whoſe head quarters 'were then at Vouſiéres, to ſupply his army with pro- 'viſions, which being refuſed by the municipality, fire 'was ſet to the village, and in a moment the blaze con- 'ſumed our whole crop, both of wheat and barley, with 'our barns, ſtables, horſes, and nearly two hundred 'houſes, with the church, were alſo deſtroyed. Their 'rage was not yet ſatisfied. They maſſacred without 'diſtinction, old men, women, and children: they 'prevented a mother from entering her dwelling, to 'ſave her three infants, who periſhed in the flames.

'They offered a pardon to any perſon who would 'deliver up myſelf and the rector; but by a road un- 'known to them, we found means to eſcape. The

'emigrants

ſhould be ſtill more imprudent and daring; if he ſhould preſume to doubt the policy, juſtice, or humanity of the war in which his country is now engaged, to call in queſtion its expediency or neceſſity, or to expreſs a belief, on the ground of evidence or facts, that it really was the deſire, as moſt certainly it was the intereſt of France to preſerve peace with us; then he has reached the ultimatum of political hereſy, and ſtands a fair chance of being denounced to Mr. R—ves, and by him, to *his* attorney g-n-r-l, as a traitor and a rebel. Alas! the generality of mankind are governed more by antient abuſes, or local prejudices

'emigrants ſatiated with carnage, and covered with the 'blood of their countrymen, at length retired; but they 'tied to the tails of their horſes, ſeveral of the inhabi-'tants, whom they dragged away as a trophy of their 'inhuman triumph. We requeſt an aid of fifty thou-'ſand livres to relieve the preſent wants of our commu-'nity, as the loſs we have ſuſtained, is eſtimated at 'more than five hundred thouſand livres.'

On a motion from Le Croix, the ſum was decreed. On the ſcore of cruelty, it would far better become us to be ſilent.

judices, than by reaſon or conviction; far more in the habit of talking than of thinking, and in this corrupted channel, opinion flows at preſent with greater violence than at any former period.

In all ſocieties, it is the ignorant or prejudiced, that form the great majority, and when their rulers are wicked, it is ſociety that ſuffers. Folly and vice triumph only for a moment, they are quickly detected, but they unfortunately leave a durable impreſſion behind them. Credulity is the ſure victim of intereſt and ambition. The torrent however rages too fierce to laſt, when it ceaſes, Engliſhmen will have only to bewail its fatal effects, and curſe the authors of this deluſion.

Our national character has undergone an entire revolution, ſtill more degenerate in politics than in morals; vice in one ſyſtem naturally infects the other. The ſage caution, the watchful jealouſy of our anceſtors, reſpecting the leaſt encroachments on popular

pular rights, are now converted into IMPLICIT CONFIDENCE in the wiſdom and virtue of miniſters of ſtate, who in grateful requital, avail themſelves of it, as an engine to increaſe the prerogative of the crown, by which they think to ſtrengthen their own authority.

Louis XIV. was held an arbitrary monarch. The noble qualities that adorn the character of George III. may poſſibly be a guarantee to his ſubjects, againſt any immediate exerciſe of deſpotiſm; yet were it not for that guarantee, ſtrengthened by our CONFIDENCE in his wiſdom and virtue, to prevent any abuſe of them by his miniſters, can it be ſaid that the enormous additional powers unknown to our conſtitution, lately granted to the crown, although a few years ago, declared by a ſolemn vote of Parliament, to have increaſed and that they ought to be diminiſhed, bear the leaſt analogy with the original ſpirit of a government, whoſe peculiar excellence

we

we are for ever told is LIBERTY *.——
That they do not render the prerogative of a king of England as formidable, as that enjoyed by the former tyrant, and which, in the hands of a prince leſs diſtinguiſhed for moderation and indifference to power, than George III. might expoſe his ſubjects to the moſt odious and abominable tyranny.

In virtue of this CONFIDENCE, miniſters will not now hear of any attempt to innovate on the part of their opponents; it ſeems rather their own object, as in the courſe of this work we ſhall prove, to deſtroy; yet in proportion as they mutilate and deface the beautiful ſyſtem of their affected idolatry, in contempt of what is called the *fundamental* laws of the land, they are implacable in proſecution of thoſe

* Perſons of a ſceptical turn of mind may probably waver from this opinion, when they conſider the nature of ſome recent proclamations, and eſpecially when they analize the poſſible conſequences of two modern acts of Parliament, diſtinguiſhed under the title of 'Alien Bill and Bill to prevent Traiterous Correſpondence.'

who avow the desire, or enforce the necessity of repairing the mouldering edifice, and of defending it against their parricidal strokes, by a strange fatality, IMPLICIT CONFIDENCE seems to increase with public calamity, ministerial corruption, and commercial misfortunes.

Time was, when a candidate for *popular* suffrage, grounded his pretension on *popular* services; on a rooted attachment to the generous cause of liberty; but amidst the delirium that now rages, he finds his surest passport to public favour, in declarations of unlimited confidence in the servants of the crown, as the genuine organs of the nation's interest, of the nation's happiness *.

To

* When the illusion is over, it will be recollected with wonder, that in the year 1793, at an election for deputy to serve in Parliament for the city of London, the successful candidate in every hand-bill circulated in his behalf, built all hope of success on the virtue of having uniformly supported for thirty years together, all the different ministers of the crown. If it be so; if there be a man, so vile a tool to interest or prejudice, as to

have

To allay this fever, and to destroy the dominion of political superstition, which this fatal confidence is intended to perpetuate, is the author's grand object.

He would enlighten his fellow citizens into a rational and dignified sense of their own felicity and importance; so far from being a leveller, he would belie Mr. B-ke's indecent barbarous description, and exalt them far above the brutish nature of swine. He would prove to their conviction the arrogant claims of artificial distinctions, the vanity of titled grandeur; he would enforce the glaring presumption and selfish nature of those who labour to support them. He depreciates the crusades and madness of war, and would expose in faithful colours the jesuitical tricks, the impudent falsehoods and far-fetched alarms, that have been eternally employed to cajole them into it.

have waded through all that quagmire of depravity and corruption, it is fair to use a French expression and pronounce him

Un tres mauvais sujet.

He would fain infuse into the marble hearts of those haughty grandees, who revel in their marble palaces, who sleep in their beds of down, a drop of pity for poor outcasts of the same species with themselves, dragging a cruel existence in the claycold huts of penury and despair. Sensible of the exorbitant price annexed to all the necessary articles of life, the natural inevitable result of our battles, our courts, our fine military establishments, &c. &c. &c. precluding poverty from the smallest share in its comforts, he dreads a calamity that must sink them still deeper in the gulph. He would awaken his countrymen from their infatuated dream, and strike the genius of truth and humanity into their souls, knowing the merciless policy of a weak unprincipled administration to seize every advantage, to persevere in any error however sanguinary or fatal on a general scale, if they deem it likely to enlarge their own influence, to distract the public mind, or draw off its attention from those necessary objects of national reform, on which ere long, it seem-

ed

ed ſtedfaſtly fixed, and which, if liberally and unequivocally accompliſhed, they were aware might put an end to that omnipotence they had ſo long enjoyed, and ſo outrageouſly abuſed, by deducting from their vile monopoly (a ſcandal and abomination to themſelves, as widening the ſphere of adverſity), and reſtoring to the popular balance, ſome of theſe juſt conſtitutional privileges, which many of themſelves once acknowledged, to have been moſt perfidiouſly raviſhed from it.

In times like theſe, when the human faculties have been rouzed from their long lethargy by the efforts of patriotiſm and philoſophy, it is the peculiar duty of us [all, as we have already obſerved, in proportion to the means we poſſeſs, to diſſeminate the principles of reaſon and juſtice. The cauſe of juſtice is the cauſe of humanity. It calls for all our affection and zeal, as it embraces the happineſs of us all. In this attempt, it becomes us not to be diſcouraged by the oppoſition and difficulties that we ſhall experience from miſ-

taken

taken men. It is their imaginary intereſt which prompts them to blacken a cauſe that is all juſtice and benignity, and their exertions have hitherto impeded its ſucceſs. The increaſing advocates of equality ſhould therefore riſe in their efforts to overcome this obſtacle. Superior to danger, let us ſharpen our intellectual ſword, and add to the general ſtock of knowledge. When the cauſes exiſting in evil governments, which have ſo long retarded its progreſs, and obſtructed the path to that happineſs and dignity, of which our nature is ſuſceptible, are removed, mankind will ſhudder at the injuſtice to which they have ſo long ſubmitted. They will diſcover the fallacy of artificial diſtinctions, and deſtroy the cruelty of that fatal monſtrous depravity, under which one claſs of the community has often languiſhed in vain for the putrified offals rejected from the tables of another; while the great themſelves have, at the ſame time, wallowed in every ſuperfluous luxury, which, ſo far from adding either to their virtue or felicity, ſerved only

to

to harden and corrupt their hearts. Let us then ſteer our courſe by the rudder of truth. Under her direction the journey may be long, and thorns may be planted in the way, but with perſeverance we ſhall be ſure at length to reach the happy haven of our hopes,

Much certainly of future tranquillity or diſorder amongſt mankind depends on the conduct of thoſe privileged orders, which now appear ſo inveterate and malignant againſt any attempt of philoſophical reform. They realize the obſervation, that no principle in nature is ſo powerful as that *eſprit de corps*, that ardour to aggrandize themſelves, which would engroſs and confine the operations of philanthropy within one narrow miſerable circle, and which tends to diſtinguiſh and divide objects, which univerſal laws have indiſſolubly united.

‘ Thus it appears, that of all impulſes
‘ to a miſerable ſelf-intereſted conduct,
‘ thoſe afforded by monarchy and ariſtocracy
‘ are

'are the greatest *;' but it is labour in vain to contend with truth. It is like striving with a mortal hand to arrest the progress of the sea. The wisest policy would be concession. It was the opinion of Fenelon, who was himself the preceptor of princes, that princes were the most unhappy and most misguided of human beings. '. Les plus malheureux & les plus 'aveugles de tous les hommes †.' Princes may have virtuous propensities, but they are misled by flatterers and parasites, who oppose the indulgence of them. It never can be the true interest of one man, or any particular body of men, to resist a system of reason and equity, which naturally implies the interest of all. The man who would urge the necessity of those scenes of misery that exist amongst us, arising from that monstrous unnatural inequality of condition, springing from bad governments (for to no other resource can it possibly be attributed), is a misanthropist

* Godwin concerning Political Justice.

† Telemaque, livre xiii.

of

of the moſt odious caſt. When we recollect the horrible ſtory which defiles the hiſtorical page, the civil and foreign wars which it relates, the bloody ſcenes which the jealouſy and hatred naturally reſulting from the diſcord of claſhing intereſts in the community, from partial immunities in everlaſting warfare with general good, have produced, can it be ſaid, that it is not high time to cloſe this hiſtory of calamity? The queſtion of truth is now at iſſue. If they will not go over to the ſtandard of political juſtice, let the advocates of ariſtocracy temporize, at leaſt, with an enemy, whom it will never be in their power eventually to overcome. The wreck of monopoly and popular ſuperſtition cannot be far diſtant, now that the ſource of enquiry is opened. The powers of deluſion are, however, at this period, triumphant; but if the rulers of nations are wiſe, they will not thence confide in a raſh ſecurity: they ought not to build with too much faith on the conduct of many wiſe and enlightened men belonging to their own order, who look to

I truth.

truth, with anxious ſolicitude, but who dare not explore it, and whoſe timidity and want of firmneſs ſerve to increaſe their imagined ſafety. Let them alſo not count too much on their own retainers and numerous dependants. They are men, and cannot be dead to their own intereſt. Their attachment is to be relied on as long as they conceive it of advantage to themſelves. The inſtant the winds ſhifts, the ſame intereſt will enliſt them on the enemy's ſide. It is now a time to carry home conviction to the breaſt of our opponents, to paint in ſtrong colours the infamy of being regarded by an enlightened poſterity as the unrelenting enemies of juſtice and philanthropy, as ſtrangling truth and the regenerated happineſs of mankind, in order to eternize the reign of general corruption and misfortune.

As friends to humanity, let us proceed to vindicate her rights, and to illuſtrate the barbarous evils by which ſhe has been for ever perſecuted.

Of

Of all the calamities that have ſcourged mankind, war is the moſt dreadful; yet, as it adds ſplendour and prerogative to courts, the miſeries of mankind have not been conſidered as a counterbalance againſt them. The rights of ſovereigns vibrate in our ears, but the wrongs of nations paſs unnoticed. Hence, Europe is now again in arms; and its inhabitants betrayed, through the falſeſt medium, to ſhed their blood in defence of an unnatural cauſe, which militates againſt their own beſt and deareſt intereſts.

It is impoſſible, we believe, to produce one war in the hiſtory of mankind, that did not in ſome way originate in thoſe three great monopolies, prieſthood, monarchy, and ariſtocracy. It is impoſſible, in the whole catalogue, to produce a ſingle example where the people have not been the eventual ſufferers.

The deareſt intereſts of mankind are ſacrificed; all the kindred feelings of nature are tortured in war. The burthens always preſs moſt heavily on thoſe the leaſt able to ſupport them. It therefore ſeems aſtoniſhing, upon firſt recollection, that mankind ſhould ſubſcribe with ſo much facility to their own miſery; but the wonder ceaſes, when we conſider the uncommon pains that are taken to keep them in the profoundeſt ignorance, to play upon their paſſions, to ſoothe their vanity, and to dazzle their ſenſes by a magnificent diſplay of thoſe gaudy trappings and pageantries, which always march in the train of military operations.

Whenever the omnipotence of courts is attacked, it is their conſtant practice to encourage the cheat, and to feed this ſyſtem of general calamity; but the day of reckoning *may* come, when the proud ſtateſman ſhall be taught humanity, and learn to acknowlegde and reſpect the RIGHTS OF MAN.

It has been already obſerved, that the moſt ſucceſsful war ever waged, although it might gratify the envy or rapacity of courts,

courts, never yet failed to aggravate the load of public miſery, both on the victor and the vanquiſhed.

Sir John Pringle, in his very accurate account of the diſeaſes of an army engaged in war, ſhews, that the annual loſs of men in the campaigns, during which he was phyſician to the army, was one out of ſeventeen, beſides thoſe who died in battle or of their wounds; but the proportion of natural deaths amongſt the ſeamen is far greater; and when the cauſes which lead to the termination of wars are conſidered, the patience of philoſophy can no longer brook the barbarous outrage committed on humanity.

'These cauſes are want of proviſion, 'want of men, and want of money. 'When the youth of a country go to war, 'the fields remain uncultivated, and con'ſequently yield little food. When every 'private family has loſt a ſon or a brother, 'levies are no longer to be made without 'difficulty;

' difficulty; and when the public trea-
' sures are given away to men who return
' nothing to the public in exchange, and,
' by the loss of their industry and labour,
' take away a great deal from it, the treasury
' is exhausted. During the war, previous to
' the peace of Ryswick, the price of corn
' was double, and in Scotland quadruple its
' ordinary rate; and in one of the years
' pending that war, eighty thousand persons
' died of WANT in the last of those coun-
' tries *.' Thus, after the wealth of a nation has been exhausted, and its natives destroyed, peace is only restored when war is longer practicable or possible, for want of those resources.

In the last German war, which begun in 1756 and ended in 1762, twenty battles were fought, and two hundred thousand soldiers were slain, when, after all that infernal havock, it was *coolly* determined *that things should remain pre-*

* Dalrymple's Memoirs.

cisely

cisely as they were at the beginning of the war.

In the war with our late colonies, for the just and honourable purpose of coercing America to the obedience of a British Parliament, in which she was not represented, our coffers were emptied of one hundred millions of the public money, and our island depopulated of one hundred and fifty thousand soldiers.

Nevertheless, such dear-bought experience has not cured the evil; the mote is not yet extracted; nations march voluntarily to the butchery, to fight the battles of courts, with as much apparent ardour as if they were really braving death for the preservation of their own liberties, or for relief from those intolerable burthens by which they are oppressed, that by the strangest fatality they are still shedding their blood to increase and perpetuate.

To

To feed this delusion is now more than ever the policy of ariſtocratic governments. When a great empire, after having groaned for many ages under the vileſt ſlavery, goaded by the ſtripes, at length was rouzed to break its chains, and opened a vein of knowledge, renouncing wars, and inviting the world to accept the olive-branch of peace *, expoſing the frauds and cruelty by which mankind had been ſo long abuſed and maſſacred; it then became a main point with thoſe governments to employ all their art and reſources to undermine the pacific ſyſtem, and to ſupport that murderous engine by which they themſelves were ſupported. The ſplendor of palaces would have been eclipſed, and the forces of corruption endangered, by the ſuppreſſion or reduction of military eſtabliſhments. National exchequers were therefore drained, and employed againſt the national intereſt, to foment treaſon and rebellion

'* La Conſtitution Francoiſe renonce à entreprendre aucune guerre dans la vue de faire des conquetes.
La Conſtitution Francoiſe, Titre vi. art. 1.

amongſt

amongſt a people that panted for peace, which, alas! they were not permitted to enjoy, and who were ſtruggling in the general cauſe of human happineſs *; to bribe citizens to

* It is now the fashion amongſt many, who with affected candour, wish to appear in the amiable character of Moderés, to commend the proceedings of the French Conſtituent Aſſembly, as a cover to their own inveteracy againſt the preſent government; but when that aſſembly decreed in the conſtitutional code a renunciation of offenſive war, it may be aſked, if any one ſtep was then taken by other powers to *pin them down* to that pacific diſpoſition, or if the leaſt deſire was expreſſed of co-operating with them in eſtablishment of it? If, on the contrary, every provocation, inſult, and outrage were not offered to make them abandon the principle? if even then, almoſt every court in Europe did not, on that account, regard them with jealouſy, alarm, and hatred? if the hireling B—ke, who thence was honoured with the heart-felt acknowledgments of the moſt amiable ſovereign in Chriſtendom, did not pour forth all his gall againſt them? if the object of thoſe courts has not been uniform, through all the ſtages of the revolution, to impede its progreſs, to create rebellion and maſſacres in France, and then alledge thoſe horrors as a pretext for all *civilized* governments to unite in one common cauſe againſt a race of *lawleſs uſurpers*, whoſe original

to turn traitors to their country, in order to perpetuate their own favourite partial ſyſtem, by which one claſs of men, for ſuch a ſucceſſion of ages, had been enabled to tyrannize with impunity over the other *. Our rulers have at laſt taken off the maſk, and as a guard and ſecurity to themſelves, emboldened by the preſent popular infatuation, have involved the country in this fatal conſpiracy; but the means adopted

original and unpardonable crime conſiſted in having afforded an example fatal to the over-ſtretched prerogative of kings, and whoſe ſubſequent misfortune it was to be eternally harraſſed by their ingenious and royal contrivances to prevent them from indulging that preſumptuous and unwarrantable arrogance which claimed a right to legiſlate for themſelves.

Here we have a brief epitome of the fair dealing, the ingenuous open practice and humanity of courts.

* To this hour, all over the continent of Germany the vaſſal is conſtrained to devote five days out of ſix to the gratuitous labour of his lord. On the ſixth, if *agreeable*, he is free to work for himſelf. In France, before the revolution, the ſame feudal ſyſtem obtained. Who then can wonder at this royal confederacy, to check and to punish ſuch an unnatural ſacriligious revolt?

for

for ſafety, ſometimes prove thoſe of de-ſtruction. Like the cruelly ingenious artiſt, who labouring with zeal and refinement to glut the barbarous rage of the tyrant Phalaris, was the firſt who periſhed in the fiery flanks of the brazen bull he had invented, they alſo may be caught in their own toils.

'Quos necis artifices, arte perire ſuâ.'

Every man who has a ſoul to feel for the felicity or miſery of his fellow creatures, muſt deplore the indifference with which at all times they have been ſeduced to butcher each other: that they ſhould be ever impoſed on by ſuch nonſenſical deluſive gibberiſh, as the dignity of the crown, the glory of our arms, the rights of ſovereigns, &c. &c. &c. under ſuch mockery, to fight againſt their own deareſt intereſts, and to inflict on themſelves endleſs and horrible calamities.

The fraudulent pretexts that betray nations into war are as flimzy and contemptible as the conſequences are ever fatal.

Sometimes it originates in the rapacity or ambition of princes, who never think they have people or territory enough to govern; ſometimes in the profligacy of miniſters who engage their country in war, *with a view to divert public clamour from their evil adminiſtration.*

Difference in opinion hath alſo coſt many million of lives; it is held a very juſtifiable cauſe of war, to invade a country after its inhabitants have been plagued by famine, ſcourged by peſtilence, or *embroiled by faction amongſt themſelves.*

' If a prince ſends forces into a nation, where the natives are poor and ignorant, he may *lawfully* put half of them to death, and *make ſlaves of the reſt*, in order to civilize

vilize and *reduce them from their barbarous way of living*. Poor nations are hungry, and rich nations are proud, and pride and hunger will be ever at variance. For these weighty reasons, the TRADE of a SOLDIER is considered the most honourable of all others, because a SOLDIER is HIRED to KILL in COLD BLOOD, as many of his FELLOW CREATURES who never injured him, as he possibly can *.

There is likewise a kind of *beggarly princes*, not able to wage war of themselves, —*who hire out their troops to RICHER PRINCES for so much a day to each man, of which they receive about three-fourths to their own share*, and from this humane traffick, they derive the chief part of their maintenance. Such are those in many northern parts of Europe; amongst whom our trusty and well-beloved cousin,

'* Military services are the *duty* of all citizens, but 'ought to be the *trade* of none.'

Machintosh, Vindiciæ Gallicæ, p. 240.

the

the L—dg—ve of H—ſſe C—ſ—l holds a very conſpicuous rank *.

—

What ſtupid barbarous infatuation that can reconcile men to the deadly inſtruments and dreadful ravages of war! Cannon, cohorns, muſquets, carbines, bayonets, piſtols, gunpowder, ſwords, retreats, attacks, undermines, countermines, bombardments, red-hot balls, ſea fights, ſhips ſunk with a thouſand men, twenty thouſand killed on each ſide, dying groans, limbs flying in the air, and to fill the climax of R-y-l valour, the mind may conceive a hundred men blown up at once in a ſiege, and as many in a ſhip, and the dead bodies dropping from the clouds, to the great diverſion of the ſpectators †.

—

It would be impoſſible by the moſt laboured argument, or impreſſive eloquence,

* There are alſo German Electors who might be named, as having no kind of objection to this ſpecies of virtuous commerce.

† Gulliver's Travels, Part iv. Chap. v.

to

to expreſs more forcibly, the folly, madneſs, and havock of wars, than by the above plain unexaggerated deſcription of them. With war, including every variety of crime, and every act of deſtruction, we become gradually familar, under ſpecious terms, that are ſeldom examined, becauſe they are learned at an age when the mind is apt to retain whatever is impreſſed. Thus for example, *when one man murders another to gratify his luſt, or any violent impulſe of momentary paſſion, we ſhudder; but when one man murders, or by his fiat, cauſes to be murdered thouſands, and ten thouſands, cities to be conſumed, and provinces deſtroyed, for the gratification of his vanity, pride, thirſt of conqueſt, or revenge, we approve and admire, we envy and applaud.*

If after having diſpaſſionately peruſed the preceding extract, the reader ſhall diſcover, that when the events it relates, have occurred in hiſtory, and of which, even now, ſenſibility is tortured with daily ſimilar accounts, that

that he felt no emotion, no pity, no indignation, and that he acquiefced in wars, which reflection affures him, have been commenced only for fuch caufes, and conducted on fuch principles, let him not condemn thofe perfons, who anxious for the inftruction and prefervation of their fellow creatures, would tear off the veil of a murderous prejudice, painting in native deformity, thofe abominations by which they are made wretched, and thofe arts by which they are deftroyed.

At this defperate crifis, whereon revolves the fate of liberty or flavery, for generations to come, when Englifhmen are expofed to the general flaughter, under feigned hypocritical pretences, not a fhadow of which now exifts, pretences that heretofore bore no fway, for when the Emperor Jofeph in the year 1786 attempted to open the river Scheldt, our treaty with the Dutch was not then deemed a matter of fuch vaft importance by the Britifh cabinet, neither when of late, the Rights of Nations were *really*

and

and moſt outrageouſly violated by the projected invaſion of France;* were they then conſidered of ſufficient weight to break in on the miniſter's ſober plans of finance, by diſturbing the peace of the kingdom; no, nor even now, when the virtuous triple alliance amidſt its warlike operations, have agreed by main force, on the partition of Poland; does ſuch an act of tyrannical rapacity, ſuch a daring infraction of *natural rights*, alarm either his juſtice or humanity. Paſs the Rights of Nations; but when the jealouſy of c—ts was rouſed, when the *ideal* rights of ſovereigns were attacked, and the haughty creſt of tyranny was lowered, long before the execution of the unhappy Louis, then the whole gang was in immediate action; the common intereſt of them all was endangered; ſome acting under ambuſcade, their ſubjects not yet ripe, not worked up to the neceſſary pitch of warlike phrenzy, others, under leſs

* Alas we ourſelves are at this inſtant embarked in a ſimilar undertaking.

reſtraint, openly directing their attacks, but all their plans well digeſted and connected with each other, the blood of citizens was not weighed in the balance. At an awful period then like this, when the ear is almoſt hourly ſtunned with the repetition of the bloody battles that have been fought, the towns which have been conſumed, the thouſands that have been ſlain, the gentle voice of charity and peace will be faintly heard. Let us however amidſt this uproar of confuſion, this wide waſte of ſlaughter and deſolation, recommend to our truly Chriſtian ſovereign, as the fountain of power and of mercy, who with his word might long ere now have conſtrained the bloodhounds of war to ſtop their inhuman career and lay the foundation of peace; let us recommend to his benignant ſoul, the following extract from a ſermon of that gentle paſtor and orthodox prelate the late Dr. Taylor.

'As contrary as cruelty to mercy, tyranny to charity, is war and bloodſhed, to the meekneſs and beneficence of the Chriſtian religion. In the goſpel it is written, Our ſwords

ſwords ſhall be turned into ploughſhares, and our ſpears into pruning hooks. I know that no tittle of God's ſpirit can return unperformed and ineffectual, and I am certain that ſuch is the excellence of Chriſt's doctrines, that if earthly potentates would encourage ſuch doctrines, Chriſtians would never war with each other.'

To engrave ſtill deeper this moral and Chriſtian duty on his royal breaſt, let us in aid of our argument tranſcribe the ſentiments of a more profane author, but whoſe philoſophy is generally pure, and whoſe genius and philanthropy were on numberleſs occaſions, eminently and ſucceſsfully exerted.

' God having endued man with a degree of reaſon, ſuperior to that of other animals; that reaſon ſhould be a ſecurity againſt his degrading himſelf to an imitation of them ; eſpecially as nature has not provided men with arms to murder each other, or with an inſtinct that reliſhes the taſte of human

 blood.

blood. Neverthelefs, this favage cuftom has fo debafed the original character of man, that two or three nations excepted, there are none which antient hiftory does not defcribe in a ftate of conftant warfare.*

'The moft determined parafite will not deny that war drags always at its heels, peftilence and famine, particularly if he has ever vifited the military hofpitals in Germany, or paffed through certain villages or towns, where fome great military difciplinarian, has had an opportunity of *leaving his mark behind him.*†

'Doubtlefs, it is a godlike fyftem that defolates whole provinces, demolifhes their habitations, and on a computation of every hundred thoufand, actually deftroys forty thoufand perfons.‡

'Myriads of men arm and attack each other, with more than mortal fury, with-

* Voltaire. Queftions fur l'Encyclopediæ.
† Ibid. ‡ Ibid.

out

out having the leaſt degree of intereſt in the diſpute; nay, even without knowledge, or enquiry into the circumſtances of it. *

'What ſignify to me the boaſted virtues, 'the piety, temperance, chaſtity of a 'prince, while half a pound of lead, fired 'at the diſtance of ſix hundred paces, by his 'order, ſhivers me to atoms, and that I die 'in the bloom of youth, in inexpreſſible 'torture, amidſt five or ſix thouſand dying 'victims.—While my eyes opening for the 'laſt time, behold my native town in 'flames, and the laſt ſounds that vibrate 'on my ear, are the piercing cries of wo-'men and children expiring under its ruins; 'and all this, for the pretended advantage 'or glory of a man, whom we never knew, 'and probably never ſaw in our lives.' †

Let kings and princes, miniſters and courtiers, contractors, commiſſaries, and

* Ibid. † Ibid.

the whole tribe of military butchers, chew on this philoſophy. Perhaps, they may diſcover as much virtue in it, as in a regular attendance at church on Sundays, or in ordaining faſts and penances, deprecating vengeance from our *national* ſins.

But all the perſuaſion of morals, philoſophy and religion, have no effect, when directed againſt the flinty hearts of intereſted, all graſping ſtateſmen, whoſe places and whoſe power, they imagine to depend on the calamity.

The people however, tired out and exhauſted by an implacable perſeverance in error and ambition, eternal victims to the paſſions, vices, and caprice of others, enjoying ſcarcely the leaſt reſpite from the ſcourge of war, may at length be rouzed to point their vengeance againſt thoſe ſatellites, who have a vile intereſt in beguiling them blindfold to deſtruction, through the mazes of fraud and miſrepreſentation, and whenever the period ſhall arrive, that *the people at large are convinced* of their dupery, of

the

the perfidy, and abuſes which have brought on their ſufferings, and of the horrible ſtratagems by which their countrymen have been beguiled and led to death, that period muſt be fatal to their betrayers.

Experience is an infallible monitor, and hence miniſters might draw a moſt ſalutary caution.

Here might our governors and their ſycophants read an inſtructive leſſon; not to build with too great ſecurity, on the tranſitory tempeſt, their *conjuration* has raiſed. If their raſhneſs was not too headſtrong and incorrigible for reſtraint, the page of hiſtory might alſo learn them, not to repoſe too unlimited faith; not to indulge their hopes beyond all bounds of diſcretion, in the dreadful anarchy that is now ſaid to prevail, and which all their arts, their reſources and treaſures are exhauſted to nurſe and foment in France. It would inſtruct them that ancient Greece with only a handful of men, defended her territories againſt three million of invaders. Plutarch would inform

form them, that at the very period, when Sylla and Marius were carrying on their profcriptions without mercy, againft their countrymen; even, while one half of the Roman people were maffacreing the other, it was even then, that they triumphed over the whole race of kings. Amidft the rage of civil difcord and tumult, that diftracted the Republic, from the profcriptions of Sylla, till the battle of Actium, in that interval, Rome conquered Gaul, Spain, Egypt, Syria, all Afia Minor, and Greece. This example was not long fince, and is ftill in a great degree moft pointedly applicable to the ftate of Great Britain, and indeed of the greateft part of Europe, in their relation to France, and if paffion did not govern, paramount over principle, in the breaft of our mafters, leaving juftice and humanity intirely out of the queftion; if the delirium of the moment did not blind them againft their eventual intereft, it would teach them diffidence and moderation, and enforce the policy and wifdom of not driving events to the laft extremity. But alas! they appear infenfible to danger.

Having

Having embarked the people, on an ocean, apparently calm and ſerene, they are not aware of the rocks and ſhoals by which it is ſurrounded: the devouring havock of war diſturbs not their immediate tranquillity; ſafe as they imagine themſelves within port, they enjoy the ſtorm, nor will they relent, till torrents of blood have again been ſluiced; millions of treaſure again conſumed, till liberty has received her mortal wound, or they themſelves lie buried in the gulph. They have atchieved a temporary conqueſt over the reaſon of their countrymen. Our misfortunes on the continent are ſtudiouſly concealed. Freſh victims are almoſt weekly embarked for the ſlaughter; error and infatuation are all alive; truſting to the phrenzy, they have ſet their all upon a caſt reſolved to ſtand the hazard of the die.

In holding this language, the probing language of truth, the author will incur the hatred, and poſſibly the perſecution of all tyrants, who, agreeably with their uniform practice, knowing the impoſſibility to refute, may resolve to punish it. But he is not of that cast to consult the narrow maxims of selfish prudence, when opposed to the dictates of his own conscience. Anxious to enlighten his countrymen, he will never prostitute his pen, to prop the baseness of hard-hearted grandeur, to depreciate the generous cause of liberty; nor will he ever vouchsafe to court the insidious smiles of fortune, or of power, by a sacrifice of his opinions or his principles.

To flatter the insensibility, to applaud the usurpations of privileged impostors, derogating from the fair and common stock of human nature; to preach the doctrine of courts, to enter into all their selfish views and distinct advantages; to flatter their odious vices, and to sooth their pride; to join in the hue and cry they excite, in order to increase popular delirium, at the expence of common sense and common honesty, and eternally to admire the *heterogeneous beauties*, the *unparagoned excellence* of a system, the constant abuse of which, they find so propitious to their all grasping grafping defires, their unfeeling luxuries, and on which abufe, their monopoly depends, is what they require from every perfon, who fhall prefume to fpeak or write on political fubjects, under dread, if they deviate from this rule, of the anathemas of government, the *torture* of law, and the perfecution of power.*

He

* The difinterefted patriotic fociety at the Crown and Anchor, felf-created as it were, to render the *harmonious difcord* ftill more ftriking, into a fourth department in the f—te, confifting of placemen and penfioners, parifh officers, and police magiftrates, and other equally independent friends of the C—t, arrogating to themfelves the conftitutional jurifdiction of licenfing the prefs, denounce to the S-c-t-ry of S—te, or to *their* Att—n— G-n-r-l, all publications that do not exactly quadrate with thofe doctrines, which it is their *duty* and *intereft* to promulgate; and the mode that they adopt, in order to enforce thefe *truths*, cannot be applauded with more gratitude than it deferves, and which in juftice, it muft be acknowledged, hitherto to have received. They publifh their own doctrines, as ORTHODOX, as LAW, although afferting the antient and once exploded maxim in England, of PASSIVE OBEDIENCE and DIVINE RIGHT, and therefore repugnant to the fpirit of KING WILLIAM's GLORIOUS and IMMORTAL REVOLUTION,

He ventures to brave all theſe dangers from a rational and profound conviction in the

LUTION, which notwithſtanding, they profeſs to revere, as the baſis of their political creed, and they circulate theſe loyal pamphlets of their applauſe, with a zeal and expence, (*doubtleſs at their own charge*) that reflect infinite honour on their liberality; while at the ſame time their candour is equally admirable, proſecuting every bookſeller, printer, or hawker, who is daring, or ignorant enough, to publiſh doctrines militating againſt their own. 'Audi alteram partem,' was formerly reckoned an eſſential principle, or rather an integral part of argumentative diſcuſſion, indiſpenſibly requiſite to the diſcovery of truth; but this worthy aſſociation not finding it convenient to their patriotic views, have laid it aſide leſt it might enlighten and raiſe the ſwiniſh multitude, above the level of their native ignorance, and thence, they have prohibited all books, whoſe doctrines do not tally with thoſe protected by themſelves, under the moſt terrible penalties of fine, pillory, and impriſonment. From this juſt, prudent, and conſtitutional monopoly, by which, publicans are alſo inſtructed in their duty:—what newſpapers they muſt allow their cuſtomers to read, what converſation they are permitted to hold, COMMON SENSE, TRUTH, and the RIGHTS of MAN are baniſhed from our houſes, and the LORD's ANOINTED ſubſtituted in their place.

What a conſummate politician is JOHN BULL, happy in his *implicit confidence*, always in *the right box*. Well

the truth, juſtice, and beneficial tendency of his theory, and while he points his juſt

Well indeed may he rejoice, when now as a recompenſe for the ſurrender of COMMON SENSE and the RIGHTS of MAN, he gains in exchange, the immediate and tutelary protection of the LORD's ANOINTED, G——e III. But to be ſerious, perſecution of opinions is always ineffectual, and ſometimes dangerous. Attempts to modify the mind of one perſon, agreeably with the fancy or caprice of another, muſt be ever vain and nugatory. Perſecute or torture truth as you will, it will in the end prevail. The capital crimes of two Britiſh martyrs, Ridley and Latimer, conſiſted in circulating Engliſh Bibles, and when for this *abominable hereſy*, theſe two champions of proteſtantiſm were burnt at Oxford, one of them exhorted the other as follows: 'Brother, be of good comfort, 'our perſecutors will be diſappointed, for our ſufferings will lead men to enquire into that, for which we 'ſuffered, and this fire will light ſuch a candle in England, as I truſt in God's Grace, will never be extinguiſhed.'

It is needleſs to obſerve, that Popery was very ſoon afterward deſtroyed in Britain, that the Bible ſtill continues to be read in Engliſh in all our churches, and that the religion of thoſe two inflexible martyrs, is ſtill our national faith.

Perſecution is and ever will be the parent and nurſe of enthuſiaſm.

ſeverity

ſeverity againſt the infamous deluſions, the bitter oppreſſions that are notorious amongſt us, his gall overflows againſt the unconſcionable all graſping minions who thrive upon them, who are now every where denouncing Bella, horrida Bella, exulting in the maſſacre of myriads of Frenchmen, nor even feeling a pang for the loſs of their own countrymen, that have already periſhed, and that may periſh, their only object being concealment, hoping thereby to enjoy a future uninterrupted ſecurity in their monopoly, from thoſe dire alarms, by which their coward hearts have of late been ſcared.

He dares at the riſque of utter ruin, to withſtand the fury of heated prejudice, and irritated paſſion: to brave the clamour of vulgar abuſe, and the far more tremendous perils of legal vengeance. Undiſmayed by the terror of example, held out by ſo many of his injured and unfortunate fellow citizens, now languiſhing in gaol, torn from their families, unprotected, many of them expoſed to the hardeſt penalties of want, deprived of liberty; loſt to ſociety, ruined

in

in their trades, for having laboured in their vocation, unconſcious of offence, he ſtill aſſerts the natural independent empire of the human mind, proving that courts and their creatures can be the only gainers by this diſaſtrous war, that it muſt inflict endleſs calamity on the people at large, and from a perſuaſion that his tenets are founded on charity and truth, it can be no ungenerous effort on his part, to ſtrive to enforce them, and infamous would it be to abandon his legitimate inheritance, eſpecially as a Briton, born in a nation for ever boaſting its freedom, to combat the infernal maxims that ſtrike at the natural, beſt, inalienable charter of man.

In the barbarous age of Attila, or when the Danes invaded this iſland, war was familiar, it was ingrafted on the general ſyſtem; civilization had made no improvements, and the bleſſings of peace rarely enjoyed, were very imperfectly underſtood; but now, under a philoſophic and merciful ſovereign, whoſe reign, owing to evil coun-

counſellors, had been already too much ſtained by the maſſacres of war, it might have been preſumed that the rage of blood had had its fill; that inſtead of plunging deeper into thoſe horrors, the remainder of his days would have been devoted to the bleſſed functions of charity and peace;—to perſonal ſacrifices, which his overflowing treaſures can abundantly afford, to the alleviation of his peoples burthens, and that he would have ſtood forth a god-like mediator to quell the vengeance of fierce inexorable tyrants, and check them in their wild lawleſs career of rapine, blood, and devaſtation.

Theſe are the offices of *true* religion, the heartcheering delights of a patriot prince, whoſe tender heart bleeds for the loſs of every ſoldier or ſailor that periſhes in his battles, miſerable victim, ignorant of the cauſe for which he ſuffers, and it is fair to hope, that at length, indulging his own natural benevolent propenſities, he will avail himſelf of the immenſe advantages, his

elevated

elevated ſtation and peculiarly fortunate circumſtances afford, to annihilate a ſanguinary ſyſtem under the malignant planet of which, ſince his acceſſion to empire, millions have been already ſacrificed in India and America; to exterminate the deſolating principles of offenſive war, and that he will cordially enliſt on the ſide of humanity, to deſtroy that ſtalking horſe of ſlaughter, which now again lays waſte the world.

> ' Oh blind to think that cruel war
> ' Can pleaſe the prince of peace,
> ' He who erects his altar in the heart,
> ' Abhors the ſacrifice of human blood,
> ' And all the mad ambition of that zeal
> ' Which deſolates the world he died to ſave.'*

Such we repeat are the ſentiments philoſophy and religion inſpire, but unfortunately, in this age, ſimilar doctrines have appeared libellous and ſeditious in the diſcriminating judgment of our Att—ny G-n-r-l, and here it is natural to point out

* Mores Percy.

the deſcription of men, who by that learned oracle, and by Mr. R—ves, are denounced to the public, and proſecuted at law, as libellous, ſeditious, and deſperate incendiaries.

They are branded and preſented as ſuch, who dare to advance, that all abuſes which have crept into the conſtitution, ought to be examined into, and immediately reformed, in order to preſerve it from ſudden ruin, or from natural decay ; they who are anxious to reſtore to their countrymen a more equal repreſentation, after the example of their illuſtrious prototypes, the Duke of Richmond and Mr. Pitt, as likely to procure the following eſſential bleſſings.

1ſt. By reducing the number of unrequited penſions, aboliſhing unneceſſary places, *where they who hold them, do nothing for the money they receive*, and by introducing the ſtricteſt œconomy into every branch of government, a vaſt annual ſum would

would be ſaved, conſequently the public burthens leſſened.

2d. By a better mode of collecting the taxes, the revenue would be more productive to the ſtate, leſs oppreſſive to the poor, and leſs injurious to the liberties of the nation.

3d. By aboliſhing tythes, and paying the clergy in ſome more eligible way, the laborious huſbandman would cultivate his land with greater ſatisfaction and profit, and all cauſe of litigation between the clergyman and his pariſhioner, would be removed.

4th. By putting an end to all unjuſt, extravagant, hypocritical, and ambitious wars, our population and commerce would be exceedingly increaſed.

5th. By providing more liberally for that reſpectable body of men, the parochial curates, religion would proſper, and their condition thus improved, they might be able out of their income to perform many charities, which a penurious pittance from 20 *l.* to 40 *l.* a year, will not admit of.

6th. By revising the poor laws, the support of the indigent and afflicted might be thrown in juster proportion on the rich, where the burthen ought to fall; to the infinite relief of the lower class of tradesmen, poor housekeepers, and meritorious hardworking peasants.

These are a few of the innovations projected by these incendiaries, through the channel of short parliaments, fairly and constitutionally elected by the people at large, as agreeable with their original principles, and subject to the control of their electors.*

These

* From the reign of Edward the First, to the restoration of Charles the Second, (the Parliament of 1640 excepted,) there were never any other than annual Parliaments, and during that long interval, the representatives never assumed to themselves, any other power then

Theſe are the deſperate incendiaries, the levellers and republicans, whom Mr. R—ves denounces as labouring to confound all order, to deſtroy all property, to eſtablish Agrarian law, while both by their words and their works, they have invariably reprobated ſuch doctrines, their avowed object being to point out the extreme folly and madneſs of unmerited *confidence*,* to

then what they derived from their conſtituents, by whom, they were *conſtantly* inſtructed, and whoſe opinions they as *conſtantly* obeyed.

For the above, we have Lord Coke's authority, who ſays, 'It was always the law and Cuſtom of Parliament, that when any new decree was moved in the King's behalf for his ſpecific aid, or the like, the Commons might anſwer, that they tendered the King's eſtate, and were ready to aid the ſame; only that they *dare not* agree without conferring with their counties.' Hence, it is evident, that ſuch conferences are warrantable by the law and cuſtom of Parliament, and that however modern delegates may arrogate the power of judging *ſolely* in all things, that arrogance is by no means agreeable to the original ſyſtem of national delegation.

* The ſole merit on which Mr. P—tt can poſſibly reſt his claim to that *confidence* he is ſo forward and vehement

to expoſe the impudent quackery of thoſe political mountebanks, who dare to impoſe ſuch a regimen, to reſtore to every man his birthright, to enforce the bleſſings and neceſſity of peace, to render our laws as amiable and beneficial in practice, as they are ſaid to be excellent in theory; to deviſe ſome plan, for inſtruction of the young and ignorant; for relief of the diſtreſſed, to eſtabliſh a comfortable aſylum for the lame and the blind, for conſolation and ſupport of the aged and infirm, thinking it far better, that an equitable and permanent proviſion ſhould be made by law, than that the chance of effecting theſe great beneficent purpoſes, ſhould depend on the precarious ſupply of private charity, or public contribution.*

Conſcious

hement to enforce, and which unfortunately has always bore too much ſway in this country, 'conſiſts in the meaneſt of all the talents of ſtateſmen,' that of harranguing in public; not on great occaſions, as the orators of Greece and Rome did, but on every occaſion; *an avocation from buſineſs, which he calls doing buſineſs*'—Dalrymple's Memoirs.

* Such are the perſons pointed out by Mr. R—ves

as

Conſcious of the injuſtice, the cruelty of torturing men for opinions ſake, it is the duty

as ſeditious levellers, and deſperate republicans. He cannot therefore complain, if in return, he is preſented with a faithful portrait of himſelf.

The *immediate* birth and parentage of this patriot citizen are enveloped in myſterious darkneſs, although he can trace his genealogy from the remoteſt ages of antiquity, being deſcended from the moſt ancient and reſpectable of all families;—the SANS CULOTTES. It muſt be confeſſed indeed, that his late conduct does not demonſtrate any very great affection or veneration for his anceſtors, but ſhould the family ever riſe to that proud equality, to which in a neighbouring nation it aſpires, he poſſeſſes a happy accommodating venality, that cannot fail to enſure him impunity and pardon from his *relations*.

Mr. R—ves appears to have made his *debut* in the political world, at the time of Admiral Keppel's trial, when he compoſed an elegant panegyrical poem, in honour of that gallant officer. Poetry delights in fiction, and at that period, our poet indulged his muſe in the bittereſt invectives againſt his M-j—ties g-v—m-t, for which heinous tranſgreſſion he has ſince made liberal compenſation, by a contrary example of well timed and moſt fervent loyalty.

The noble minded H—kſb-ry is known, whenever it ſuits his purpoſe to exert it, to inherit the happieſt and moſt extraordinary genius, in working metamor-

phoſes

duty of all good and enlightened citizens, to perſevere in this rugged part of reform, againſt

phoſes on the human mind. He has moreover, a kind of peculiar inſtinct, a *manual touch*, whereby he inſtantly diſcovers thoſe pliant ſupple diſpoſitions, that any ways ſympathize with his own. By this ſympathy, however far aſunder their original diſtance, theſe congenial ſouls were drawn together. The times were deemed critical, and critical ſervices were required. A very few minutes converſation was all ſufficient to explain mutual intentions, and the uſual forms of delicacy and etiquette complied with, under the all puiſſant recommendation of his noble patron, our *poetipolitical* SANS CULOTTES, (for ſuch then, he almoſt literally was) was introduced to the m—t—r as a *perfect maſter of all work*; *ready for any ſervice*; only ſubject to one reſtriction. He never ſerved *gratis*. The journeyman is worthy of his hire. It was neither expected or deſired that he ſhould; the patriotiſm of Mr. R—ves, like that of his maſter, derives recruited zeal, in proportion with the rewards beſtowed on it, and when wages are abundantly paid, ſervility is more certain. His pulſe was accordingly felt, and it beat in perfect uniſon; ſo that now, no longer a SANS CULOTTES, he was at once put in poſſeſſion of an annual income, the fruit of anticipated ſervices, to the amount of 2000 l. and amongſt other precious ſinecures that he holds, he is Chief Juſtice of Newfoundland, the ſalary

againſt a treacherous time-ſerving coalition
of

lary of which is ſaid to be *only* 1000 l. per annum; altho' there cannot be any duties annexed to this appointment, requiring a local reſidence, ſince he himſelf is ſo actively and ſo honourably employed in the *administration of juſtice at home*.

A *gentleman*, thus reſpectable in fortune and connections, independent of the nation, if not of the c—t, was in every point of view a fit arbiter of the property and liberties of Engliſhmen, peculiarly qualified to defend them againſt the ſo-much dreaded violence of levellers and republicans. Our miniſter therefore of implicit confidence gave him his cue. The bait well gilded was thrown out. John Bull, as uſual, bit freely: the Crown and Anchor became the focus of loyalty; within that centre all the *confidence* of the kingdom was collected, and Mr. R—ves's aſſociation gave birth to thoſe patriotic prodigies we have witneſſed; thoſe Alien Bills, and *treaſonable* Bills; to thoſe ſeaſonable and humane proſecutions againſt drunken journeymen, printers, and bill-ſtickers, whereby the preſs, as it has been already ſhewn, is wiſely monopolized by two branches of the legiſlature, to the excluſion of the other, and the crown acquires an addition of prerogative, that muſt for ever ſecure it againſt all danger of Plebeian invaſion. He is the idol of P—tt, the *friend* of H—kſb-ry: with theirs, his name will be tranſmited *pure* to poſterity.

of rival parties; † to ſave, if poſſible, this adored

Mr. R—ves, to his other tried virtues, adds the moſt amiable candour and untainted veracity. He declares, 'that he is perfectly ſatisfied with the ſtate of the nation, and that every other perſon *ought* to be ſatisfied alſo;' yet, if it be fair to judge from the London Gazette, the Gazette de la Cour, of *ſacred authority*, from the tremendous liſt of bankruptcies there announced, a part of the mercantile world *is not* perfectly ſatisfied with the actual ſtate of things; but when a *gentleman*, no leſs diſtinguiſhed for the conſiſtency and independence of his principles, than for the pure nature and extent of his ſervices, thus deigns to announce *his* ſatisfaction, it would be equal hereſy and ingratitude in the people, were they heard to murmur or repine. In his accurate and impartial definition of the laws; for the energy and vigour he has infuſed into our councils; correcting popular errors; cruſhing the ſedition of diſaffected reformers; for his virtuous example in reeceiving and propagating anonymous calumny as a ground of criminal proſecution; calling forth all the latent patriotiſm in the country, ſtill further to extend the increaſed and increaſing influence of the c—wn, as ſolemnly recognized by a vote of Parliament, he alſo extorts our *confidence* and gratitude; and it muſt reflect

† It inſpires a moſt exalted idea of parties, when one conſiders the late tergiverſation of the Honourable, and

adored conſtitution from a total decay, by proving

fleĉt immortal glory on the preſent age :—the bright example will flouriſh a perennial monument of the ſenſibility, *conſiſtency*, and wiſdom of Engliſhmen, that in the year 1793 of the Chriſtian æra, J—n R—ves, *Eſquire*, wrought a total change in our national character;—that it was a hireling I-f-m-r who modified, and gave an entire new bias to the political ſyſtem of the B—t-ſh G-v—m—t.

---

and Right Honourable, the Noble, and moſt noble Seceders from the Whig Club. For a long time it was a mortal ſtruggle, *un combat à mort*, between them and their more happy rivals, each panting *to cut the others throat*, eſpecially B—ke, who having been once permitted for a ſhort time to ſip of the delicious fount, diſplayed all the ſymptoms of a Maniac in his rage: both parties glowing with impatient ardour; one to preſerve *the good things* already in their poſſeſſion;—the other *to turn* thoſe out already in poſſeſſion, and to get at them themſelves: But when the principle itſelf was threatened; when jealous of the French revolution, they apprehended *theſe good things* to be endangered; that the expenditure of courts would be reformed, their civil liſts reduced, the fountain of corruption in ſome degree dried up, and thus all their expectations deſtroyed; then theſe enraged antagoniſts, theſe furious *cut-throats kiſſed* and embraced, uniting in proving the danger to which its principal element is now more then ever expoſed, from the undermining encroachments of the moſt formidable enemies, concealed under the dark diſguiſe of inſidious affected friendſhip.

It might be dangerous to arraign the genuine ſpirit, the *immortal* part of the Britiſh conſtitution; but let us exert ourſelves to correct thoſe corroding ulcers that threaten its *immortality*. Let us guard againſt the treachery of falſe friendſhip, and apply a ſafe and healing cataplaſm to the wounds, which old age and corruption have engendered in the body, leſt at length they mortify, and reach the heart.

cloſeſt bonds of amiable *fraternity*, to protect the common miſtreſs of their fondeſt affections from the rude unhallowed violation of baſe democratic raviſhers. It has ever been the wretched fate of England to be ſplit and torn to pieces by theſe parties and cabals:—to be gulled by the affected patriotiſm, the plauſible moderation of one, or inſulted and ruined by the open, avowed, practical corruption of the other.. Both running to the ſame goal.

Taking

Taking for granted the vaunted excellence of our happy form of government, it ought not to blind us againſt its practical errors; neither ſhould it throw us off our guard againſt thoſe deſperate monarchical ſtrides, daily encroaching, which, unleſs ſucceſsfully reſiſted, cannot fail to undermine it altogether; nor ought it to render us unjuſt towards another nation, emulous of our *original* example, to improve its own; and as Solomon has told us, 'there is nothing new,' ſo there is nothing perfect under the ſun; the very nature of man is imperfect, and after ſo many dear and abortive efforts, to eſtabliſh that pure and ſimple reform in their monarchy, which they at firſt projected, but to which the prejudices, pride, intereſt, and paſſions of their privileged orders would never ſubmit, and which all the crowned heads, ariſtocracies and hierarchies in Europe, were either ſecretly or openly combined to counteract, ſurely the French were not blameable, under ſuch circumſtances, for aſpiring to a degree of perfection in a new government, hither-

to

to unattained by any nation either ancient or modern. Their antient ſyſtem, by its violent exceſſes, had exhauſted patience and worked its own diſſolution; and how far the ſyſtem that ſucceeded *was* excellent—how far the practice of it would be eaſy and beneficial, compatible with the purity of its theory, or incompatible with the depravity of man, nor calculated to correct it, is ſtill a myſtery. Alas! the active malice, the claſhing intereſts, and everlaſting jealouſy of thoſe intereſted to oppoſe it, prevented the world from a fair trial of its efficacy; and it will ever remain a lamentable reflection for humanity, if the liberties of a regenerated people, who had laid down an illuſtrious example of peace and brotherhood, but who never were allowed to enforce it, whom the combined and *open* force of all the tyrants in Europe was unable to conquer, after the torrents of blood that have been ſluiced, ſhould fall at length a ſacrifice to the blackeſt, moſt unexampled treachery, the

tyranny,

tyranny, and diabolical corruption of courts.*

It has been often ſtunned in our ears with an affectation of candour, 'Oh, we admit the juſtice and neceſſity of the principles on which they ſtarted, (although even then we well remember the ariſtocratic clamour which they excited,) but they have loſt all right of them, and have degenerated into the moſt barbarous ſtate of anarchy, regicide, and bloodſhed.'

Alas! was it their fault, if they have perforce abandoned that ſyſtem they at firſt

* It will not require an infinity of penetration, to decide, whether B—t-ſh gold was employed in this honourable traffic, when it is recollected, that the parole of rallying, uſed by the chiefs of the Inſurgents in Brittany, was 'vivent les Anglais,' long live the Engliſh; and its magic was ſo powerful, that even the peaſants, who had certainly the greateſt intereſt in the new order of things, deſerted in bodies to the rebel ſtandard. It can hardly be imagined that the parole itſelf had ſufficient virtue to operate on a French clown, unleſs accompanied with a more ſubſtantial temptation.

laid

laid down, not only unſupported by other governments, but either ſecretly or openly attacked by them all, finding the impoſſibility of contending againſt ſuch a hoſt of perfidious and powerful enemies, united to interrupt its progreſs, and for the ſake of weakening it, to ſplit the country into a thouſand different factions? Did their unhappy king ever join in cordial ſincerity with them? Did his perturbed brain ever enjoy the ſhorteſt interval of reſt, under the curtailment that his once unbounded prerogative had ſuffered? Has he not been *proved*, to the conviction of all, but ſuch as are impenetrable to *proof*, to have adopted every ſtratagem, either he himſelf or his confidential diſappointed adviſers could invent, to overturn that conſtitution he was ſworn to defend, but which in his ſoul he execrated and abhorred? How then could a government proſper? How could it continue its march, while the executive power was hoſtile to it, eternally fruſtrating the operations of the legiſlature?

Did

Did the accurſed jealouſy, the revengeful turbulent ſpirit of prieſthood, nurſed in prejudice, ſoured by diſappointment, ever ceaſe, either directly or indirectly, to conjure up the dæmon of rebellion, and to excite civil war in the nation, panting to wade through ſeas of blood, if in ſo doing it foreſaw the moſt diſtant proſpect of regaining thoſe treaſures, or of recovering that omnipotence which the church had ſo long enjoyed, under no more virtuous or equitable claims than thoſe of fraud, monopoly, and uſurpation, and which policy, wiſdom, juſtice, and above all, the public good, demanded ſhould be reduced? Oh no! their clergy were ſtrangers to the meek and beneficent ſpirit of true religion; they were unacquainted with the virtue of ſacrifices; and founding their own dominion on the baſis of ignorance, tyranny, and ſuperſtition, how could they be imagined ever to feel the divine glow which a love of liberty inſpired? Obſtinate till the laſt, unrelenting and vindictive, we now behold them ſunk in the deepeſt abyſs of wretchedneſs, lingering out a loathſome exiſtence in foreign ſtates, on the precarious alms of vain arrogant oſtentation, and of cold ariſtocratic charity, with no other proſpect to their parricidal hopes, than what they derive from the threatened deſolation and eternal ſlavery of their native country; and the nobles, cramped in their foul habitual luxury, curtailed of their privileges, their empty titles and diſtinctions gone, have they not (with few exceptions,) by the moſt deſperate treaſons, inceſſantly laboured, alas! too ſucceſsfully; and are they not now diſperſed all over Europe, either in hoſtile courts, or in hoſtile armies, or in open rebellion at home, braving the laws, inſtigating and aiding the vengeance of enraged and mercileſs tyrants, to render the land that gave them birth, which they heſitated not to renounce, rather than ſubmit to thoſe ſalutary reforms that reduced them more to a juſt level with the reſt of their fellow citizens, one wide waſte of blood and carnage?

Can therefore the moſt bigotted prejudice affect to deny; (in his heart no man can,) that after ſo many fruitleſs attempts to eſtabliſh a limited monarchy, on principles that did not deſtroy, although they abridged the prerogative of the king, and confined the power of the clergy and nobles within proper rational limits, the people were not *forced* to get rid of this vaſt coloſſus of oppoſition, that had ever ſhewn itſelf callous to every requiſition and duty of patriotiſm? They therefore ſubverted altogether the old government, the modifications of which the privileged orders, as we have before remarked, however well affected they might at firſt appear to them in their diſcourſe, were by their actions labouring night and day to prevent, and they wiſely exerted themſelves to erect a new form of government, more perfect, and better adapted to general happineſs, on the ancient ruins?

The people had, they could have no other alternative, unleſs they would conſent to repeat the doſe of their former wretched ſervitude.

It has been often and juſtly obſerved, that the alteration which the French have made in their government is the true criterion, the very touchſtone of the heart, ſtriking at particular diſtinctions, at the ſelfiſhneſs and arrogant preſumption of men, who for the moſt part, having only the ſpurious dignity of birth or title wherewith to conceal the want of every intrinſic merit, inceſſantly labour, by every artifice and violence, to perpetuate the galling *yoke*, by which the bulk of mankind have been ſo long enſlaved to their purpoſes. The French Republic is a machine, that in an inſtant winds up the whole royal and ariſtocratic corps to a pitch of exquiſite painful ſenſibility; the moſt virtuous m——ch in Europe, whom far be it from us to include in the above ſelfiſh crew, cannot hear it mentioned without betraying the moſt viſible and affecting emotions; but we would exhort him in the cheering language of our heavenly poet,

'*It is* a knaviſh piece of work, but what 'of that; your majeſty and we have free 'ſouls, it touches us not, let the galled jade 'wince, our withers are unwrung.'

Why then ſhould the harmony of his r-y-l mind be diſcompoſed? Why ſhould he *wince or whine* at the licentious exceſſes of deſperate free booters, of the ſwiniſh multitude, ſans culottes, whom the royal confederacy are about to ſweep from the earth? Why ſhould he be afflicted, whoſe conſcience is pure; 'Integer vitæ, ſceleriſque purus,'* and whoſe long and otherwiſe glorious reign, if too deeply ſtained in the purple tide of war, it can be imputed only to the malignant influence of evil counſellors, or to the ſtill more irreſiſtible force of *dire neceſſity*; and whoſe immenſe treaſures, † if

* Horace.

† If it be fair to judge from Mr. Doddington's Diary, and it is impoſſible to doubt his ſources of information, no perſon enjoys the eligible and enviable felicity

if they have never yet been applied to the support of charitable institutions, to the relief

felicity of riches to such a superlative degree as our amiable and truly œconomical sovereign.

Mr. Doddington tells us, that in a conversation that passed between him and the late Princess Dowager of Wales, 'She talked much of his majesty's (Geo. II.) 'accumulation of treasure, which she estimated at four 'millions. I remarked, what was become of it, how 'employed, where, and what was left; I did not pre-'tend to guess, but that I computed the accumulation 'to be from 12 *to* 15 *millions*; that these things with-'in a moderate degree, perhaps less then a *fourth part*, 'could be *proved beyond all possibility of denial.*'

Doddington's Diary, p. 167 and 290.

Mr. Doddington relates also a conference between Mr. Pitt and the Duke of Newcastle, in the year 1755, which proves how a *certain* nation has been gulled, and to what extent a *certain* family must have been enriched since its establishment in a *certain prosperous* island.

The Duke mumbled 'that the Saxon and Bavarian 'subsidies were offered and pressed, but there was no-'thing done in them;—that the Hessian was perfected, 'but the Russian was not concluded. When his Grace 'dwelt so much on the K—g's *honour*, Mr. Pitt asked 'him what, if out of the *fifteen million which his majesty 'had saved*, he should give his cousin of Hesse 100,000l. 'and the Czarina 150,000l. to be off from those bad

bargains,

lief of public burthens, it must be remembered, the numerous and hopeful family, for

'bargains, and not suffer suggestions so dangerous to 'his own quiet and safety of his family to be thrown 'out, which would, and must be insisted on in a debate 'of this nature, where would be the harm of it? The 'Duke had nothing to say, but desired they might talk 'it over again with the Chancellor. Mr. Pitt replied, 'he was at their command; but that nothing could 'alter his opinion.'—Ibid. p. 173.

It appears evident, from the above faithful extract, that the constitution in its practical operations under the Br—w—ck family, is as propitious to kings as it is to the people, perhaps more so; for the royal purse certainly does not *decrease*, as the public burthens *increase*; since every addition to the revenue naturally adds to the revenue and patronage of the c—wn.

An accurate, but unfortunate author, whose writings have attracted the notice of our delicate, vigilant, and susceptible g-v—m—t, applies the following pertinent and close observations to the preceding extracts:

'Thirty-seven years have now elapsed (says he) 'since G——e II. had saved *fifteen millions sterling from 'the civil list*. It has been said, that a sum at five per 'cent. of compound interest, doubles itself in fourteen 'years, but the calculation is not quite exact; and 'where a topic *so delicate* as the civil list is concerned, 'the

for whom it is his duty hereafter to provide, over and above that provision, which his faithful and never failing commons, agreeably

'the most scrupulous accuracy should be observed, and 'therefore it is necessary to premise, that in 14 years, 'one hundred pounds produce about a fiftieth part less 'than a second hundred; that is to say, 97 l. 18s. 8d. 'Now at this rate, these fifteen millions in 37 years, 'would have multiplied to more than ninety-one million and a half.

'It is true indeed, as Mr. Doddington observes, 'that we are ignorant what became of this money, how 'or where it was applied; but this we know, no part 'of it was ever applied to the service or relief of the 'people of this country, from whom it was derived. '*We have since paid several arrears into which the civil* '*list* had fallen, and 100,000l. in the superabundant 'generosity of Parliament, have been added to the royal 'salary; when at the same time the nation has been 'borrowing money to pay that sum, *nominally*, at three 'and a half or four per cent. but *in reallity* at six or 'eight per cent. Hence, properly applied, the fifteen 'million sterling of G——e II. instead of increasing to 'ninety-one million and a half, would at seven and a half 'per cent. have extended to nearly one hundred and 'thirty million seven hundred and fifty thousand pounds, 'which would at present buy out more than one half of 'our

bly with their wonted gratitude, may judge fitting to ſupply his liberal munificence towards

'our national debt; and ſave the country from an an-'nual burthen of four million and a half.'

Vide Political Progreſs of Brittain.

Theſe are *home truths* to be ſure. The ſecrets of the *charnel houſe* are here divulged, and hence the people of England may be apt to entertain an exalted idea of the fidelity and œconomy with which their repreſentatives, eſpecially during later reigns, have executed their truſt. But to be ſerious: On reading the above, will the moſt inveterate ſlave to the ſplendor, corruption, or avarice of c—ts affect to deny the juſtice, the neceſſity of their reform? And how muſt ſenſibility and honour revolt when the perſecution is conſidered to which individuals are expoſed who venture to enforce that neceſſity? What muſt be the nature of that ſyſtem which cannot endure the mention of its abuſes? What the real character of a government that caſts a man into dungeons, who, animated with the pureſt patriotiſm and philanthropy, labours to correct them?

It is fair to conjecture, that part of the enormous heaps *thus oeconomiſed* has been tranſmitted to Germany; yet, even ſuppoſing it, ſome imperfect notion may thence be formed of the immenſe wealth enjoyed, after his long reign, by the frugal and virtuous prince who continues to yield ſuch ſatisfaction, comfort, and ſolid advantages to this *flouriſhing* kingdom; and ſince

the

wards that family; from all which impartial conſiderations he now ſits enthroned in
the grateful hearts of his loyal, diſcriminating, beloved, and loving ſubjects.

It

the country is now again engaged in war, it cannot be doubted that a patriot king, ſo much better able to afford it, will follow the example of one of his illuſtrious predeceſſors, Queen Anne, who for four years together gave one hundred thouſand pounds from her civil liſt to ſupport the war againſt France. Under the preſent circumſtances it would be impious to ſuſpect the liberality and civiſm of a ſovereign who loves his ſubjects far better than his money, and who will be anxious to ſurpaſs that princeſs in the extent of his donations, as much as he exceeds her in riches and all other reſources. From ſuch a ſublime example what glorious effects may we anticipate! Then will the miniſter's aſſertion, "that gentlemen pledging their lives and "fortunes in ſupport of the preſent war were not "terms of courſe, but ſuch as they would moſt chear-"fully abide by." The generous aſſertion ſhall then be verified; he himſelf will be the firſt to throw in the profits ariſing from the Cinque Ports, that comfortable little proviſion with which he lately rewarded himſelf; Dundas, Grenville, and all his patriot friends will unite in imitation of his generoſity; and the innumerable band of ſinecure men, penſioners, and placemen of every deſcription, by the noble ſacrifice

of

It is the nature of truth to challenge en-quiry; and ſuſpicious indeed muſt be held any

of their incomes to relieve the public of its burthens, will realize the reputation of diſintereſtedneſs and patriotiſm, for which their right honourable maſter and benefactor, with ſuch admirable gallantry, pledged his veracity.

Foremoſt, amongſt this diſintereſted crew, the noble Earl of Mansfield will preſs moſt anxiouſly forward, eager to throw in his mite for ſupport of a war, the principles of which he ſo truly and zealouſly approves; for it cannot be ſuppoſed that his Lordſhip, who from hereditary and acquired wealth, together with other ſinecures, is perhaps the richeſt individual in his Majeſty's dominions, will hold it conſiſtent with the dignity of AN ENGLISH EARLDOM, however compatible he might have held it with Scottiſh prudence or a Scottiſh peerage, *any longer to keep a ſhop*, to deal, under the firm of Mansfield and Way, in ſlips of parchment, ſelling them to the poor in moments of their greateſt diſtreſs. In general, the profits ariſing to the principal partner from this buſineſs are computed at 3000l. a year, but in times of extraordinary demand, like theſe, it is impoſſible to eſtimate the income.

This is one of the trades which authoriſed Mr. R—es and a learned Judge to publiſh the *conſoling truiſm*, that juſtice in this country is equally within the reach of every deſcription of perſons; a *truiſm*, how-

any moral or political ſyſtem which ſhuns that enquiry. In all other ſciences its virtue is unanimouſly admitted. In agriculture, commerce, and navigation, the mind is conſtantly progreſſive, looking forward to improvement. The demonſtrations of Newton were conſidered as the moſt ſublime and beneficial diſcoveries, and the GEORGIUM SIDUS of Herſchell immortalizes at once the philoſopher and the patron: But in politics, the queſtion where, of all others, human nature has the deepeſt ſtake, on which its felicity wholly depends, deſpotiſm forbids man to exerciſe his reaſon, the divineſt faculty of his nature; humanity is not permitted to profit by its exertions; the beſt gift of heaven muſt be rendered null to favour the impious

ever, which ſome men are ſtill incredulous enough to deny; but in the preſent inſtance, as in many others, the *truiſm* is fully illuſtrated. The juſtice ſhop is open, and all may buy it, if they have only ready money to pay for it. Nevertheleſs, many months have paſſed ſince the miniſter's prediction, but we have not heard of a ſingle inſtance hitherto in which it has been verified.

and

and cruel policy of ſocial inſtitutions. It muſt be confeſſed, that hitherto fraud has been the characteriſtic of almoſt all governments. It appears as if it were the uniform plan to impoſe falſe notions on the underſtanding of the people, and then to govern them accordingly. For example, in the ſummer of 1792, when his *Serene* Highneſs the Duke of Brunſwick publiſhed his manifeſto, in the name of their Imperial and Pruſſian Majeſties, denouncing the projected invaſion of France, and the horrible deſign of carrying fire and ſword into that nation, and of ſlaughtering all citizens who ſhould have virtue to refuſe to turn traitors to their country, and to aid and aſſiſt their barbarian invaders, ſuch conduct appeared ſtrictly juſt, honourable, and humane to the pious monarchs of Europe; but when theſe tyrants were unexpectedly driven out of France, when the invincible energy of men ſtruggling for their rights, engaged in the cauſe of liberty and truth, compelled them to flight, and when afterwards, fluſhed with ſucceſs, they purſued the plan of retaliating juſtice, and

in

in their turn carried their arms into the territories of the enemy, inviting all nations to fraternize *with* them againſt that royal fraternity which had united *againſt* them, then the hue and cry was raiſed; all Europe muſt take up arms againſt the French; they were deſcribed as anarchiſts, monſters, devils, labouring to ſubvert all legal government, to confound all order, levellers of property, and to fill the climax, as enemies of all Kings. Thus, what ſeemed perfectly honourable on one ſide was conſtrued into unwarrantable invaſion, robbery, and ſacrilege on the other. At ſuch a criſis, to ſtop the circulation of truth, that paſſions and prejudices might have full ſcope, it became neceſſary that an embargo ſhould be immediately laid on the preſs; that ſacred Palladium of freedom was invaded by the moſt rigorous proſecutions; government ſtooped ſo low, was ſo cowardly in its fears, as to attack even bill-ſtickers and hawkers, ſome of whom are ſtill languiſhing in gaols. Aſſociations were formed by minions of the court, to prevent aſſociations amongſt the people. Every unfair

advantage

advantage was taken of that torrent of prejudice which had been raiſed; legions of ſpies and informers were ſet looſe on ſociety; magiſtrates employed theſe ſatellites to purchaſe obnoxious pamphlets, and then brought them forth as witneſſes to ſupport proſecutions againſt the innocent publiſher; * liberty of opinion was violated, and a particular bias attempted to be impoſed on private converſation. Such, let it be remembered, (it may one day be brought home to him,) was the infamous practice which prevailed in England under the adminiſtration of W——m P-tt, during which period every ſpecies of falſehood and treachery was protected and enforced by the authority of political government. The old iniquitous politics of Verſailles were to be engrafted on the conſtitution of Britain. But all prejudices and falſehoods have their

* On Eaton's trial, for publiſhing Paine's Letter to the Addreſſers, the evidence on which the proſecution was founded was on the information of a man ſuborned by the Chief Magiſtrate of what we are eternally told is the firſt city in the world, to buy the pamphlet. The informer with viſible reluctance gave his evidence; but he was bound to obey the inſtructions of his maſter.

æra

æra of detection; truth must eventually triumph over every adversary; let its sluices be once thrown wide open, its victory cannot fail to be compleat. Goverments that had the happiness of their subjects really in view, that were anxious above all things to inspire them with a love of independence and virtue, would be the most averse from imposing the least restraint to prevent an explicit avowal of their sentiments. Truth is uniform; and of all the different forms of government that exist there must be one best, and that best can only be the one where the advantages and comforts of life are most equally administered; and if an equal share of nature's benefits be desirable and good in itself, it must be so for you, and me, and all mankind. Can it be asserted that the actual system answers this description?

If there be a nation in the universe where its rulers have any other object than to render the people sober, just, and wise; —where it is required that they be *jockies*, *debauchees*, and *gamesters*, rather than men;

men; "*where the lover of truth and justice would be held in scorn and derision, and exposed to the severest penalties and punishments*; such a nation may be ripe for the chains of despotism;—but if there be not, then, liberty must every where be preferable to slavery, and the government of *impartiality*, better than that of random, tyranny, and caprice."* In this boasted land of liberty, however, strong symptoms of arbitrary power have lately shewn themselves. To illustrate this position.

If when pressed for an opinion, my lips should cowardly belie my heart, and meanly condescend to praise a system, which on a comprehensive survey of things, conviction tells me was partial and oppressive, although in so doing I should be both a hypocrite and a lyar, yet in lieu of being despised for my baseness, such is the happy temper of the present times amongst us, that I should be esteemed an honest and truly loyal subject. But if, on the contrary,

* Godwin on Political Knowledge.

I had courage to oppoſe the prejudices and paſſions of my hearers, and to promulgate my real ſentiments, to declare unequivocally in favour of liberty and equality, and to expreſs a very rational and warrantable doubt concerning the utility of Kings! then, the man who preſſed me to confidence, turns an informer againſt me; government encourages the information; a ſpecial jury appointed by an officer of the c-wn, the c-wn the plaintiff, is prepared, I am brought to trial, convicted, and my Judges on ſuch honourable and ſubſtantial proof of *guilt*, are ready in an inſtant to condemn me to their Baſtille, and to expoſe me on a pillory, to the wild fury of an infatuated rabble, that probably may be hired for the purpoſe of accompliſhing my deſtruction; and all this for what? for having exerciſed my own free judgment, and having preſumed to anſwer a premeditated queſtion, in what I conceived the language of truth. Again, when I am told from the moſt *reſpectable* authority; from thoſe who have an intereſt in ſaying ſo, that the Britiſh conſtitution

tion comprises within itself all that is wise, all that is excellent, all that is great and conducive to the public welfare; that it was matured to this ne plus ultra of perfection by the incomparable skill and ability of our omniscient and infallible ancestors; that the wisdom of antiquity precludes all possibility of further melioration, as if it were the miserable nature of man to degenerate, and not to improve; or as if the human mind was to be bound down by the chains of an eternal quietism, without another effort to enlarge the sphere of general happiness;—when I hear these pompous strains, I am apt to look around for living vouchers to confirm them; when alas! on a general survey, the picture is entirely reversed, symptoms of partiality, injustice and oppression are every where visible. Luxury and magnificence in one quarter, the most abject penury, and disease its attendant in another, temptation, irresistible to want, every where; and finally yielding to the impulse of conviction, if I should exclaim against such barbarous imposture, my truth is pronounced heresy and libel, and for the heinous guilt of speaking it, probably I shall soon be condemned an inmate of the above mentioned Bastille. There indeed, the evidence rises in still stronger energy; there, all doubts, if such there could be, become confirmations strong; there, on one side, sensibility sheds a benignant unavailing tear, over hundreds of young unhappy females, many, the deserted victims of brutal aristocratic lust, cast for transportation, some for seven years, some for fourteen, and others for their natural life, lost to society, cut off thus early from the enjoyments of the world, blaspheming their God, piercing the very walls with their shrieks, and imprecating curses on their merciless unrelenting persecutors. On another, we behold innumerable ferocious felons, still less savage then their ferocious keepers, rendered cruel from oppression, sacrifices to want, ignorance, and temptation, clashing their chains, and grinding their teeth in anguish, resentment and despair. In one melancholy secluded spot, we behold the solitary dungeons, where the patient ſacrifice condemned to die, in calm reſignation awaits the dire execution of inexorable law. In another quarter, we view numberleſs inſolvent debtors, groaning in hopeleſs miſery, abandoned to the caprice and malice of relentleſs diſappointed creditors.

Now in contemplating the happy effects of ſuch a ſyſtem, who can deny the juſtice of puniſhing thoſe who wantonly dare to recommend its reform, or to enforce the neceſſity of innovating on a government that generates ſuch bleſſed and glorious fruits? Here, however, let us pauſe.—It is not our deſign (we again repeat, well aware of the danger,) to queſtion the fundamental principles of this conſtitution; we keep at awful diſtance and revere its *wiſe* and *liberal* maxim, noli me tangere; but tremendous as the juriſdiction now exerciſed over the preſs may be, (although from ſome recent inſtances that have occurred, it appears that the people are awaking from their long ſlumber, and are at length about to aſſert their ſenſes, as well as their rights,) it ſhall not prevent us from freely pointing out thoſe vices, with a view to their correction, which can have no relation with a conſtitution, founded, as ours is ſaid to be, on the immortal principles of liberty;—vices which mutilate and deform it, ſo that it is no more like its original ſelf, (as Hamlet ſays) than I to Hercules. We wiſh to repair the mouldering edifice, on which the freedom, proſperity, and lives of citizens depend. Does it ſeem conſiſtent with the principle of juſtice, which we are eternally told is a grand characteriſtic of our conſtitution, and which ſhould form the baſis of all ſocial inſtitutions, becauſe one claſs of ſociety revels in luxury and ſuperfluities, enjoying all the advantages of knowledge, which education can beſtow; that another claſs ſhould be condemned for ever to wallow in the loathſome ſties of indigence, plunged in the depeeſt abyſs of brutiſh ignorance, expoſed to all thoſe dangerous temptations, which a conſtant ſpectacle of unbounded wealth and ſplendor neceſſarily

holds

holds forth to others reduced to the saddest extremities, some perhaps even wanting bread to support their existence? Ought there to be no medium between such violent extremes, as a preventive against those fatal consequences that must naturally be expected to result from them? Would it not be an outrage on common sense to aver, that the former class should have a right to constitute themselves as umpires, to arrogate a power of deciding in their own cause, on the excellence of a government, which yields to them all these exclusive benefits? Surely it would not be straining our argument too far, to admit, that a thief, when set on his defence for having burglariously entered the well-stored larder of a wealthy citizen, and for having taken from thence a fine fat capon or turkey, might, with more than equal propriety, plead his right, on the principle of hunger, to take what the rich man had *no occasion for*, to satisfy his own craving appetite, *that was famishing for want of it.* But here, folly and insensibility would vociferate,

rate,

răte, "Oh, in that caſe there is an end to all order; no ſecurity for property; all government is at once deſtroyed." No. The remedy is ſimple and obvious. Heſitate not to throw ſome little indulgence into the ſcale of poverty and labour. *Exalt* MAN to the rank, of which nature is ſuſceptible, reform your governments, and without confounding all gradations together, *reduce* them to a more juſt and equal level. Then, every inducement to ſuch violence is immdiately removed.

"Sublatâ cauſâ, tolletur effectus."

In our reverence for the original fabric of the Britiſh conſtitution, it does not follow that we are bound to indulge a blind rage of ſuperſtition, and to idolize thoſe polypuſes and rotten excreſcencies that have grown upon it. We are not thence tied down to venerate the corruption and profligate eſtabliſhment of courts, to approve thoſe unjuſt confederacies with foreign princes that now arm this nation againſt the rights of nations, or to grant the ſanction of praiſe

to

to the insatiate overbearing prerogative, under the vain qualification of the dignity of c—wns. As lovers of our constitution, we should be more jealous of its excellence, more anxious to preserve it free from blemishes, and fervent as our affection may be for pure representative governments, it is not to be deduced as a corollary, that we are attached to a system of representation, which depends on the nod of a court or its minions, where in the very teeth of an Act of Parliament, 12 William III. C. 2. that decrees, 'No person who holds an office of place or profit under the king, or receives a pension from the crown, shall be capable of serving as a member of the House of Commons,' in direct violation of that act, the House of Commons consists chiefly in persons of the above description, and where the duration of Parliaments is protracted to the length of seven years, although, conformably with the original constitution, annual Parliaments were the people's right.

The love of our conſtitution does not command us to reſpect the prevailing practice in regard to libels, and the criminal mode of proſecuting them by information, bearing not the leaſt analogy with its primæval ſpirit ; a barbarous practice that grew with the accurſed Star Chamber. All the learning *forced* upon us, de libellis famoſis, was borrowed, or rather tranſlated from that ſlaviſh Imperial law, commonly called the Civil, or Juſtinian Law. In our legal authorities, higher than the time of Elizabeth and Sir Edward Coke, nothing of it is to be found.

The love of our conſtitution does not call upon us to approve the doctrines of tythes, or to extol the injuſtice of our game laws, that vile relique of feudal tyranny, ſpringing from the foreſt laws of William the Norman ; in virtue of which, if a half famiſhed peaſant deſtroys a hare that devours the laſt ſolitary cabbage in his half rood of garden, intended as a ſcanty griping meal for himſelf and family, he is

ſubject

ſubject to a penalty of five pounds, or in default of payment, dragged inſtantly to gaol, there to linger, till he makes it good; while the privileged Squire, or ſtill more triumphant *my Lord*, may not only kill the hare in this cottager's garden, but may alſo purſue a fox with horſe and with hound to his very threſhold; breaking down all thoſe fences the poor man's induſtry had raiſed, as a ſecurity to his miſerable hovel. All this the great may do with impunity, to the utter ruin of the honeſt labourer, from the ſweat of whoſe brow their luxuries are ſupported, without expoſing themſelves to any penalty whatever. Yet theſe are the bleſſed *equal* laws which a learned Judge in the *ſincerity* of his ſoul tells his Grand Juries at Weſtminſter, know no diſtinction, the ſame to all; to the pooreſt and proudeſt. The falſehood is proved by the fact, and accumulates inſult on oppreſſion, but public credulity has given birth to the moſt monſtrous impoſitions. A candid ſtatement of *ſtrong facts* againſt *groundleſs aſſertions*, can never be conſtrued as a defamation of our courts.

Does the conſtitution ordain that we ſhould proſtrate ourſelves before the blood-ſtained altar of Moloch, and implore benedictions on the arm that ſmites us?—that we ſhould idolize a government, which expoſes myriads to the unneceſſary and deſperate hazard of famine or of ſlaughter, madly precipitating its ſubjects into the horrors of an aggreſſive and exterminating war, rather than wound the delicacy of regal pride by negociating with the executive council of an independent nation, that had, by the ſolemn and unanimous voice of its repreſentatives, *impartially* and *incorruptly* elected, aboliſhed royalty, and that ſtill ſmarting through the injuries which it had inflicted on them, had conſtituted themſelves into a REPUBLIC, formed on the nobleſt baſis of FREEDOM, and EQUALITY of RIGHTS.

Can our conſtitution require us to violate the eternal laws of nature and of juſtice, that we ſhould coaleſce with a banditti of Vandals to *force* on France a government,

vernment, which, after the fulleſt delibera-tion, ſhe had rejected; or otherwiſe, as is now the caſe in Poland, to diſmember and divide it amongſt themſelves, thus diſſolving the politicians charm; and what is inexpreſſibly more dreadful, aiding and abetting every ſpecies of robbery, violence, and tyrannous *uſurpation* *.

In

* Miniſters will conſider, and may poſſibly treat this publication as a libel, becauſe it ſerves to render their favourite WAR odious and unpopular. The author avows and glories in the motive, to check the career of injuſtice, and prevent the effuſion of blood. They may torture its advocate, but they can never alter the nature of TRUTH. The war begun in hypocriſy, it ſeems likely to end in ignominy and diſappointment. The pretended object in the beginning, in order to cajole the people into it, was the relief of our allies. It was natural therefore to conclude, that the end accompliſhed, negociation would follow; but it became neceſſary to aſſume another tone; we then were told, that it was too late to recede, that we had paſſed the rubicon, and that the dignity of the crown as well as the honour of the nation compelled us to yield every moſt effectual ſupport to the exterminating principles of our new allies, and that the war was to be proſecuted with the *utmoſt vigour* till we had obtained ample ſatisfaction and indemnity for the enormous expence we had thus volun-

In tenderneſs for our beloved conſtitution, where three *diſcordant* parts, of which it is compoſed, form one *harmonious* whole, it is natural to regard with ſuſpicion the eſtabliſhment of vaſt ſtanding armies, which the wiſe policy and patriotiſm of our anceſtors were wont to hold in ſo much jealouſy and terror, as inimical to the ſpirit of free governments. Their opinion was, 'That ſlavery followed a ſtanding army, as ſurely as the ſhadow follows the body.'* The whigs at the revolution remembered, (and they profited by the remembrance) the attempt of Charles I. and the ſucceſs of Cromwell to overthrow the conſtitution by means of an army—the plans of Charles II. his ſucceſſor, to accompliſh the ſame end with the ſame engine; and it had not eſcaped their obſervation,

voluntarily and gallantly incurred. Alas! the period of indemnity ſeems far diſtant, and it is to be feared the ſad reſult will be the intire ruin and ſlaughter of millions, and an additional load of taxation, wringing the laſt hard-earned morſel from the jaws of poverty and labour.

* Dalrymple's Memoirs.

that

that almoſt all the ſurrounding nations, one after another, had loſt their liberties in conſequence of the dangerous power that ſtanding armies conferred on princes. So rooted were they in this grand conſtitutional principle, that in the year 1699 they diſbanded all the troops in England, except 7000; nor could all the direct ſupplications, or indirect manœuvres of King William, notwithſtanding his popularity, engage the Parliament of that day to depart from its reſolution. In our times, Parliaments through the magic incantations of the c—wn, in virtue of *implicit confidence*, are far better trained to loyalty and obedience.

In our conſtitution, we learn to abhor, the vexation and tyranny of exciſe laws,* where the quiet, property, and liberty of a citizen, are left to the diſcretion of ruffian invaders, armed with legal authority; while

* The lenity of exciſe laws may be well imagined, by tracing the derivation of the word exciſe, to the latin verb, 'excidere,' which literally ſignifies, 'to cut up by the roots.'

the

the citizen, whofe dwelling at the dead midnight hour has been ranfacked, is precluded from all benefit of a trial by jury, that noble inftitution, fo excellent in theory, fo abufed in practice, and thus cut off from all hope or chance of redrefs.

The love of our conftitution does not authorize the patriot to give his fanction to the fubfidizing of foreign troops, to thofe contracts formed with Serene Princes for the purchafe of human flefh ;—to the horrors of a flave trade ; nor are they thence obliged to acknowledge the equity of paying five or fix pounds for an habeas corpus, which we are told is the peoples' legitimate birth-right, free of all expence whatever.

It is not congenial with our conftitution, that we fhould declare a blind approbation of laws, bearing no analogy with its fpirit ; laws, which from their prolixity and tautology, one hundred folio volumes are far unequal to contain, and which from their intricacy (where the fwinifh multitude are told

told their peculiar excellence consists) the clearest genius cannot unravel, (although it is a legal and humane maxim, 'Ignorantia Juris neminem excusat,) and in definition of which laws the learned Doctors themselves generally disagree, so that from this glorious uncertainty, which creates prolific diversion for our courts, an unbounded field is opened for fraud and extortion; and our legal processes, from the enormous expence and delays attending them, unknown to a similar degree in all other countries, frustrate every purpose of equity, totally depriving the poor man of all the means of obtaining it.*

The love of our constitution does not warrant an approbation of those unintelligible statutes, that like the sphynx of anti-

* The constitution expresly says, that justice without delay and free of expence shall be denied to no man.' The candid reader must decide how far the practice agrees with the principle.

quity, ſpeak in parables, and then devour the wretches who are unable to comprehend them; nor of thoſe draconian laws, that inflict death for very trivial offences, which have their origin in the vices of our political inſtitutions;—for letting fiſh out of a pond, cutting down an apple tree, for *privately* ſtealing five ſhillings, &c. &c. The queſtion is not how often, or how ſeldom theſe laws are executed; the fact is, they are always ready to be executed, ſo that we are left to the mercy of the King, for that to which we have an undoubted right, in virtue of our conſtitution, which declares, "that exceſſive or cruel puniſhments ſhall not be inflicted."

There exiſts no obligation in our regard for the *conſtitution*, whereby we are to approve thoſe modern ſtatutes that deprive citizens of their natural and *conſtitutional* rights, not ſuffering them to leave the kingdom without the licence in due form of his Majeſty and the privy ſeal; 'ſuch offence to

be

be deemed a misdemeanour, *punishable at discretion.*' *

In whatever light such statutes are considered, they strike us as a direct attack on the liberty of the subject, establishing a tyrannical extra judicial power in the Privy Council, superior to the laws, unknown to the constitution. They are a violent encroachment on Magna Charta, where it is enacted, 'That it shall be lawful for every one to go out of this kingdom, and safely to return by land and by water, &c.' Thus they at once annul the contract which existed between the Kings of England and the people, and violate the fundamental law of the land.

These comments in this age may be deemed libel; but if they be so, Magna Charta is a libel, for it is from thence that they are drawn.

* Vide the Attorney General's Bill for preventing Traiterous Correspondence.

We have already fully ſhewn, that while it is held unlawful and dangerous to attempt the leaſt innovation in favour of the liberty of the people, it is perfectly lawful and right to violate the original principles of the conſtitution itſelf, in order to increaſe the prerogative, and ſtrengthen the powers of the c—wn. But without daring to impeach the *original* excellence of our heterogeneous conſtitution, an intention we have uniformly diſclaimed, the wiſeſt men have acknowledged its errors.

Lord Buchan tells us, that in a converſation which he held ſeveral years ago with the late Lord Chatham, aſking what at laſt would become of poor Old England, ſo ſtupidly infatuated to the imperfection of her own government, the latter replied, 'Oh my dear Sir, the gout will diſpoſe of me ſoon enough to prevent me from feeling the reſult of this infatuation; but before the end of the preſent century, either Parliament will reform itſelf from within, or it will be reformed with a vengeance from without.'

Lord Buchan then makes this brief comment, ' Pythonic ſpeech, ſoon to be verified.'

To praiſe is one thing, to deſerve it another. The ſureſt indeed, the only criterion of judgment that can be formed on any ſyſtem, depends on the comparative benefits or injuries which it yields. The Britiſh conſtitution certainly owes much of its reputation to a compariſon with the deſpotiſm of other European governments, and thence ſtill further increaſed by the partial report of foreign writers. But it ſhould operate as a conſiderable drawback on our national enthuſiaſm, when the calamities in which this country has been eternally involved, under her ſo much boaſted government, are remembered. When we reflect, that ſince the revolution of 1688, we have been ſix times at war with Spain, and ſix times at war with France; not to mention two rebellions at home, with the black and endleſs catalogue of murders in America and the Eaſt Indies; from which infernal

infernal causes, originate the distresses and prodigious number of our poor, for whose support, two millions sterling, even in times of peace, appear a very inadequate provision,* the consequent enormous public debt, all contracted since the above period, producing an intolerable weight of taxation, that at once impoverishes, and by means of depression, enslaves the people. † It ought to awaken our country from

* If in times of profound peace, two millions annually did not suffice for the maintenance of our poor, should the present system be allowed to continue, what must the increase very soon be from the swarms of mechanics and manufacturers thrown out of all employment?

† There are selfish, hard-hearted wretches who will tell us, "that the *greatness* of Brittain grew with, and still depends on their debt," curse on such greatness, that consists in the deleterious splendor of foreign conquests, atchieved by the slaughter and ruin of millions, for no other purpose than to increase the revenue, to swell the power, or gratify the ambition of Kings; while an enormous addition of impost is thereby inflicted, drained from the sweat of hardest labour, and which creates that fund of poverty and wretchedness through the country amongst the lower classes, unfelt only by the vile pandars of a court, or by those blood-suckers who flourish and press on the miseries, which their favourite system produces,

its

its dream, to ſtagger that ſuperſtition with which it has been ever wont to bend before its idol, when on a fair eſtimate it is evident, that the number of perſons maſſacred in thoſe deadly quarrels, have, on the whole, exceeded twenty millions, which may be rated at two hundred thouſand acts of homicide a year; all which victims, contrary to the voice and intereſts of humanity, have been immolated, to feed the vanity, avarice, ambition, or revenge of courts. 'In Europe alone; (leaving the preſent mad and guilty war wholly out of the queſtion) the number of perſons that periſhed in thoſe battles, amounts at leaſt to three million; thus cut off in the bloom of life, whoſe deſcendants in the progreſs of domeſtic ſociety, muſt have ſwelled into multitudes beyond calculation.'*

All theſe examples, however, added to the many already deſcribed, have been ſtill inſufficient to cure the madneſs of war. The

* Political Progreſs of Brittain.

nation

nation that had laid down in her conſtitutional code, the principle of peace, anxious to deliver it as a grand example to the preſent age and as an ineſtimable legacy to poſterity, was not allowed to practice it. Such an innovation would have been dangerous to the ſplendor and deſpotiſm of royal and imperial palaces. The *virtue* of courts depends for ſupport on the *virtue* of vaſt military eſtabliſhments.

In the courſe of this work, whoſe object is to enforce truth, as the ſure antidote againſt all thoſe evils which embitter human life, to awaken Engliſhmen from thoſe fatal prejudices which pervert their underſtanding, making the worſt appear the better cauſe, to animate their ſenſibility, and to open their conviction, we have ſtated facts in oppoſition to aſſertion, and conſcious, however violent the torrent of deluſion and prejudice has been, or ſtill may be, that the cauſe of truth muſt ultimately prevail, if ſeconded by zeal and perſeverance in its advocates, it would be

cowardice

cowardice to desist. Neverthersess, certain it is, that things at present amongst us flow in a polluted channel, but all error from its nature is perishable.

What must be the degraded, the real character of a Senate, which constitutes one capital branch of a government, where vice is seen to triumph over virtue, where consistency and patriotism are held in scorn and mockery; the basest apostacy protected and advanced to the highest office in the State?—Where the sacred glow of eloquence which truth inspires from the lips of a Lansdowne or a Stanhope, strikes no other sensation than *extreme cold** on the already frozen breast of impenetrable lawyers? where a ———— indifferent to principle, ever at command of that cause, or of that party, where he imagines his interest to consist, confident in his numbers,

* An expression applied by ———— to Lord Stanhope, in one of his speeches towards the conclusion of the Sessions of P?rliament, 1793.

assumes a lofty tone of superiority, and openly as insolently scoffs at and derides all that is great, all that is virtuous, in that assembly? while the vast difference between these men, rests in the most opposite extremes. One derives his whole fortune from the vices and miseries of his fellow creatures;* the fortune of the others is uniformly employed in labours to correct the system which generates those vices, and in most benevolent exertions to remove their misfortunes.—When the fences of reason and truth are thus broken down; what public good can be expected to result from the deliberations of such a senate? What national evils may not be expected, so long as this reign of delusion shall last?

To pursue the argument still further. If enveloped in the full majesty of wig,

* The Chancellor of England has fourteen guineas for every commission of bankruptcy which he signs, and for several months past they have amounted on an average to fifty per week. Is it then to be wondered at, that his disinterested Lordship should be so sincere and zealous in his approbation of the actual system?

and

and ſtudiouſly dreſſed out in the impoſing paraphernalia of office, wherein all his wiſdom and virtue generally conſiſt, when a Judge delivers from the bench, the moſt glaring falſehood, aſſerting (as we have already had occaſion to obſerve the fallacy cannot be too often or too indignantly ſcouted,) 'That the laws of England know no diſtinction; that they are alike favourable to all, the richeſt and the pooreſt;' if I inſenſible to the virtue of that wig or of thoſe venerable robes, preſume to analize his aſſertion, and thence convict him of this falſehood; not by the production of fallible evidence, but from poſitive ſtated FACTS proving the reverſe; that theſe laws are altogether in favour of the rich, oppreſſive and grinding to the poor, who from the ſcandalous expence attending their adminiſtration, are neceſſarily deprived of all benefit from them; that preſs warrants and the game laws are a violent and barbarous encroachment on the rights of the latter, fatal to their lives and their liberties; that tythes and taxes fall infinitely the heavieſt on them, who in ſtrict juſtice, ought to be exempt from their operation, ſince they had no ſhare in the cauſes which inflicted them, derivable ſolely from the profuſion, inſenſibility, and ruthleſs ambition of courts, or from the rapacity of churchmen. That teſts, excluſions and reſtrictions are impoſed on the diſſenters, who are in general the moſt enlightened and meritorious members of the community. When alſo it is notorious, that the poor, even ſuppoſing them to inherit every eminent quality, are ineligible to the duties of citizenſhip, that they are precluded from the ſatisfaction of ſerving their country in the ſenate, or of exerciſing the right of ſuffrage in favour of the perſon they would prefer for their repreſentative, thus evincing no reſpect for patriotiſm, genius, or talents, but rendering every other conſideration ſubſervient to wealth, on which the qualification of citizenſhip is made to depend. What muſt be the degraded condition of ſociety amongſt a people, where on ſuch principles, a Judge ſhall be extolled and looked up to as an ORTHODOX SAINT, for having propagated a falſehood, while I am proſcribed, and condemned to the pillory and a dungeon, or perhaps baniſhed from my country, as a libelliſt and a rebel, for having aſſerted the truth?

Can there be imagined, in complete refutation of this GREAT JUDGE's aſſertion, a more deciſive teſtimony of unequal laws, a more violent ſtretch of tyranny, than to call men together for the purpoſe of electing a delegate, and at the ſame time to prohibit them from conferring their ſuffrages on him who to them appears beſt qualified for the truſt? Such excluſion aſſerts man to be of leſs value than his property. 'It tells him, your moral and intellectual qualifications may be tranſcendantly great, but you have not enough of the means of luxury and vice. To the non-elector, it holds a ſtill more deteſtable language. It ſays, you are poor, you are unfortunate; the inſtitutions of ſociety oblige you to be eternal witneſſes

of

of the ſuperfluities of others; becauſe you are ſunk thus low, we will trample you ſtill lower; you ſhall not even be reckoned in the liſts for men, you ſhall be paſſed by as thoſe, of whom ſociety makes no account, and whoſe welfare and moral exiſtence, ſhe diſdains to recollect.' *

In ſuch caſes, all the ſacred maxims of reaſon and equity are outrageouſly violated, but it would ſeem as if they were held as crimes in a government, where their moſt zealous champions are expoſed to the ſevereſt puniſhments.

In thus vindicating their cauſe, I ſhall excite the ſtupid clamours of ignorance, and may poſſibly draw down on myſelf, the vindictive rancour and perſecution of deſpotiſm; but ſhould that be my fate, I ſhall ſubmit without a murmur, and with heartfelt ſatisfaction, if from my exertions or my ſufferings, any ſuperior degree of

* Godwin concerning Political Knowledge, vol. ii. p. 682.

hap-

happineſs may finally reſult for the reſt of my fellow citizens.

The conſequences of this temporary infatuation, this monſtrous perverſion, that have been deſcribed, are now writing in the blood of our ſlaughtered ſoldiers abroad, and in the intire ruin of numbers of our deluded unhappy countrymen at home.

Affairs every hour aſſume a more tremendous aſpect. Bankruptcies of a moſt alarming nature, unbounded in their extent, multiply through the nation, and they muſt continue to multiply, as long as the war ſhall be continued, till the whole community will be affected by the iſſue. The preſent unexampled price of proviſions is not only intolerable to the poor, but is ſenſibly felt by the middle claſſes, and it will neceſſarily increaſe, while the wages of induſtry and labour muſt of courſe be lowered, from the unavoidable ſtagnation in every ſpecies of commerce. Thus, the indigent and laborious are driven to the climax

climax of wretchedneſs, which may find vent in the moſt violent acts of rage and deſperation. Already by theſe bankruptcies, (ſpite of the miniſter's impudent aſſertion) the conſequence of this war, thouſands of artizans, labourers, and manufacturers, are deprived of all employment. We daily hear of the moſt deſperate ſuicides being committed. Every day produces new inſtances of the fallacy and miſchief of our HEAVENBORN STATESMAN's financial ſpeculations; but an alien to ſenſibility, he has not a ſoul to feel for the confuſion, deaths, and ruin, he has created.—For the numbers, whom thro' their infatuation to his plauſibility and deceptions, he has reduced from affluence to want;—for the myriads he has nailed to the very center of deſpair. The traitor of public confidence, as he ever has been from the beginning, ſo will he continue to the end, affecting to trace theſe misfortunes from other cauſes, ſtill throwing out the bait, to catch freſh gudgeons, his inſatiate appetite not yet gorged with the multitude he has devoured.

What

What muſt be the effrontery, the apathy of that man, while his conſcience ought to groan under the weight of reflection and remorſe, who, in an hour like this, his country engaged in the moſt critical, deſperate, and eventful war, with a view to extend his impoſitions ſtill further, to ruin more credulous and ignorant men, to reconcile the nation to his horrors, was inſolent and daring enough in open ſenate, to eſtimate the revenue for the enſuing years, on an average of the four laſt years, when it was ſwelled beyond all probability, by a variety unforeſeen events ? by the diſtractions in other parts of Europe, by many years of peace at home, all the enjoyments and bleſſings of which that might have been ſecured, he has now madly abandoned, and by the encouragement which he afforded to the fictitious opulence of circulating paper ?

In taking ſuch an average, he is guilty of wilful premeditated fraud, adapted merely to the temper of the times, to the ignorance

rance and credulity of IMPLICIT CONFIDENCE, the ſandy foundation on which his empire reſts. How in the name of common ſenſe is it poſſible to take the average of four proſperous years of peace, as the calculation of his eſtimate for the current year? With what ſincerity or prudence can he rely on ſuch calculation, we leave for the ſober judgment of rational and impartial men to decide. During the above period, England was the general magazine of almoſt every commercial nation, and her manufactures, conſequently the revenue in all its branches were increaſed to a vaſt amount, particularly by the ſpecious, but eventually ruinous circulation of paper, beyond its capital, bearing a productive ſtamp, which the preſent war has entirely deſtroyed. Thus, one chief favourite ſource of the revenue is at once cut up, and can it be imagined that we ſhall have more of the carrying trade, when the flower of our ſeamen is otherwiſe employed? Will our manufactures be encouraged with more alacrity and vigour, as money

becomes

becomes ſcarcer? Will the demand for theſe manufactures be increaſed, in conſequence of an almoſt general war, which muſt naturally produce a general inability to pay for them? Or will an intire prohibition of them in France augment the conſumption.

In a word, notwithſtanding his unfair deluſive ſtatement, he is obliged to eſtimate the war expence for the current year at above ſix millions, to be raiſed by a *moderate decent* loan bearing *only* eight per cent. premium. Let the iſſue therefore be as favourable to his *juſt* and *honourable* deſigns, as the moſt ſanguine or perverted imagination can anticipate, what advantage are the people of England to reap in compenſation, for a wanton ſacrifice of their countrymen's blood, and for all this conſumption of treaſure? It may, agreeably with the r-y-l ſyſtem, conduce to the glory of our arms; but it cannot fail to aggravate the miſeries and wants of the nation, and if the preſent loan bears a premium of 8 per cent. ſhould the war be protracted,

 we

we believe the minister, skilled as he is in prophecy and calculation, would be puzzled to foretel the terms to which he will be reduced in the next.

Perhaps, in the mean time, misfortune may operate a change in the public mind, when the people will discover they have been duped, and will be lost in amazement at their own weakness and facility, in having yielded to the infamous schemes of pretended necessity, disguising the real views of avarice, jealousy, ambition, and revenge.

The dire effects of this war in which the r-y-l fraternity have now precipitated Europe, and the obligations for which we are indebted to them, have been candidly stated. The principle that originally formed this honourable league is obvious, but there has arisen another grand object ultimately to be atchieved.

It were folly to ſuppoſe that his IMPERIAL MAJESTY would regard with indifference the aggrandizement of his neighbours, by their uſurpations in Poland, unleſs he anticipated an ample indemnity for his complaiſance, in being permitted hereafter to enjoy a capital ſhare in the rich ſpoils of conquered France; nor is it to be preſumed that the prudent cabinet of England would remain a calm obſerver of ſuch robbery, if it did not look forward to an increaſe of revenue and of influence in a ſimilar compenſation, probably in being allowed peaceably to enjoy a future poſſeſſion of the preſent French colonies in the Eaſt and Weſt Indies. But may all ſuch infernal confederacies end as they ought to do, in defeat and diſappointment.

The cauſe of truth to which peace and happineſs are attached, muſt be eventually victorious, and may the RIGHTS of MEN fix an invincible ſtandard on the wreck of VANQUISHED DESPOTISM. Whenever the ſcience of government ſhall be extricated

extricated from its preſent intricate and myſterous forms, truth will ſhine forth, and the real happineſs of man abſtracted from all metaphyſical perplexity or legal ſophiſtry, be ſhewn to conſiſt merely in the ſimple principle of obedience to the pure decrees of reaſon and juſtice. Had legiſlators been half as judicious in propagating virtue, or in removing the temptations to vice, by the formation of more equal ſyſtems, as they have been ingenious in diſcovering the means of depraving mankind, the world at this day, inſtead of a butchery, might have been a Paradiſe.

The author animated by the pureſt intentions, has communicated his thoughts with freedom. He has endeavoured to illuſtrate and give energy to his arguments, by the ſtrongeſt examples, by irreſiſtible facts, and as a protection againſt the baſe and numerous herd of courtiers and their ſatellites, that will be ready to pour forth their gall againſt him, and perhaps to cruſh him with their power, he ſhall endeavour to to ſeek a ſhelter under the authority of an illuſtrious patriot, the IMMORTAL LOCKE.

'He who labours to blind the people and to keep them from inſtruction; may be juſtly ſuſpected of ſedition and diſaffection; but he who makes it his buſineſs to open the underſtanding of mankind, by laying before them the true principles of government, cuts up all ſedition by the roots.'

FINIS.

POSTSCRIPT.

AN attentive reader will diſcover ſome trifling anachroniſims in this publication; but they no ways affect its general plan. The beginning, as far as relates to Dumourier, was written ſome months ago. The remainder was undertaken and finiſhed within the ſpace of the laſt ten days.

July 31, 1793.

PEACE AND REFORM,

AGAINST

WAR AND CORRUPTION.

[Price Two Shillings and Sixpence.]

PEACE AND *REFORM*,

AGAINST

WAR AND CORRUPTION.

IN

ANSWER TO A PAMPHLET,

WRITTEN

BY ARTHUR YOUNG, ESQ. ENTITLED,

"The EXAMPLE of FRANCE, A WARNING to BRITAIN."

"I ſhall always have the Satisfaction to have aimed ſincerely "at Truth and Uſefulneſs, though in one of the meaneſt Ways."

LOCKE.

LONDON:

PRINTED FOR J. RIDGWAY, YORK STREET, ST. JAMES'S SQUARE.

MDCCXCIV.

PEACE AND REFORM,

AGAINST

WAR AND CORRUPTION.

AN attentive perufal of many political Pamphlets, produced in the beginning of the prefent year, and an opinion that it would not be difficult to expofe the fallacy of the arguments upon which were founded the moft popular of thofe written againft the Caufe of Freedom, led me firft to think of attempting their refutation; and fome leifure during the autumn months, enabled me to try what I had previoufly wifhed to have feen done by any abler hand. I have efpoufed that fide which is, for the moment, the leaft popular; and obfcure as both this Pamphlet and its Author may be, I am therefore prepared to expect fome fmall fhare of that obloquy, which is now fo largely beftowed on all thofe who prefume to queftion the wifdom of the meafures of government. Secured from danger by power, and uncontradicted by reafon, becaufe of the danger, the advocates of Corruption have of late exulted, almoſt unoppoſed, in their triumph. The moſt moderate Favourers of Reform have been blended with the moſt inſane Zealots for Revolution; Toleration and Atheiſm; Peace and Regicide, have, by the ſupporters of abuſes, been wickedly deemed, and by the multitude weakly believed, to be ſynonimous terms.

The national underſtanding thus miſled and prejudiced; the temper of a very great majority of the People rendered furious and vindictive; the partizans and the partakers of Corruption bold, active, and cruel; the current has been, from neceſſity, ſuffered of late to run wholly in favour of the moſt abſolute Toryiſm. Few men would enter on a labour ſo perilous and unacceptable as that of expoſing the Deluſion. To incur odium from the many for the approbation of the already approving few; to write cramped up as much as if pinioned in the Pillory, leſt it ſhould actually be the reward; to oppoſe reaſon to paſſion, and be certain of being unſucceſsful, whether right or wrong, were conſiderations ſufficient to intimidate Prudence by the danger of the attempt, and by its hopeleſsneſs, even to ſilence the moſt honeſt Zeal in the cauſe of Freedom.

Accordingly the Preſs laſt winter was much more occupied by Tory or High Church and King opinions, than two years before it had been by thoſe of an oppoſite deſcription. Their abundance was even greater than the harveſt which followed the labours of Mr. Burke; and although their arguments may be futile and ridiculous, they cannot fully be anſwered, while

New-

Newgate and the Pillory are called in to support them.

The firſt Pamphlet that ſuggeſted to me the idea of endeavouring to expoſe theſe exploded, inconſiſtent, miſchievous, Doctrines, was, that of Mr. Arthur Young. Several reaſons induced me to think it a proper object of animadverſion; for, although on the firſt peruſal it appeared to be ſuch a jumble of contradictions, falſehoods, and even libels on that Conſtitution which it profeſſed to defend, that I did not believe common ſenſe could endure it; yet on reading the approbation of Mr. Reeves, and finding it had been circulated with great induſtry, I concluded it might be of ſome uſe to refute what I thought ſo ſuſceptible of refutation; and while the apparent eaſineſs of the taſk ſeemed to ſet its accompliſhment within my reach, an object ſo inglorious did not promiſe to provoke a Rival. Mr. Reeves has, by his approbation, adopted its opinions as his own, and, however worthleſs it may be in itſelf, it no doubt derives ſome conſequence from being thus promulgated as the Manifeſto of his Committee.

Its deſign is to deter us from making a Parliamentary Reform, by exciting our horror at the atrocities which have taken place in France; theſe atrocities Mr. Young falſely aſcribes to the principles of Liberty; and aſſerts, that Engliſhmen would be equally guilty with their neighbours, if once they began political improvement. With *Reform* he connects *Property*; and attempts to eſtabliſh as a fact, that a government more purely repreſentative than our own is at preſent, could not long exiſt without an Agrarian Law;

 thus

thus, deceitfully alarming all men of wealth and advising them to join in the war against the French, as the only means of preserving whatever they hold dear. To follow him regularly through every falsehood and absurdity would neither be entertaining nor useful. I shall therefore begin with some specimens of his unfairness: I shall shew that the crimes of France, so far from having any natural connection with her principles, are the very same which the rage of Faction has led the Friends of War and Corruption in England, if not to perpetrate, at least to recommend in support of Principles directly opposite; and which, if admitted to be proof against the principles of French Liberty, must also be proof against the principles of Mr. Young, and the other English Tories, as the blind advocates of each system equally applaud them. After having discussed these preliminary matters, I shall proceed to the consideration of the two great questions of Reform and Peace, against which Mr. Young and his fellow-labourers have raised so many prejudices.

His disingenuousness is evident at the commencement of his book, the very foundation of which is laid on palpable misrepresentation. He owns himself to have been a "warm friend" to the first Revolution, yet the chief part of his industry is employed in condemning Mr. Paine, Major Cartwright, &c. for their writings in defence of it. He reprobates them for having done what he himself did, yet he does not own he did wrong. Had he like others repented his mistake and made his recantation, he then, with a better grace, might have attacked those with whom he formerly had agreed; and, like Mr. Pitt in the laſt debate on Parliamentary Reform, might have maintained, that conſiſtency was a proof of a want of judgment, and that it was always to be preſumed thoſe were in an error who did not change their opinion.

"The Revolution before the 10th of Au-" "guſt" (ſays Mr. Young), "was as different" "from the Revolution after that day as light" "from darkneſs; as clearly diſtinct in prin-" "ciple and practice as Liberty and Slavery." "The ſame principles which directed me to" "approve the Revolution in its commence-" "ment, the principles of *real Liberty*, led me" "to deteſt it after the 10th of Auguſt." Here he aſſerts his approbation of the Revolution *up to* the 10th of Auguſt, which he acknowledges was conducted, till that period, on the principles of *real Liberty*; and he alſo ſays in the ſame page, "How little reaſon therefore" "to reproach me with ſentiments *contrary* to" "thoſe I publiſhed before the 10th of Auguſt;—" "I am *not* changeable, but ſteady and con-" "ſiſtent."

Compare this with page 21, where, in ſpeaking of the Revolution, he affirms, "it has" "brought more miſery, poverty, devaſtation," "impriſonment, bloodſhed and ruin, on France," "in *four years*, than the old government" "did in a century."—If the "*principles* and" "*practice* of the Revolution up to the 10th of" "Auguſt were conformable with real liberty," how could they have brought miſery, poverty, &c. on France for *four years?* How comes it that he approves the devaſtation, bloodſhed, and ruin *before* the 10th of Auguſt and yet diſapproves of them afterwards ?—But it is in fact the old Deſpotiſm he contends for, which (p. 33) he calls " the mildeſt and moſt benignant go-" vernment in Europe, our own only excepted; " a government cruelly libelled in the cha-" racter given by one of our reforming " Orators."—Mr. Young, however, libels it ſtill more in his own Travels, publiſhed long after the Revolution, where, ſpeaking of the natural richneſs of the country, he ſays " the diſpenſa-" tions of Providence ſeem to have permitted " the human race to exiſt only as the prey of " Tyrants, as it has made pidgeons for the prey " of hawks."—" Oh! if I were a legiſlator of " France, I would make ſuch great lords ſkip " again!"—Yet this is the government which he now calls " regular and mild." *—I would not quote theſe paſſages, if Mr. Young had owned his approbation of the firſt Revolution had been miſplaced: But, on the contrary, he affirms he is " ſteady and conſiſtent."

Mr. Paine's works he treats as if they had been written and publiſhed ſince the 10th of Auguſt, 1792. The panegyrics contained in " The Rights of Man" on the Conſtitution of 1789,—A conſtitution of which Mr. Young declares his unaltered approbation, are falſely and artfully tortured into panegyrics on the Convention, and the events that have taken place ſince the deſtruction of monarchy. For inſtance, he gives part of a ſpeech of Marat in January 1793, wherein the Convention is called

* P. 49.

" a ſcandalous

" a ſcandalous ſpectacle—an aſſembly of mad-" men and furies," and immediately follows it by obſerving, that " Paine is of a contrary " opinion, he ſaid they debate in the language " of gentlemen; their dignity is ſerene, &c." Theſe paſſages in Paine were publiſhed long before the 10th of Auguſt; and with equal juſtice might the eulogiums of Mr. Burke, on the character of the French people, prior to 1789, be quoted as eulogiums on the maſſacres of the ſecond of September.

But Mr. Young's reaſonings are not more inconſiſtent with the opinions he pretends to entertain, than they are with each other, for " The example of France, a warning to Britain" may not improperly be called " the example " of France an example to Britain." It reproaches the French with deſtroying the Liberty of the Preſs, and adviſes the very ſame thing to be done in England; it condemns the principle of arming one claſs of men againſt another, and ſoon afterwards ſets forth the neceſſity of following the example here, by arming the rich againſt the poor; and the violation of the freedom of election at Paris is held up to deriſion, while corruption and preſcriptive election in England are applauded as the true foundation of national proſperity. Indeed he is not ſingular in theſe blunders, for bloodſhed and rapine would be equally practiſed in this country as in France, if we may take the *will* for the *deed*. Here the theory has been inſtilled and admired; there the practice has been adopted. And the only difference between the French and Engliſh Marats,—a difference which

does

does not diminiſh their guilt,—is, that the one would aſſaſſinate all who deny, and the other would aſſaſſinate all who maintain the ſovereignty of the people.

The faults of the Convention, of public bodies, and even of individuals, are carefully collected and detailed as the deliberate acts not only of thoſe who rule in France, but of the whole nation. The moſt falſe aſſertion or the moſt wicked counſel, though coming from an inſignificant fool, or diſregarded madman, is ſufficient to excite Mr. Young's execration, and to criminate a whole people. How little leſs guilty can the reaſonable part of mankind think this kingdom, if their judgment is formed in the ſame manner. Crimes equally deteſtable have been preached and vindicated in this country, by perſons of eminent ſtation; and if the ſanguinary ſcenes of Paris have not been repeated in London, Mancheſter, and Birmingham, it is not for the want of Britiſh Marats, and Roberſpierre's to inſtigate and protect the inſtruments. If aſſaſſination is to be committed, it is indifferent to me who are the objects, or what are the motives;—whether the victim be a plunderer of the poor induſtrious Swiniſh Multitude, or of pampered tyrannical Nobles, and lazy miſchievous Prieſts. The offence is as heinous in the one caſe as in the other; and juſtice might be as much violated, were Marat or Roberſpierre, as if Windham or Burke were to be murdered with impunity.

As a companion to Mr. Young's ſhocking picture of France, I ſhall give the outline of a propoſed one in England. But if my colouring is not ſo bold as his, it muſt be accounted for by the peculiar circumſtances under which I write, rather than in the weakneſs of my ſubject. What he ſays of Chabot, Roberſpierre, or Danton, it may be dangerous to ſay of a prieſt, a counſellor, or a judge in England. He might decorate his tales with the moſt glaring falſehood and rancorous calumny, and be in uniſon with the nation and in favour with the government. The diſapprobation of the firſt, and reſentment of the ſecond, might be my lot, were I to indulge equally in much better grounded invective. His reaſoning is enforced by aids which it would be imprudent, probably dangerous, for me to uſe; for when it is difficult to demonſtrate his argument, or ſuſtain his aſſertion, he attacks humanity with a pike, a dagger, or a guillotine, and, addreſſing himſelf to the feelings, inſtead of the underſtanding, triumphantly exults in his abſurdity and falſehood.

If "Marat's grand ſpecific of cutting off "* 150,000 heads" be compared with Mr. Reeves's "exceſs of virtue to exterminate the "Diſſenters,†" which ſhall, we think, moſt criminal? There are more than 150,000 diſſenting heads in Britain, therefore Mr. Reeves outdoes Marat; but, on the other hand, we muſt recollect that he does it in a more delicate manner. Marat ſpoke roundly out; Mr. Reeves only *inſinuates*. Marat's, however, were words,

* Young p. 69.

† Vide the *original* publication of Thomas Bull to John Bull, owned and apologized for by Mr. Reeves; and alſo the Comments of Mr. Fox in his Speech, Dec. 13, 1792.

and might have been the ebullition of the moment, but Mr. Reeves's was a deliberate act, which, from its nature, must have been considered and approved by a body of men, the Crown and Anchor Committee. In whatever way we compare these two circumstances, we shall find them nearly on a par; but their effects in this country were very different. Marat's advice has been the theme of horror in every company, though it did not extend to them; on the contrary, Mr. Reeves's has been little noticed, though there are very few persons who have not some friends among the dissenters, and consequently were affected by it. The more we examine the characters of these two gentlemen, the greater similarity we shall find between them. How far they have been justly rewarded, I shall not pretend to decide: Mr. Reeves, besides enjoying about half a dozen places under government, has lately been paid between three and four thousand pounds—Marat has been assassinated.

Mr. Reeves, in his "reflections on the present crisis," says, "it would be well if those who dislike the English Constitution would remove to another region." What decree of the Convention would occasion emigration more certainly than this sentiment, if it had the power? And Judge Ashhurst, in his charge to the grand jury on the 19th of November, 1792, at the very moment the decree of fraternity was passing in France, declared, "there have, however, under the best systems of government, been found men of corrupt principles, who, having forsaken honest industry, wish

"wiſh to throw every thing into confuſion, and "to live by rapine and plunder; when that is "the caſe, it is become neceſſary for the coer- "cive power of the ſtate to lend its reſtrain- "ing hand, and to puniſh offences of ſuch a "flagrant nature. There is no proſpect of "reformation, till ſuch *corrupt members* be "*cut off* *." The wide ſenſe which would be given to the laſt expreſſion by the inflamed populace, among whom this charge was liberally diſtributed, it is not very difficult to imagine.

The Faſt Day, inſtead of being paſſed in conformity with its profeſſed purpoſe, in humiliation before God, in prayers for the converſion of unbelievers, the reformation of ourſelves, and the general peace and happineſs of mankind; inſtead of a day on which every prieſt made an extraordinary exertion of his powers in imploring the benevolence of the Almighty to enlighten the minds, to ſoften the hearts, and to ſpare the blood of his people, it was chiefly celebrated by the moſt dreadful maledictions. The Supreme Being, who, true religion tells us, enjoins brotherly love, forgiveneſs, humanity and virtue, was addreſſed by our divines as if he had been more mercileſs and blood-thirſty than any divinity that ever diſgraced paganiſm; and the temples of the God of Peace were made to reſound with imprecations, from which even our anceſtors would have recoiled when engaged in the worſhip of their ferocious Odin, whom they revered as "the terrible and ſevere God; the active "roaring deity; the father of ſlaughter; the

* Vide the miniſterial Gazette, the Times of November 30th, always very correct in its law reports.

 "God

" God that carrieth deſolation and fire, and
" nameth thoſe that are to be ſlain *."

The ſolemnity of the ſcene was well calculated for rouſing and miſleading the paſſions, and every artifice was employed to excite hatred towards the French, and provoke us to fury. The prieſthood as well as the princes felt themſelves intereſted in the cauſe, and their zeal ſhook the pulpit with exhortations to vengeance. The Biſhop of Glouceſter, before the Houſe of Lords, thus ſpoke of that nation;—" Infatuated and
" remorſeleſs people! The meaſure of your
" iniquities ſeems at length to be full; the hour
" of retribution is coming faſt upon you! Drunk
" with the blood of your fellow citizens, you
" have dared to ſpread your ravages abroad;
" rouſing the ſurrounding nations, in juſtice to
" themſelves and the common cauſe of hu-
" manity, to confederate againſt you, *in order*
" *to execute the wrath of God on your devoted*
" *heads*." His lordſhip, however, might have been reſtrained from ſuch raſh denunciations of divine judgment, by the awful admonitions of the founder of that religion which he pretended to preach."

" And Jeſus anſwering, ſaid, ſuppoſe ye theſe
" Galileans were ſinners above all the Galileans,
" becauſe they ſuffered ſuch things? I tell you
" nay,—But except ye repent, ye ſhall all like-
" wiſe periſh."

" And thoſe eighteen on whom the Tower of
" Siloam fell and ſlew them, think ye that they
" were ſinners above all men that dwelt in Je-

* See the Edda.

"rusalem? I tell you nay: but except ye re-
"pent, ye shall all likewise perish*."

The other Fast Day Sermons were in unison with that of the bishop of Gloucester, with a very few exceptions. The Rev. J. Gardener, at Taunton, said, "Shall we not labour to "bring such persons" (as the French, and Reformers in general) "to a proper sense of their "duty, *or exterminate them and their opi-* "*nions?*" and the Rev Mr. Bromeley, at Fitzroy Chapel hopes "that the reckoning which God "will make will not be long delayed against a "nation," (France) "which is certainly be-"hind no other whose measure of iniquities "has in any records of time *called forth his* "*vengeance to erase it from the earth* †." These are the sentiments of our high church pastors: Such is the religion, the benevolence, the humanity, they teach! To exterminate for opinion! What more did Marat ever desire! To be the instrument of God in executing his vengeance, Mahomet used the same plea for all his murders and rapine! To erase a whole nation from the earth!!! Neither Mahomet, Marat, nor Roberspierre, have equalled this! How limited and insignificant have been their proscriptions compared with those of our own pious pastors, who would "seal on the fore-"head as the servants of God ‡," all those who make war against France; who would "send

* St. Luke, c. xiii.

† These passages are taken from the sermons published under the names of those divines.

‡ Vide Revelations, c. vii. v. 3.

"myriads

"myriads of locusts, with crowns like gold upon "their heads, and faces like men, invested with "scorpion power, to torture the unsealed" enthusiasts of that distracted nation, and "let "loose the angels of the Euphrates to slaughter "a third of mankind * !"

Similar passages from the sermons preached on that *Christian* day would fill a volume. Most of them tend to inflame the people to a war of extermination, and insinuate the destruction of those who desire a Parliamentary Reform. Surely our divines cannot be so much mistaken as to imagine these harangues gratifying to the Head of the Church? Their affection towards the crown, indeed, is natural. The Bishop of Durham's promotion has taught them the road to preferment; and my Lord of Gloucester has been long looking for a translation: but not such as Elijah's: His present ambition looks no higher than Canterbury.

Nor were the sermons publicly preached more inflammatory than the writings anonimously published by our High-Church Men; one of which, in Birmingham, under the fictitious name of Job Nott, thus speaks of those whom he calls "New-fashioned, restless "Dissenters," and the members of a society instituted on the principles of Mr. Pitt and the Duke of Richmond for procuring a Reform of Parliament. "Do be off—only think of the "New Drop—you may be recorded in the "Newgate Calendar—transportation may re- "form you—*you deserve to be highly exalted*—

* Vide Revelations, c. ix.

"Did

"Did you ever ſee the New Drop?" and concludes with wiſhing that theſe Diſſenters and Reformers, whom he deems factious, "tied in "their garters may ſwing." Yet this elegant author calls himſelf a friend to conciliation and unanimity, a *moderate* man, a man of *peace!* He may be ſo for a *Birmingham* man; but if ſuch are the friends to peace and moderation in that town, can we wonder at the atrocities which have taken place there, and ſtill may be repeated, while Job Nott and ſuch publications are publicly ſold with a bookſeller's name to them, and are even boaſted of by their authors*?

Members of both Houſes of Parliament have acted in uniſon with the church, and have alſo repeatedly inſiſted that a war of extermination is the only thing which can ſave this country. The defence of the riot at Mancheſter equals the exhortations of the pulpit. We not only find riots indirectly recommended, but openly vindicated. Unlawful violence againſt a man for his political opinions is juſtified in the Britiſh Houſe of Commons! Here the "Sacred duty of inſurrection" is preached as unequivocally as ever it was in France, where actual and exceſſive danger is in ſome degree a palliation of criminality. But in England no juſtification of ſimilar atrocities could be ſhewn, except in the unfounded apprehenſions artfully excited by a falſe and pernicious alarm.

* One very curious article contained in Job Nott, deſigned probably to give confidence to the Church and King Partizans, is, "that Sir Robert Lawley never is kept waiting by Mr. Pitt, *when* he ſends in word it is on *Birmingham buſineſs*."

Mr.

Mr. Reeves's Committee detected in their outſet, inſinuating it to be an exceſs of virtue to exterminate the Diſſenters, did not alter their courſe, though they more carefully concealed their proceedings. The ſtreets were over-run with the moſt violent inflammatory libels; the war-whoop againſt Diſſenters and Reformers was ſung at every corner; and, if aſſaſſination was not committed, it was not for want of prompters. Some of the hand-bills and ballads in circulation laſt winter would even have ſhocked Mr. Burke! And it is fortunate that the lower had more diſcretion and humanity than the higher ranks of perſons who encouraged ſuch publications, otherwiſe we might have had a Tory *Second* of *September* in England; and the bloody anniverſary, a diſtinguiſhed *red* letter day in the "Church and King" Calendar, might have been celebrated by our Bigots.

Not one of the authors or diſtributors of thoſe incendiary papers was even ſeized, much leſs puniſhed: but a poor bill-ſticker, who could not read, was tried and impriſoned for poſting up bills in favour of Parliamentary Reform; and Holt, the printer, at Newark, has been convicted of a libel for re-printing a paper on the ſame ſubject, which was firſt circulated under the auſpices of Mr. Pitt and the Duke of Richmond, when they contended for that meaſure; and which it is not improbable was originally written by his Grace, as it ſtrongly contends for Univerſal Repreſentation.

I ſhall not comment on what Mr. Young repeatedly inſinuates, though he does not plainly deſire,

desire, by such passages as " The King of " France died on the scaffold, because he would " not shed the blood of Traitors, Conspirators " and Rebels ; he listened to those who peti- " tioned for Reform ;" and I shall also pass over the many oral threats of assassination made by individuals, the anonymous letters to the same effect, one of which at Staines, threatened the house and life of Mr. Fox, and conclude this slight sketch, of the desire of some men, to see " Church and King" massacres in this country, by giving as an epitome of the others, an extract from a hand-bill, circulated at Exeter, in December last. " Our noble King hath made a " fine speech from the throne to his Parliament, " as must be acknowledged by every well-wisher " to his country, and as for them that do not " like that and the present CONSTITUTION, let " them have their deserts, that is a HALTER " and a GIBBET, and be burnt afterwards, not " as PAINE hath been, in effigy, but in body " and person. To which every loyal heart will " say Amen !"

These facts, I think, are sufficient to justify me in asserting, that the assassinations, and other crimes in France, are not detested by certain persons in this country on account of their enormity, but that those who execrate most bitterly, only wish to imitate them on a different class of victims. Marat's fall was regretted, by our Tories, because he laid the eggs of mischief; and the death of the King of France, was declared in the House of Commons, by a member of Administration, to be, in some respects, a fortunate circumſtance in rouſing the Britiſh Nation to War.

The animating ſoul of Mr. Young's book, being the atrocities of the French, which he falſely aſcribes to their principles, I have thought it neceſſary at my commencement to ſhew, that, according to his own reaſoning, he condemns his own principles, ſince the ſame atrocities have been recommended by the advocates for his opinions; and, that if I might indulge in the ſame furious execration, I could find cruel doctrines enough in England to balance againſt him:—to miſlead and inflame thoſe who ſwallow aſſertion for fact, and invective for argument. I do not, however, defend the crimes of the French, although I think, as far as crimes can be excuſed, no people in the world ever had more to plead in extenuation, becauſe no people in the world ever were ſo irritated by internal treachery, and alarmed by external danger.

But, proſcription and cruelty, are not the only parts of the conduct of the French which have been imitated in this country. We had our Tory Jacobin Aſſociators at the St. Alban's Tavern, and our more furious and degraded Club of Cordeliers in the Crown and Anchor Committee. If in Paris " Perſons have been impriſoned by order of individuals," others, at home, have been voted in a ſtate of accuſation, upon the authority of anonymous letters tranſmitted to Mr. Reeves. The affiliated Jacobin Clubs of the French Provinces have been made the model of the Reeveſian Aſſociations and Committees againſt Republicans and Levellers at home; and in the

Engliſh

English Parochial, as well as in the French Popular Meetings, the Conſtitution, as declared by Reeves, Pitt, and Co. has been formally approved. Every Preſident or Chairman of theſe Conventions becomes a Municipal Inquiſitor: Sir Joſeph Banks makes his *viſites domiciliaires* in the pariſh of St. Anne, and keeps a regiſter of the complexion, age, employment, &c. of lodgers and ſtrangers. The ſection of St. James's *denounce* for *inciviſm* every houſekeeper who does not oblige his ſervants, workmen, and apprentices, to ſign their acceptance of the Conſtitution. No tradeſmen is to be employed, who has not been fraternized by the officers of his diſtrict; no publican is to be licenſed, who has not reported *ſuſpected perſons.* Every man is called upon, more palpably than in France, to declare our Conſtitution glorious and unreformable; and if any one is more conſiſtent than Mr. Pitt and the Duke of Richmond, and ſignifies a wiſh for the removal of abuſes in the conſtruction of the Houſe of Commons, he is branded as a Jacobin, and if poſſible, utterly ruined. Is not this governing by the very ſame means, ſo much execrated in the French: by mobs, by terror, by popular coercion? The great maſs of the people, from the higheſt to the loweſt ranks, are ſummoned to conſtitute themſelves into partial arbitrary tribunals to acquit and to condemn.

The dread and regret with which the inſtitution of theſe English Primary Aſſemblies was beheld by the rational Friends of Freedom, found ſome conſolation in the hope that they would not be of long duration. It was imagined when

 the

the temporary alarm was paſt, that they would not only be diſuſed, but the public would contemn the deluſion, and give the government of the country to thoſe who conſtitutionally ſhould poſſeſs it, and whoſe reſponſibility is a check upon their intemperance, the King's Miniſters. But inſtead of this, we find our Tory affiliated Societies, converted into the inſtruments of the Church and King Jacobins, and executing without authority or reſponſibility, thoſe meaſures which adminiſtration deſire, but cannot with decency tranſact. They denounce all who wiſh to petition the King or Parliament, contrary to the ſentiments of the Placemen and Penſioners at the Crown and Anchor Tavern; the inhabitants of Glaſgow have been threatened with Church and King vengeance for preſuming to complain of that which is daily ruining them,—the War; and our Parochial Clubs are knocking down the Conſtitution, in imitation of the Clubs in France, by voting contributions to ſupport the army. Every perſon may ſoon be obliged, under pain of denunciation as a traiterous Jacobin, to join in theſe patriotic gifts; and by ſuch proceedings, the neceſſity of calling Parliament together, may be ultimately ſuperſeded. Such an alteration in the Conſtitution would, no doubt, be highly agreeable to the Alarmiſts.

To condemn opinions or inſtitutions for crimes which are committed by their real or pretended ſupporters, is both groſs fallacy, and flagrant injuſtice. The moſt clear principles, and the moſt ſalutary inſtitutions, are open to the attack of ſuch ſophiſtry. Suppoſe I were inclined to condemn the Britiſh Government in Church and

State

State, becauſe the riots and exceſſes in Birmingham were in behalf of Church and King, would any man of ſenſe admit ſuch events as full proof that our Conſtitution is fundamentally vicious? Yet, if I were to argue thus, I would only imitate Mr. Young. I might like him ſay, "the "*theory* of the Engliſh religion is *peace*, but the "*practice* is *riot*;—the preachers of it, tell us "to have good will towards our neighbours, yet "they inſtigate a mob to fire and plunder them. "As for their kingly government it is ſtill worſe. "The people pay about twenty millions annually for *protection*, but at Birmingham the "rabble are permitted to *burn* and *rob* for a "week together; and if it ſo happens that "they have deſtroyed your whole property, "and you have not a long purſe to go to law, "you can have no redreſs:—If you are completely ruined, you are completely excluded "from juſtice.—Such is the Britiſh Government—Such is their glorious Conſtitution!—"But in preference to it give me the ſimple "deſpotiſm of Pruſſia: At Spandau I may go "to ſleep in ſafety:—at Birmingham I may expect to be awakened amidſt the flames of "their helliſh Church and King Government."

In 1780, Mr. Young might ſtill have condemned the proteſtant religion—not more juſtly—but more ſpeciouſly. If he had written on the 6th of June, in that year, he might, with the ſame fairneſs with which he treats the French, have ſaid, "The proteſtant religion is "a bayonet in your breaſt, or a bullet in your "boſom. In *theory* it teaches to do unto others "as you would have them do unto you; in

" *practice*,

" *practice*, it teaches fire, plunder, devasta-" tion and bloodshed. The Protestants *entreat* " redress *by petition*, and assault, wound, and " threaten those who are to grant it: They " pray for their enemies, and burn the houses " and chapels of those who do not offend them: " They declaim against drunkenness, and get " so beastly drunk that they are consumed in " the diabolical flames of their own kindling: " they recommend honesty and mercy, yet " empty the goals of felons and murderers " whom they make their associates. Their " *theory* instils *virtue*, but their practice ap-" proves only of *vice*. They enlighten mankind " by a general conflagration, and send souls to " heaven by bludgeon and halter worship. Such " is the protestant religion! Give me paganism. " Among the Tartars I may sit in safety under " my own fig-tree. No sanguinary rapacious " protestant, with the creed in one hand and a " bludgeon in the other, will, in Thibet, de-" mand money at my door and threaten to burn " my house: THERE I WOULD BE IN SAFETY." In this manner Mr. Young might condemn the British government and religion, by blaming them for the crimes committed in popular commotions, which the best of governments cannot always prevent; and from these as reasonably draw conclusions unfavourable to them, as he has done to the French Revolution, by applying the crimes of individuals, or the temporary accidental confusion and mischief in France, to the principles which actuate the mass of the people.

Our Alarmists have not only adopted the French system of ruling by Clubs and Proscriptions,

tions, but our own, and the other governments in Europe, have discovered much that is worthy of imitation in the conduct of the unanointed executive Council. If the French affiliated Brabant by the point of the sword, have not the allies bullied, insulted, dragooned every neutral power? Sweden, Denmark, Venice, Switzerland, Tuscany, and Genoa, have had their independence violated. I dare not, indeed, speak in adequate terms of the conduct pursued with the two latter powers, whose towns were threatened, with tolerable plainness, to be given up to military execution, if they did not declare War against France! Is there no resemblance to be found between the decree of the 19th of November, and the conduct of our Generals and Admirals in the West Indies and Toulon, where they have offered assistance and fraternity to all Frenchmen who would renounce obedience to the mother country, and accept of TRUE liberty, as modelled by those who have just bestowed it on Poland? The more the proceedings of the Belligerent Powers are examined, the more it will be found that France, which formerly set the fashions of dress, now sets the fashions of government over Europe; and that the people of England in particular, have adopted their political conduct, with more eagerness, than ever they adopted the stilo of a cap or a coat. The objects, indeed, are, different; but the means taken to obtain or secure those objects, and which alone excite indignation, are the *very same*:—Nay, the objects of the French people, the establishment of the Liberties, the Peace, and the Happiness of Mankind, are *good*, admitting the means to be bad: But

the

the objects of the Tory Jacobins, perpetuating the ignorance of the poor, arming the rich against the poor, the suppression of the Freedom of Speech, and the Liberty of the Press, together with the justification of every vice of government, are *bad*, and their means are *equally bad* also.

It will be found, upon a candid examination of facts, that instead of the crimes which have disgraced France, being the consequence of her principles, they have been produced and wilfully instigated by the German Princes, in hopes of rendering odious those very principles, as they dreaded that their establishment in France, would ultimately destroy all tyrannical governments in Europe. The French were by no means the authors of the present War; on the contrary, they did all in their power to prevent it. It was the Courts of Austria and Berlin, and a few profligate emigrants, that provoked the rupture, which has now involved Europe in calamity. France confined herself within her own territories, and to her own domestic concerns, till she was exasperated by a combination against a government recently settled, approved by her inhabitants, and which promised to establish a peaceable and lasting limited monarchy. Before the ferment of the first Revolution was allayed, and the dregs it had stirred up were sunk to their proper obscurity, the King, by his flight, proved his connection with the Princes who were plotting against the Constitution. Their hostile intrigues at foreign courts, became too manifest and provoking: they deserted their country to procure its invasion, and

left

left the field compleatly in possession of the Republican party, whose credit they strenghtened by their own treachery, and taught the people to believe the Nobles naturally and irrevocably their enemies; and to conclude, that security for their Liberties was to be looked for, in their own interference and activity, rather than in the generosity or justice of the higher ranks of society.

In September 1791, the manifesto from Monsieur and the Comte d'Artois to the King of France, announced their success in persuading the Emperor and the King of Prussia to hostilty against the new Constitution: and those Monarchs gave it under their hands, signed at Pilnitz, that they required all the powers in Europe to assist them in this War, for "the Rights "of Sovereigns." The Princes also affirmed, that "the *other* European Courts had the same "dispositions with those of Vienna and Ber-"lin."—The speedy confirmation of what they had asserted, respecting the Emperor and King of Prussia, procured belief to the other passages of their declaration, particularly as they remained uncontradicted by those to whom they made allusion; and it was necessarily concluded, that all courts, and even that of St. James's, wished well to the concert of Princes. But how did France act in this situation?—Not like England last winter. She did not precipitate herself into a War, although provoked by the most flagrant violation of the Rights of Nations. She negociated;—for eight months she negociated:—till finding it impossible to obtain either satisfaction or explanation for the Pilnitz Conspiracy, and that the Despots of Germany were resolved on hostilities, and were only delaying their commencement till fully prepared, she submitted to inevitable compulsion; and to shew that she was not dismayed or terrified, she proclaimed War, which on her part was indisputably *defensive by anticipation.* But notwithstanding hostilities had been effectually declared by the Emperor and King of Prussia, in August 1791; and she did not resolve on a rupture till the April following, many persons have had the effrontery and folly to assert, that France invited the War!

It is neither to their new principles, nor the natural cruelty of the French, that we are to ascribe the atrocities which have lately disgraced that nation. It might as well be said, that the principles of the Protestant Religion inculcate murder and rapine, because such doctrines have lately been recommended from the pulpit; or that they produced the riots in 1780, as that the Principles of Liberty which have animated the French are the cause of the crimes committed by some of them. It is to the foreign combination against the people, and the resistance of the rich to the establishment of their Liberties at home;—" It was that hateful out-" rage on the rights and feelings of human " nature, that wretched tissue of pride, folly, " and inhumanity; it was the Duke of Bruns-" wick's Manifesto that first steeled the heart and " maddened the brain of all France; which pro-" voked those it had devoted, to practice all

" the

" the cruelties it had impotently threatened to " inflict; which sharpened the daggers of the " assassins of the 2d of September, and whetted " the axe suspended over the unfortunate Mo- " narch *." That infamous manifesto produced the 10th of August; the treacherous surrender of Longwy provoked the horrid massacres of the 2d of September; the inevitable War with Britain and Holland hurried the unfortunate Louis to the scaffold; and the loss of Valenciennes proved the forerunner of the trial, and the delivery of Toulon the signal for the execution of the Queen. The success of the combined powers has invariably occasioned the very reverse of their professed object; it has always made more enthusiasts, united the people more firmly, and removed the prospect of re-establishing Monarchy and Nobility to a greater distance. Since all Europe has joined in the cry of erasing France from the list of nations, she has only retaliated by vowing the destruction of all Despotic Governments. The monsters of France have been begotten by the monsters of Germany. The Duke of Brunswick first taught them proscription and murder; their only choice was, whether they should assassinate, or be assassinated;—whether the Duke of Brunswick should preside over another St. Bartholomew, or Marat over a 2d of September.

We shuddered at the news of the 2d of September, yet the *merciful* doctrines preached at home, did not even excite a murmer. On the

* Vide Mr. Sheridan's Speech, Dec. 15, 1792.

Royal-Exchange the gallows was openly talked of, as neceſſary to extirpate the favourers of Peace and Reform. If then, Engliſhmen, by a falſe alarm, could be guilty of wiſhing for the blood of perſons whoſe only crime was difference of opinion, why ſhould we condemn the French, in whom every evil has been realized, which here was only dreaded? If Engliſhmen, merely becauſe they were *told* they were in danger, could endure ſuch ſanguinary language, what might not have been their acceſſes if ſome of the principal perſonages in the kingdom had brought an hundred thouſand German robbers to deſtroy our valued Conſtitution and eſtabliſh Deſpotiſm? If they had taken poſſeſſion of Yarmouth and Norwich, and threatened to give up the city of London to "military execution," what mad or wicked theoriſt might not then have been liſtened to? Mr. Young, by warning Britain againſt the example of France, does in fact acknowledge, that in ſimilar circumſtances, Engliſhmen would be guilty of ſimilar enormities. If they would not, what occaſion is there for *warning* them? The inhabitants of France are not naturally more cruel than thoſe of this country, and were the enemies of that nation to ceaſe to goad and exaſperate her by their forces without, and their treacherous and incendiary agents within, a fair experiment might then be made on the undiſturbed operation of French principles; it might then be ſeen, that from the forced ſtate in which France is held by the confederacy of Deſpots, ariſe thoſe crimes, and that impunity which have been falſely and wickedly aſcribed to the Principles of Liberty. She might then, indeed, be an example, instead of a warning to other nations: and nobody foresaw this more clearly than the Despots themselves; for when the Constituent Assembly declared in favour of a pacific system, against conquest or offensive War, the whole fraternity on the continent were alarmed for their *trade*. Abolish War! Abolish the means of gratifying our ambition, of plundering our subjects and perpetuating our tyranny!—Abolish War!—Then we must make War on you to prevent it. We will give a stab to your pacific system in its infancy, and by driving you into excesses and horrors, convince the world that War, our Trade, is necessary to the Happiness of Society.

I cannot close the whole subject of the War between France and the other continental powers better than by quoting what Lord Mornington said in the House of Commons, May 7, 1793, of the War in which England was engaged immediately after the revolution of 1688: his words may very justly be applied to the present contest, if instead of Louis XIV, we read the Triumvirate, the Empress of Russia, the Emperor of Germany, and the King of Prussia. "The Wars which "immediately followed the Revolution," (said his Lordship,) "were absolutely necessary for the se-"curity of that auspicious settlement. The re-"cent establishment required protection, not "only against the abdicated King, and those "who supported his cause at home, or who "had followed his fortunes abroad, but also "against the pride and jealousy of Louis XIV. "*He could not suffer a LIMITED* MO-

"NARCHY,

" NARCHY, *FOUNDED* ON THE LIBERTIES " OF THE PEOPLE, to grow up and flouriſh *in* " *peace* ſo near his Throne. He naturally fore- " ſaw that ſuch a Conſtitution muſt become a " *continual reproach* to the tyranny of his go- " vernment, and an inſuparable obſtacle to the " progreſs of his ambition. It was, therefore, " his policy to attempt the deſtruction of ſo for- " midable a neighbour, by every means both of " open force, and *ſecret machination.*"

Next to the crimes committed in France, which have artfully been miſrepreſented as the conſequence of French Principles, the word *Equality* has been falſely deemed to mean an Agrarian Law : thus at once exciting horror, and creating an alarm for property. Mr. Reeves, in the publication already alluded to, ſays, Equality means, that all men ſhall be equally tall, equally wiſe, and equally ſtrong, as well as equally rich. This may be fit for Mr. Reeves to ſay, but not for me to anſwer. I do not doubt, however, of its having prejudiced the vulgar, who would naturally believe the French could be guilty of any thing, after being gravely told, that they had roaſted alive, baſted with oil, and eaten many of the Swiſs and Nobles ; that others they had made into pies and cried them about the ſtreets*; and that they " were drunk " with the blood of their fellow citizens †." Mr. Young makes a better uſe, for the Tory Jacobins, of the word Equality, by conſtruing it to mean an equalization of property ; " for,

* Vide the accounts of the tranſactions on the 10th of Auguſt, publiſhed ſoon after that day in the Times.

† Vide Biſhop of Glouceſter's Sermon.

ſays

ſays he, " that all were equal in the eye of the " law, was decreed by the Conſtituent Aſſembly, " and why call the year 1792 the fourth of " Liberty and firſt of Equality?"—All were not equal in the eye of the law by the decree alluded to, or even previous to the 10th of Auguſt. One whole branche of the Legiſlature, the King, was above the law; and although I am ready to admit that it was childiſh to make the diſtinction in dating the year, yet, when I find ſome reaſon for it, and none in ſupport of Mr. Young's aſſertion, that " Property was glanced at," I think it is proper to take that reaſon, however ſmall, as the fair explanation, rather than put a conſtruction upon the word which no circumſtance juſtifies, merely becauſe Mr. Young aſſerts " it " either meant that (equalization of property) or " it meant nothing;" becauſe he acknowledges that he does not underſtand it, ſhall we receive as fact what he wiſhes, and for that reaſon ſuppoſes it to mean? The King was not amenable to the law, therefore, ſtrictly ſpeaking, there could not be perfect Equality. On the queſtion of Royal inviolability I give no opinion.

It is not neceſſary to ſay much in anſwer to the common miſrepreſentations of Equality. No candid intelligent man, either in France or England, could ever underſtand it to mean otherwiſe than an equality of reſponſibility to, and protection from the law; and of this, no nation in the world was ever more in want than France previous to the Revolution in 1789. The expence of law-ſuits conſtitutes the only grievous inequality in England. It is impoſſible for a poor man, with his own means, to obtain re-

dreſs

dreſs by a courſe of law in this country* ; and, even a prudent man of ſmall fortune, will ſubmit to an injury, rather than riſk his ruin by entering into a conteſt with a wealthy litigious opponent. Many an inſtance of injuſtice, accompliſhed and maintained by riches, may be found in the Memoirs of a northern Nobleman, who has long been the tyrannical oppreſſor and plunderer of the poor, and middling claſſes, in that part of the kingdom, which is curſed with his reſidence.

It is to what *he calls* the French Equality, that Mr. Young aſcribes a ſyſtem of rapine and plunder, which he affirms exiſts in that nation. He concludes a number of his paragraphs with "This "is Equality! Rob the farmer! Plunder the "landholder and divide his land! Equality of "property! An Agrarian Law, &c. According "to French principles, the firſt beggar I meet, "may ſabre in one hand, rights of man in the "other, demand a ſhare of what is my own, "my property, my land at Bradfield." And in this manner he proceeds, arguing, as if an equalization of property had actually taken place in

* It has been ſaid, even from the Bench, that our laws are equally open to the poor as to the rich, becauſe if a man cannot fee an advocate, the court will provide him one gratis. This, like ſome other parts of our Conſtitution, was excellently intended, and, no doubt, at its firſt inſtitution, proved highly beneficial; but like many more inſtitutions, Time, that great innovator, has reduced it to a mere ſhadow. The fee of a counſellor is the leaſt expence of a law-ſuit; nor can his ſervices be of much utility to his client, if he is unacquainted with his caſe, till after the trial has begun; and even then moſt probably, he cannot, from the ignorance of the poor man, rightly underſtand it.

in France; or at least as if some notorious and undeniable proofs had occurred of robbing a man of his estate, and dividing it among "Beggars."

The only instance, however, which he attempts to produce in support of this, (and if more or better could have been found, he has shewn so much industry in collecting the crimes of the French, that he certainly would have brought them forward), is, an unauthenticated one in the Clermontese, where an estate was seized from the proprietor, who was, no doubt, an emigrant, as Mr. Young owns, "*he lived at* "*a distance*"; and where some of the tenants who talked of retaining their farms, because those who laboured should not pay money to those who did nothing, were, most probably for so doing, obliged to quit, and the property was ultimately held in trust for the nation. But this story rests wholly on Mr. Young's bare assertion, who has not quoted even the authority of a newspaper, which he invariably does on all other occasions; and whether it is true or false is immaterial, because it proves nothing like a general principle of equalizing property. In the present state of France, no doubt, many atrocious robberies are committed, which would be punished or prevented, if the German Plunders would allow the government to act, as it certainly would do in tranquillity, with rigorous justice. In any country in a similar situation, similar crimes would be perpetrated; and at all events they can have no connection with the Principles of Liberty and Equality.—Because the northern Lord to whom I have just alluded, has, by dint of wealth, plundered every man in his neighbourhood who had any thing to loſe, are we therefore to conclude, that it is a principle in the Engliſh law that the rich may rob the poor?

Inſtances, and ſtrong authenticated inſtances, to confute Mr. Young's aſſertions reſpecting an Agrarian Law are on record, and cannot be denied. About the very time he was writing his book, when all the horrors and anarchy, on which he continually rings, were reigning, the Duc de Penthievre died, where he had long lived, in the heart of France. He poſſeſſed immenſe wealth both in land and moveables; was the father-in-law, but enemy, of the duke of Orleans, from whom his daughter had been long ſeparated; and he was even ſuppoſed to be unfriendly to the Revolution. He was an amiable and beloved man; he never interfered in politics; amidſt every violence and change, his property and perſon were untouched, and many a poor man's tear bedewed his grave. No beggar, ſabre in hand, demanded a ſhare of his property, either during his life or at his death. Here then, is a direct notorious proof, that the property even of an *eminent nobleman* is not violated, while he does not oppoſe the exiſting government; and undoubtedly every man, who conducted himſelf like the Duc de Penthievre, was equally unmoleſted. It was incumbent on Mr. Young to give proofs, that men had been plundered in France for no other offence than that of being rich, before he pretended to be ruled by "Events" which never took place, to be guided by "Experiments" which

never

never were made, and to follow a "Practice" which never had any exiſtence, but in his own credulity or miſrepreſentation.

It is, however, highly probable, that the French Government, ſince it has no ally to pay the expences of defending its own territories, and is ſo hemmed in and inſulated by its enemies that it cannot borrow, will be obliged to have recourſe to ſome extraordinary meaſures which may be no further juſtifiable than on the hackneyed plea ſo often uſed by its preſent invaders, "State neceſſity!" But whatever may be done in the preſent ferment and alarm, when France, inſtead of thinking of ſtrict juſtice, has to ſtruggle for her very exiſtence as an independent nation, will be no proof that ſhe would not have been, if permitted to remain in peace, and yet will be, when peace is reſtored to her, as equitable as her neighbours. Should the Government ſeize a part of the effects of the wealthy for the defence of the country, that will give no more reaſon to expect an Agrarian Law, than raiſing twenty Millions annually in Britain gives reaſon to expect it will be afterwards equally divided among the people. Mr. Young well knew that there is a decree, making it death to propoſe an Agrarian Law, which has long been and ſtill is in *full force*, but it did not ſuit his impoſture to notice it. Whatever may be done in France, ought not to be aſcribed to the principles or rapacity of the people, but to the unparalleled exigency of the times. To ſupport her Liberties, indeed, the rich will probably be forced to pay what the poor cannot; and to this Mr. Young will not object, as he admits, p. 123, "In taxation, ſpeaking at large of "a nation, to quantum *paid* is not ſo much "the object to regard as the quantum *left* after "the taxes are paid."

But while I deny that any thing like proof can be produced of an Agrarian Law having taken place in France, I own that an extenſive and awful confiſcation has been made! What has been the occaſion of it?—Not a deſire to plunder and divide Property. It has been the folly, weakneſs, or wickedneſs of thoſe who have ſuffered; ſome of whom openly declared againſt the Conſtitution, and excited the invaſion of the country; others had made their hoſtile diſpoſition too manifeſt to be ſafe at home, therefore they fled; and the ruling power in Paris, finding the Emigrants were drawing out the wealth of the nation in order to make War upon it, ſeized the eſtates of all thoſe who did not appear within a limited time. Such as were friendly to the Conſtitution could have no objection to appear at their poſt, becauſe they were in no danger; and thoſe whoſe hoſtility was aſcertained by their abſence, deſerved to loſe their property; deſerved to loſe it on the principles of the Britiſh Government, which ſeized the property of the Rebels in 1715 and 1745, as greedily as the French Convention; and whoſe tremendous confiſcations in Ireland during the Commonwealth, (afterwards *confirmed* by Charles the IId.) and in the reign of William the IIId. ſurpaſs all that has hitherto been done in France; where, if mens' minds were reſtored to tranquillity by peace, and their country ſecure, the vengeance of enthuſiaſtic fury would aſſuage,

aſſuage, and probably moſt of the fugitives would be reinſtated in their ancient inheritance and ſequeſtered property.

Beſides general pictures of French exceſſes, and miſconſtructions of the word Equality, Mr. Young continually maintains "Experiment," "Practice," and "Events," to be the only wiſe rule of conduct; and, alluding to the experiment of perſonal Repreſentation being attempted in France, for I deny that it has been made, he ſays, (p. 56) "The thing is tried; that method "of drilling has been experimented and found "good for nothing; the crop did not anſwer." But if two neighbouring farmers were to try a new theory, and the children of the one were to drive beaſts into their father's field, to nip the firſt ſhoots, to trample and deſtroy the corn as it ſprung from the earth, and his crop did not anſwer; while that of the other farmer, whoſe field was unmoleſted yielded an abundance beyond all expectation, could it, in ſuch a caſe, be juſtly ſaid the experiment failed? The farmers are France and America; the children are the Emigrants, and the beaſts are the Germans. The experiment of Repreſentative Government has not been allowed a ſufficient period to be made in France; for even if the field had been unmoleſted, the corn has not had time to vegetate, much leſs to fill and ripen. In America, the field was as much diſturbed, during ſeveral years, as in France, and accordingly produced nothing but weeds. But the theory was known to be good; it was perſiſted in, and when fair play was given to the ſoil, the crop was aſtoniſhing. So it will be with France, which at pre-

ſent,

ſent, in reſpect to Government, may be called a neglected or barren ſoil; for there is a more important duty than cultivating the field; the natives muſt defend it, or they will have no field to cultivate.

But ſays Mr. Young, the experiment has not finally been tried in America. No! Eighteen years is no experiment in America, though ſix months is a compleat experiment in France! "But America has ſuch a plenty of land that "ſhe has no poor; it is not her Repreſentative "Government that prevents there being any "poor, but it is the plenty of land. When ſhe "has a numerous indigent poor, her Govern-"ment will tumble to pieces; the mob will "not poſſeſs the Sovereign authority and re-"main hungry," continues he. I deny that it is her extent of territory alone that prevents her being burthened with a numerous indigent poor. Look at almoſt every country in Europe, not even excepting Britain and Ireland, and acres enough will be found to make thoſe who are now poor as comfortable as the American farmer,—I do not mean by an Agrarian Law; I mean by properly employing the waſte unoccupied lands. Look at the vaſt tracts in Germany, Hungary, and eaſtward towards the Black Sea, whoſe native fertility is doomed, by a barbarous policy, to feed wild beaſts inſtead of man; where whole countries, that would render millions happy, are made a blank on the earth by the reſtleſs deſolating ambition of bad Governments, or perhaps, to afford amuſement to one Tyrant. In Spain, the example of pride and indolence in the Nobles, has occaſioned ſuch a contempt and neglect of Agriculture in the lower classes of society who ought to attend to it, that population has decreased, and the nation become insignificant in the scale of Europe compared with what it formerly was. The natives live chiefly on the natural productions of the soil, one of the richest in the world, which if properly cultivated, might maintain in greater plenty than at present, six times the number of inhabitants. "The extent of ground is of so little value "*without labour*," says Mr. Locke, "That I "have heard it affirmed, that in Spain itself, a "man may be permitted to plough, sow, and "reap, without being disturbed, upon land he "has no other title to, but only his making use "of it. But on the contrary, the inhabitants "think themselves beholden to him, who by "his industry, on neglected, and consequently "waste land, has increased the stock of corn "which they wanted."

It would be superfluous to point out similar evils in the other European nations. With regard to France, under its old Government, which is more immediately interesting to the question, I desire no more to be said in support of my opinion than what is contained in Mr. Young's own travels. It will there be found that it was not the great population of that country which occasioned the poverty and wretchedness of the multitude, but that it was the monopoly of the land by a dissolute tyrannical Nobility and Priesthood, whose possession operated effectually to diminish the produce of the soil, and to blast with sterility those plains upon which nature had lavished her richest bounty. The arbitrary and enormous

enormous exactions of the Agents of the Government aggravated the diſtreſs of the people, among whom lay acres ſufficient to make them as happy as the American farmer. It is the miſerable policy of Governments that makes ſo many poor in Europe; and what is the cauſe of the people being in general much more happy and wealthy in Britain than in Germany? Not "Corruption," as thoſe who fatten by it would make us believe. It is becauſe we have much leſs of the old ſyſtem remaining; becauſe men are more enlightened, induſtry encouraged, and property better ſecured; becauſe our anceſtors have wrung from the hand of power and bequeathed us more Liberty than is enjoyed under any other Monarchy; nor can theſe bleſſings be preſerved but by that ſpirit which acquired them.

But it may ſtill be ſaid, America has more acres in proportion to the number of its inhabitants than any country in Europe. I ſhall not diſpute this, becauſe it is of no importance to my argument. I contend that there is a ſufficiency of acres in Europe to make every man as comfortable as the American farmer, and that the extent of territory in the New World does not alone prevent indigence among the people. It is the ſpirit of their Government, which encourages not only Agriculture, but Manufactures and Commerce, and diſcourages War. Look at Holland! The number of poor in Holland is perhaps as ſmall as in America, and certainly much leſs than in any other European nation; yet Holland contains very few, and thoſe very unproductive acres. It is the moſt populous ſpot in Europe, and, leaving her poor out of

the

the calculation, is twenty times more populous than America. How happens it then, that with ſo few acres, and ſo many inhabitants, the multitude of the Dutch are even more wealthy and comfortable than the American farmer? Because, though her Government is very defective, its ſpirit encourages induſtry, commerce, and œconomy, and always avoids War, unleſs forced into it by ſome inſidious friend. It is the encouragement given to Manufactures and Commerce, as well as Agriculture, rather than the quantity of acres, that makes a people rich and happy. Dr. Smith, and all profound political œconomiſts, affirm, every Artizan, Manufacturer, and Labourer, to be as valuable to a ſtate as acres of land, and that the greater the population, if Government animates and properly directs induſtry, the greater will be the riches of the country, and enjoyments of the people. It is wicked pernicious policy alone that proves, and ſuch ſhallow, or deluded politicians, as Mr. Young, who aſſert, that population is the cauſe of poverty, and that the richeſt man who ever lived, was Adam, becauſe he alone exiſted, and was landed proprietor of the whole world.

The view Mr. Young takes of America, with regard to paying taxes, is equally unfair with his "*Speculations*" reſpecting her Repreſentative Government. He ſays, that a Farmer in the Back Settlements may have plenty of beef, mutton, corn, wool; he may be rendered quite eaſy and happy, by a ſuperfluity of the neceſſaries of life, but for want of Circulation, of Commerce, he will not be able to pay a ſingle Tax; and therefore when America is involved in a War, and called upon for Taxes, ſhe will be ruined. *When* ſhe is involved in a War!—But her Government will not every few years alarm, miſlead, and madden the people into one, becauſe the Government emanates *from* the people, *for* the people's benefit, and is not directed by an ambitious or ſelfiſh junto:—And it is unjuſt in Mr. Young to eſtimate the power of America to pay taxes by the farmers in the *back ſettlements*. He owns, that the duties laid on the diſtilleries in Scotland, do not pay for the collection, and ſays, that the expence of collecting taxes from the farmers in the back ſettlements, would alſo be more than could pay for their collection: would it not, therefore, be as fair to conclude, that Britain cannot pay taxes, becauſe the Scotch diſtilleries cannot, as to conclude that America cannot pay taxes, becauſe the farmers in the back ſettlements cannot? A little conſideration will ſhew us, that America, like Britain, has circulation and commerce; like London, Liverpool, Briſtol and Glaſgow; it has Philadelphia, Boſton, Charles-Town and New York:—theſe laſt, indeed, may not be ſo extenſive and rich as the former; but, two hundred years ago, London was not a fourth part ſo wealthy and populous as at preſent; and is not America daily increaſing her commerce, manufactures and population?

Thus, I think, Mr. Young's "Experiment," "Practice," and "Events," as applied to America, are wholly illuſory. Repreſentative Government has ſtood in Peace, and flouriſhed in

America

America twelve years. “ Yes,” ſays he, “ but “ it will be deſtroyed when ſhe has a numerous “ indigent poor.”—*When* ſhe has an indigent poor ;—but, that will never be, more than at preſent, while the ſpirit of her government prefers, as it now does, Peace and Induſtry, to War and Corruption. He would condemn Repreſentative Government from the “ experiment” of a few months attempted in France, in the midſt of the moſt dreadful warefare ever known ; but in America, “ Experiment,” “ Practice,” and “ Events,” which he ſays, ought to be the only rule of conduct, he would ſet wholly aſide, becauſe *there* he finds they are ſtrongly againſt him, and that he cannot hold up a *terrifying example* of what *has* happened. He would condemn RepreſentativeGovernment in America on “ ſpeculation” and “ theory,” which he a thouſand times ſays, ought never to guide us ; he would condemn it by predicting, what *will* happen, not by ſhewing, what *has* happened. On the contrary, in France, the experiment of a few months, is to be our only guide, and theory and ſpeculation we are totally to diſregard ; in America theory and ſpeculation are to be our only guide, and the experiment of twelve years we are totally to diſregard ! ! !—How Mr. Young can reconcile theſe palpable contradictions, or how any man, of the leaſt underſtanding, could be duped by them, is beyond my comprehenſion. It may juſtly be aſked of him, in his own words, “ what “ inducement have we, therefore, to liſten to “ *your ſpeculations*, that condemn what all” *America* “ feels to be good ?”—(p. 85)

Hence, I think, I may fairly affirm, that in America, there is a noble instance of the blessings flowing from Representative Government. The Revolution there, was at first, as much execrated as that of France now is. In 1777 the same invectives may be found in the proclamation of general Burgoyne, that in 1792 were brought forth in the manifesto of the Duke of Brunswick: "He appealed to the suffering "thousands in the provinces, whether the pre- "sent unnatural rebellion has not been made "a foundation for the compleatest system of "Tyranny that ever God, in his displeasure, suffer- "ed for a time to be exercised over a froward "and stubborn generation. Arbitrary im- "prisonment, confiscation of property, perse- "cution, and torture, unprecedented in the "inquisitions of the Romish Church, are among "the palpable enormities which verify the "affirmative. These are inflicted by assemblies "and committees, who dare to profess them- "selves Friends to Liberty, upon the most quiet "subjects, without distinction of age or sex, for "the sole crime, often for the sole suspicion, "of having adhered in principle to the govern- "ment under which they were born, and to "which by every tie, divine and human, they "owe allegiance. To consummate these shock- "ing proceedings, the profanation of religion "is added to the most profligate prostitution of "common sense; the consciences of men are "set at nought, and multitudes are compelled, "not only to bear arms, but also to swear sub- "jection, to an usurpation they abhor." Here is an epitome of all that has been said and written againſt the French, and why ſhould we not ſuppoſe, that were they left to themſelves, they would ſoon become as orderly, peaceable, flouriſhing, and happy, as the Americans? France has the natural ſources to make merchants like Holland, manufacturers like Britain, and farmers like America. And, I believe, the concert of Princes, was firſt formed againſt her from a knowledge that a few years Peace, would make her people ſo wealthy, comfortable and happy, that inſtead of being a terrible warning, ſhe would be a ſeducing example to ſurrounding nations; that the Deſpots of the continent ſaw ariſing from the ruins of French Deſpotiſm, the fabrick of human felicity, and conſequently the harbinger of their deſtruction, and therefore they wiſhed to ſtrangle it. At preſent, France is neither an example, nor a warning; ſhe is in a ſtate of madneſs, occaſioned,—not by perſonal Repreſentation, as Mr. Young continually aſſerts, for he might as juſtly ſay, the ſhocking yellow fever which has juſt broke out in Philadelphia, is the effect of RepreſentativeGovernment in America; but, by the infamous invaſion of the Duke of Brunſwick, and the treachery and alarm raging in her boſom. I therefore affirm, that an admirable proof of the utility of Repreſentative Government exiſts in America, and deny, that the experiment of perſonal Repreſentation has been even *tried*, much leſs "*compleatly made*" in France, or that ſhe ſhould either encourage, or deter us, from ſalutary Reform. France would not Reform till it was too late:—may her example, in that reſpect, be, indeed, a warning to Britain.

Having

Having ſhewn Mr. Young's fallacy in condemning Repreſentative Government in France upon " experiment," and in America upon " ſpeculation ;" and having eſtabliſhed the experiment of America in my own favour, I ſhall now notice a few of the moſt miſchievous falſehoods, and abſurd contradictions, which he has advanced againſt Reform, but without ſtopping to examine every groundleſs aſſertion, and trivial argument. I ſhall take his leading reaſons only; the moſt unfounded and atrocious of which is, where he maintains, " that the " example of the King of France ſhould deter " all other Kings from liſtening to the com- " plaints of their ſubjects ; he wiſhed to Re- " form ; he was the firſt Monarch who was " deſirous of making his people happy, and *he* " *died for it on a ſcaffold*."—It is difficult to ſay, whether the falſehood contained, or the Tyranny recommended in this paſſage, ſhould moſt provoke indignation ! The falſehood is ſo well known, that none but Mr. Young could have had effrontery ſufficient to have aſſerted it ; and the ſentiment conveyed is more dangerous to the liberties and happineſs of Britain, than all the works of Mr. Paine and the " Jacobin Societies." The King of France *did not* die on the ſcaffold becauſe he liſtened to Reform ;—it was becauſe he would *not* liſten to it till it was *too late* ;— till he was *compelled*. Inſtead of liſtening to Reform, he liſtened to evil Counſellors ; he ſuffered himſelf to be guided by perſons who laviſhed the puplic money on uſeleſs placemen and penſioners ; on favourites, paraſites, and the moſt pernicious of all traitors, *regular-bred*

courtiers,

courtiers, who, to ſupply their prodigality, loaded the people with Taxes ; and finding, at laſt, their profligate extravagance was on the eve of ruining them, agreed to Reform as their only chance of ſalvation. They firſt threatened the Parliament of Paris if it did not comply with their demands ;—did that look like a wiſh to Reform? They next tried the ſhift of the Notables ; but like their conduct with the Parliament of Paris, it alſo proved ineffectual ; and after many other vain expedients, they were at laſt forced to call the States General, in hopes that they would cover their paſt iniquities, and grant a new leaſe for plundering the Nation. In that hope, however, they were alſo miſtaken. The people had long ſmarted with patience under the Tyranny of the Nobles, and extortions of the Government ; they were now menaced with large additional burthens, and the general danger created a general alarm. The ſpirit of the country was rouſed by the infamy of the Adminiſtration ; and finding the Court only ſtooped to conceſſion, to hide its miſmanagement, and inſure its future robberies, rather than from a ſincere wiſh to Reform and make them happy, the people reſolved no more to truſt to thoſe who had invariably betrayed them ; the cauſe of the people triumphed ; the rapacious views of the courtiers were defeated, and the old Deſpotiſm ſtripped of its riches and grandeur, was too feeble, ugly, and corrupt, to protract its exiſtence. Such was the commencement of the French Revolution. It was not the deſire of the King to *Reform*, but the deſire of his Miniſters to *rob*, that brought him to the ſcaffold.

All

All the calamities with which France is afflicted, are ascribed, by Mr. Young, to personal Representation, and the same are predicted in England, if any Reform of the House of Commons takes place. Accordingly, a number of his paragraphs conclude with "Such is the "monster, personal Representation:"—"Such "the result of that Constitution founded on "personal Representation:"—"Power, in the "hands of the people, by means of personal "Representation, has ruined France:" &c.—And thus he proceeds, asserting, that all the misfortunes in which that nation is involved, are the consequence of the will of the people, being supreme. In answer to this, which is the *sole object* of his book, I shall shew, first, that he contradicts himself, and that the very reverse of what he so often repeats and labours to establish, may be proved by his own words; and secondly, that the experiment of Personal Representation has not been attempted in France, till *after* the downfal of Monarchy, and, therefore, it *cannot* justly be blamed with producing that event, or the transactions which preceded.

P. 91, he says, that "if the House of Commons "were such Representatives" (as in France) "they *would be guided* by the folly, madness, "and passions of the people." Seven pages further on, however, he thinks quite differently, and that "Representation destroys itself, and "generates with infallible certainty an oligarchy "of mobbish demagogues, till of all other "voices, that *least heard* is the *real* will of the "people."—Again (p. 106.) he maintains, that

"a Par-

" a Parliament conſtituted on perſonal Repre-" ſentation *can* act *no otherwiſe* than by the " *immediate impulſe* of the people." But this, he ten pages before, affirms to be wrong; He thinks, " a word however, might be ſaid on " the point of perſonal Repreſentation, rendering " the will of the people *ſupreme*. The *futility* " of the idea is demonſtrated, in the Aſſemblies *ſo* " *choſen*, in France; their firſt merit, on Jaco-" bin principles, is, that of ſpeaking the ſove-" reign will of the people, by which expreſſion, " is always underſtood the Majority: But, ſo " truly abominable, is this ſyſtem of Govern-" ment, that there has not been a ſingle in-" ſtance of great and marked importance, in " which the *Minority*, and commonly, a *very* " *ſmall Minority*, has not, by means of terror, " carried all before them."—Thus, he at one time affirms, that the will of the people " *would* " guide" perſonal Repreſentatives, and yet, that among ſuch Repreſentatives, the will of the people would be " *leaſt* heard."—That perſonal Repreſentatives " can act *no otherwiſe*, than " by the *immediate impulſe* of the peo-" ple," and that every inſtance, of great and marked importance, in France, has, by means of terror, been carried by the will of a *very ſmall Minority!*—Theſe contradictions are fatal to all Mr. Young has written, and are a juſt illuſtration of the whole *fairneſs* of his book.

His inconſiſtency, in condemning perſonal Repreſentation, might be farther expoſed, but it will ſhorten the ſubject much to ſhew, that the caſe of France is wholly inapplicable, and is neither an example, nor a warning to Britain,

 with

with regard to Reform, particularly as applied by Mr. Young. The Aſſembly which framed the Conſtitution of 1789, was not elected by univerſal ſuffrage, nor agreeably to any new ſyſtem of Reform. It was elected according to the rules, and under the direction of the French Monarchy; according to a ſyſtem eſtabliſhed for centuries. Reform, or Perſonal Repreſentation, therefore, are no more to be blamed for what it did, that was blameable, than they would be, if our Houſe of Commons were to exterminate every Friend to Liberty, and eſtabliſh Deſpotiſm in England. The Conſtituent Aſſembly was elected according to the old " Mild benignant" French Monarchy; according to a ſyſtem, " The work of the wiſdom of ages; yet it was that very Aſſembly which Mr. Burke reprobated, and Mr. Paine applauded, and againſt which the Convention at Pilnitz, the foundation of the preſent War, was formed. It was the authority of that Aſſembly which the Britiſh Government would never fully recognize: It is that Aſſembly which Lords Auckland and Hood, and even Mr. Young deſcribe, when they mention " The miſcreants, who, for *four* " *years*, diſtracted France." Then why ſhould the tranſactions of that Aſſembly deter us from Reform, ſince it was elected according to the Conſtitution of the Old French Deſpotiſm? It ſhould rather be an argument *in favour* of Reform, becauſe, according to Mr. Young and others, it produced much miſchief, and it was an old UNREFORMED Aſſembly.

The ſecond Aſſembly was not elected by univerſal ſuffrage, and of the third Aſſembly, it is uncandid

uncandid to ſpeak, for, during its exiſtence, it has rather been the Council of War of a great Army, than the ſeat of Peace and temperate Legiſlation: and it might as reaſonably be concluded, that the Britiſh Government is deſpotic, becauſe, for the ſake of diſcipline, Deſpotiſm muſt be exerciſed in the Britiſh Camp under the Duke of York, as to conclude that Anarchy, Confuſion, and Deſpotiſm, are the certain accompanyments of French Principles of Liberty, and will always be exerciſed by the Convention.

Having now ſhewn the inconſiſtency with which Mr. Young would build up his "Warning" againſt perſonal Repreſentation, by which he always means Reform, having alſo ſhewn that the French Revolution, and the calamities afflicting that country, did not ariſe *from* perſonal Repreſentation, which has neither had time nor opportunity to operate there; and that therefore the tranſactions in France have no analogy whatever with Parliamentary Reform in this kingdom; I ſhall, for a while quit French affairs to examine what Mr. Young ſays of the Britiſh Conſtitution, and particularly of the Houſe of Commons.

"But" (ſays he, p. 92) "the Houſe of "Commons are corrupted and bribed. And "if the nature of ſuch an Aſſembly demands "to be corrupted in order to purſue the public "good, who but a Viſionary can wiſh to re-"move Corruption?" Muſt not an Aſſembly, conſtituted for the public good, be of a moſt *deteſtable nature*, if it demands to be bribed in order to diſcharge its duty? Again, "In-"fluence, or, as Reformers call it, Corrup-

 "tion,

" tion, is the oil which makes the machine of " Government go well." And p. 171. " Ex" TRAVAGANT COURTS, SELFISH MINISTERS, " *and* CORRUPT MAJORITIES, are ſo " intimately interwoven with our practical " Freedom, that it would require better poli" tical Anatomiſts, than our modern Reformers, " to ſhew, on fact, that we did not owe our " Liberty to the identical Evils which they " want to expunge." Could the whole National Convention more groſsly Libel the King, the Miniſters, and the Parliament, of this Country? Surely, Mr. Young muſt have known, that he was writing the moſt bitter and dangerous ſatire on our Government, when he ſaid, that extravagant Courts, Selfiſh Miniſters, and *Corrupt Majorities*, were intimately interwoven with our Freedom, and yet aſſert, that this is " that glorious Conſtitution which is the inhe" ritance and pride of Britons!" I appeal to every candid man whether the friends to the Liberty of the Preſs, or Mr. Young, ſeem moſt diſpoſed " *to publiſh the Corruptions of the* " *Conſtitution*, in other words, *to write it* " *down*. (vide p. 163.)

In anſwering this frontleſs avowal of Corruption, I muſt ſuppoſe the Houſe of Commons compoſed of either good or bad men. If they are the former, and are ſuffered to exerciſe their own diſcretion, they will purſue the public welfare without Corruption, unleſs it is preſumed they cannot ſee it without the explanation of a Bank Note. If they are bad men, they will be bribed to do evil as readily as good. It may indeed be ſaid, that influence is often neceſſary to

make

make a virtuous man do a virtuous action; and that is true: For, although a virtuous man will act virtuously when he does act, yet there are occasions where he is not called upon by duty to act at all: But on the contrary, a Member of Parliament *is in duty bound* to act, to take either one side or another; and if he is a good man, he will act for the best, according to his conscience, without either Corruption or Influence. It is an absurdity to say, that a man can be *corrupted* to act *virtuously*; because if he acts from a corrupt motive, he is equally vicious whether the action be good or bad, and will not much consider whether he does right or wrong, while his primary object, Corruption, is obtained. The same reasoning will apply to the assertion, that "a man may be bribed to act "wisely;" unless the man is supposed to be a fool. Nor do I understand how a man can be *influenced* to do good, for, in a case, like that of the House of Commons, where he *must* act, he must be predisposed to do evil before he can be influenced to do good, and consequently he must be a bad man: And all the arguments in favour of Influence, do, in fact, go to prove, that the Members of the House of Commons, are traitors to the State, who would ruin it if they were not influenced to the contrary. As Mr. Young has quoted Dr. Johnson's definition of "*Principle*," I will take what the same author says of "*To Influence*," which is, "to modify "to *any* purpose." If Influence, therefore, can modify to *any* purpose, (which it certainly can, or else it is no longer Influence;) and if our House of Commons is, as Mr. Young asserts, directed

directed by Influence, then it is the mere creature of the Executive Power which possesses that Influence; and it is a mistake to suppose that it makes laws, or does either a good or a bad action: It is the King's Ministers, who, holding the Influence that directs it, ought to be wholly blamed or thanked for whatever it does; because, they may *influence* it to the most wicked, as well as the most wise measures; and it would be better, if the "Monster," as Mr. Young calls it, were annihilated, for then morality would not be wounded; Government would be carried on at a less expence, and with more ease and vigour; and Ministers would be much more responsible for their conduct.

But while I maintain influencing or corrupting the Representative Body by the Executive Power (which in this country, is not, I hope, the case, notwithstanding Mr. Young's assertions) to be the most pernicious of all Policy, and the blackest of all Treason; I am far from maintaining that Members of Parliament should not be rewarded for their trouble: On the contrary, I think they should be openly paid a regular, ample stipend; but it should be paid merely as a reward for their trouble, and not as an equivalent for their honesty; they should publicly receive a certain sum, and not secretly take a recompence which they are ashamed to own. If it were the custom, that our Ambassadors should receive no pay from our own Government, and were permitted to take as much as they could procure from the Courts to which they were sent, can it be doubted that they would sacrifice our interest for that of those from whom they expected a reward? In like manner, it would be folly to suppose that a Parliament pensioned by the Government, would guard the interests of the people against the Government.

I am at a loss to conceive how the Corruption of the House of Commons can be deemed the *cause* of our prosperity and happiness, nor have I ever seen any fact produced tending to prove it. It is asserted, that we are prosperous and happy, and admitted that Corruption does exist; and, therefore, it is inferred, because Corruption is a part of the system which makes us prosperous and happy, *that it is the cause* of our prosperity and happiness. But nothing can, I think, be more false than this inference: It might as justly be inferred, that a mixture of weeds, among the corn, is the cause of a plentiful harvest; that the dross mixed in the ore with gold and silver, is the cause of their value; or that insects and locusts are the cause of a luxuriant herbage. Would a tradesman ascribe his accumulation of wealth to the pilfering of his till by his shopman? Corruption may, indeed, be a *part* of a system, good upon the whole; but it is a *bad* part, and ought to be removed. It is not to Corruption we are to attribute our prosperity and happiness, but to the spirit and industry of the people.

I shall now consider the question of Reform under four distinct heads, and in doing so, shall aim at brevity, and endeavour, as much as possible, to avoid a repetition of the many arguments which have been advanced in favour of it. I shall examine

The

The neceſſity of Reforming the Houſe of Commons.

How far a Reform can be made in conformity with the ſpirit, principles, and practice, of the Conſtitution.

The time for making a Reform.

What the nature of the Reform ſhould be.

Of the NECESSITY of Reform, the removal of Mr. Young's *ſalutary* Corruption, is, the ſtrongeſt proof; for Corruption, if practiſed, muſt deſtroy the whole original deſign of the Houſe of Commons, which, even according to to himſelf, was to *adviſe* the King in important matters of State. Now, as advice does not mean aſſent, but muſt often be contrary to the opinions and wiſhes of thoſe who aſk it; and as it is well known, that the King cannot act contrary to the advice of his Commons, it is, in fact, a controul, a command. If, therefore, Corruption or Influence makes them adviſe the King to whatever he recommends, their controul is loſt, and the King is as abſolute as the Empreſs of Ruſſia, ſo long as he poſſeſſes the means to *influence*. "If "Courts *can* be perfidious, you are to ſuppoſe "they *will* be ſo; and if you have not ſo pro-"vided as to turn that perfidy to the benefit of "the people, you confeſs at once, that your "Conſtitution is viſionary," ſays Mr. Young (p. 68,)—If ſo, what proviſion is there againſt the perfidy of the Britiſh Court, while it dictates to Parliament by its Influence? With Corruption and Influence, then, our Houſe of Commons muſt be an illuſion, and a dangerous illuſion; becauſe, it is not reſponſible, and takes off all reſponſibility from the Crown. It muſt give a falſe appearance of ſanction, and bind the people to whatever the Crown propoſes, and pays for with the money taken from the people: It would be as if a Court of Law were to grant to a highwayman a licenſe to rob, upon condition that he paid into it a part of his plunder. With Corruption, our Houſe of Commons, would be both *uſeleſs* and EXPENSIVE; but I am far, very far from believing, it is governed by Corruption, and I think it my duty here to remark, on the ſhameleſs effrontery of Mr. Reeves, in thanking Mr. Young for aſſerting, that we are governed by extravagant Courts, ſelfiſh Miniſters, and corrupt Majorities (vide p. 171.) and alſo, to expreſs my ſurpriſe, that the Houſe of Commons has not addreſſed the King, or that the Attorney General has not been commanded to proſecute in his book, that which in Mr Horne Took's petition, reſpecting the Weſtminſter Election, was, by all parties, deemed the moſt groſs and ſcandalous libel that ever came before them.

Mr. Young aſſerts, and, indeed, it is the common doctrine of all thoſe who coincide with him in opinion, that the Houſe of Commons was always deſigned to repreſent, not the people at large, but the people of property, in the kingdom. Admitting this to be a fact, let us ſee how far its preſent ſtate agrees with the deſign. Are the paupers of Stockbridge, Barnſtable, Seaford, all the boroughs in Cornwall, and a majority of the boroughs in the kingdom, the men of property? Why are the wealthy Inhabitants of St. Mary-le-bonne, and other pariſhes in London, who in point of property, are able to buy the electors of a majority of the House of Commons, excluded from sending Representatives? Why are the wealthy Merchants and Manufacturers of Manchester, Sheffield, Birmingham, and even of London, denied their right of voting? But, it will probably be said, a rich and commercial man, may, at the expence of five thousands pounds, procure a seat in Parliament, if he desires it, and this shews the utility of the rotten boroughs, and proves that property, predominates in the House of Commons: To this I ask, will a commercial, or any other man, lay out five thousand pounds without the prospect of a return? If we see a rich avaricious man, expending immense sums, to obtain the influence over a borough, we cannot mistake his object; it must be with him an adventure, a speculation, which he hopes, will, in one way or another, return a proportionate profit. And the mischief is, that the traffic may not be merely confined to British subjects, but may, by foreign Princes, be converted into the means of ruling our Councils, and ruining us as a nation; for, if Mr. Pitt spoke truly, when he declared, " it was notorious " that the Nabob of Arcot had fifteen Mem- " bers in that House, and that they did not act " upon an identity of interest with the people," why may not any other Prince send in his members, and by expending a million sterling, take the money out of Englishmen's pockets, and force them to fight his battles? If it be said, though the Electors are poor, the Representatives are wealthy, I answer, that we not only find beggarly boroughs, but needy members

sitting

ſitting for them. And as to " the property of the kingdom being in the hands of the mem- " bers *," I will aſk where is the property (diveſted of their places and penſions, and other political emoluments) of Meſſ. Pitt, Dundas, Jenkinſon, Long, Roſe, Steele, Addington, and Burke? Theſe are the leading men in Parliament, yet, according to Mr. Young's argument, they muſt lead to miſchief, becauſe they have little or no property.—Look at the oppoſition :—See, (according to Mr. Young's argument again) what ample ſecurity we have that they will act for the public good, becauſe they have large poſſeſſions. Meſſ. Grey, Whitbread, Lambton, Byng, Wharton, M. A. Taylor, Baker, Lord Wycombe, &c. &c. either poſſeſs, or are immediate heirs, to large eſtates; and Meſſ. Erſkine and Sheridan are of all others, intereſted in the peace and proſperity of the country, as their lucrative incomes from the bar and the theatre, would be the firſt ſpecies of property likely to ſuffer from a convulſion.—Go up to the Houſe of Peers, and ſearch for the property (places and Penſions excepted) of Lords Grenville, Hawkebury, Chatham, Auckland, and Loughborough. Compare the leaders of adminiſtration and oppoſition throughout, and it will be found, that the former are poor, and the latter are wealthy;—Nay, take the aggregate of the number, and fortunes of " the Jacobin Society of the " Friends of the People," and compare them with the Houſe of Commons, (places and pen-

* Young p. 84.

ſions excepted) and they will, perhaps, be found to be as wealthy and reſpectable, as that pure body. If, as Mr. Young aſſerts, property were to be the foundation of our confidence in public men, there would inſtantly be a change in adminiſtration, and a Reform of Parliament. I therefore deny, that in the conſtruction of the Houſe of Commons, there is any operating principle or controul, which ſecures the protection of property, more than there is among a club of ſtock-brokers, whoſe primary object always is their own immediate advantage, whether it be connected with the welfare of the nation, or not. Hence, if we are to be guided, by what Mr. Young affirms, of the Houſe of Commons, that *it is a Repreſentation of property*, a Reform becomes as indiſpenſible as upon any other principle. What, though ſome members are men of property, they may conſent to invade the poſſeſſions of the rich in general, becauſe they may receive a private compenſation that will not only reimburſe their own perſonal loſs, but plentifully reward them for betraying the intereſts of men of property at large, who have no more controul over them, than the Swiniſh multitude of Mancheſter and Birmingham. Diſtribute the elective franchiſe, equally among men of property, and I am content, becauſe I believe ſuch a diſtribution would render the Houſe of Commons independent of the Government, which is the true object of any Reform.

It may, perhaps, be ſaid, our Conſtitution, originally, recognized only as men of property the owners of landed eſtates; that they all now

have

have votes, and therefore the ancient ſpirit is preſerved. Without enquiring into the abuſes of County Elections, or ſhewing the futility of the expectation, that eighty county members, could ſecure us againſt four hundred and ſeventy-eight from cities and rotten boroughs, I ſhall content myſelf at preſent with aſſerting, that the ancient ſpirit, principles, and "*Practice*," of the Conſtitution, recognized as men, who had a right to be conſulted in the National Councils, all who were of CONSIDERATION, whether by Landed Property, as at firſt was the caſe, or by Manufactures or Commerce, which afterwards occaſioned Citizens and Burgeſſes to be called to Parliament, and which now are of much more importance to the kingdom than all its land. I ſhall ſhew this more fully when I conſider how far a Reform can be conſtitutionally made. At preſent, I ſhall only aſſert, that according to the original principles, and practice, of the Conſtitution, and according to Mr. Young's definition of what the Houſe of Commons *is*, (a Repreſentation, not of Perſons, but of Property), a Reform is abſolutely neceſſary, becauſe it neither agrees with what it originally was, and now ought to be, nor with his deſcription of it; for Property is not even ſo much repreſented in the Houſe of Commons as Perſons.

Such, upon the principles of the Anti-Reformers, is the neceſſity of reforming Parliament; and if the practical evils ariſing from the defective Repreſentation are conſidered, they will be found ſtill more urgent in favour of that meaſure. It is, I believe, univerſally admitted, that the prosperity of this country has arisen from the superior portion of Freedom enjoyed by its inhabitants, above those of the surrounding nations: If that be the case, the continuance of our prosperity must depend on the continuance of our Freedom; and, if we find the House of Commons easily agreeing to narrow the latter, we cannot expect that the former will have a very long existence. The ready acquiescence to laying on additional burthens; the profusion of the public money, and the invariable, enormous accumulation of debt, demonstrate the certainty, that at some time, we must reach the summit of the borrowing system: And even before this natural death of our public credit, the flames of some unnecessary War may melt the waxen wings, on which, like Icarus, we have towered to such an unnatural heighth. But what is more immediately alarming, the most arbitrary laws are found necessary, and are enacted, to ensure the collection of the Revenue: Those Laws are destructive of Freedom, and consequently must destroy our prosperity, for they openly and unequivocally invade our Liberties, and tend gradually to abolish and totally to annihilate them. The Right of an Englishman to a Trial by a Jury of his equals, has long been esteemed the dearest he possesses; but this, in certain cases, which, with the increase of our debt, are annually accumulating, is compleatly abolished. It is not that justice is done between man and man that constitutes Liberty, so much as that justice is done between the Government and the People. In the most arbitrary and tyrannical

rannical Monarchies, ſtrict juſtice is generally adminiſtered between individuals; nay, it is more eaſy to be obtained, perhaps, than in Britain, becauſe the expence is leſs. All men act juſtly, unleſs they have an intereſt in acting otherwiſe: Deſpots, therefore, can have no intereſts in deciding partially between individuals: On the contrary, they will be eager to do rigid juſtice, in order to palliate their own robberies. Of what importance, then, is it, that we have Juries to try actions between John and William? Theſe might be as fairly decided, if there were no other Jury than the twelve, or four Judges. It is in caſes between the Crown and People that injuſtice is to be guarded againſt. Yet, we find Parliament yearly ſanctioning in the Exciſe, Stamp, and other Revenue Laws, the gradual Abolition of the Trial by Jury; becauſe, according to the late Earl of Chatham and Sir George Saville, their Corruption involved us in the American War, which brought a debt of an hundred Millions on our heads; and, according to Mr. Young, they are now to add another hundred to deſtroy a combination of Reformers; i. e. to preſerve to Lords Camelford and Egremont the privilege of ſending Members to Parliament for the Sheep Cots of old Sarum, and the Stones of Midhurſt! And to preſerve "Extravagant Courts, Selfiſh "Miniſters, and Corrupt Majorities!!!" (vide p. 171.)

The oppreſſive operation of thoſe Revenue Laws, particularly of the Exciſe, has often been ably demonſtrated. During the preſent Adminiſtration, they have been eagerly extended.

What

What can be more vexatious than that the Stamp Office ſhould keep in its pay Informers, who, before they will be ſuch, muſt have loſt all ſenſe of ſhame or honeſty; who muſt have abandoned all hopes of ever being reſpectable in ſociety, and who, conſequently, muſt hate, and become the enemies of mankind, becauſe they know mankind deſpiſe and deteſt them? What can be more vexatious or deſtructive of Freedom, than that one of theſe reptiles may go into a tradeſman's ſhop, purchaſe a pair of gloves, and by quirk or perjury, (for the oath of ſuch a miſcreant, is ſufficient, and is taken in preference to that of the moſt reſpectable tradeſman) fine the vender in ten guineas, half of which goes to himſelf? Is this tried by a Jury? No. Who tries it? A Magiſtrate, or two, appointed by, and receiving a ſalary, from the proſecutor, (the Government;) it is tried by men who ſubſiſt on the fund to which the other half of the penalty is carried, and who, therefore, in a certain degree, have a common intereſt with the Informer. For additional inſtances of this kind, beſides the Exciſe, Farming of Taxes, &c. conſult the Hatters, Perfumers, and many other Shopkeepers. Liberty, which animates the induſtry and enterprize of the people, and is univerſally allowed to have been the cauſe of our proſperity, can no more exiſt under a continual extenſion of theſe laws, than ice in a furnace; and when once the cauſe is removed, the effect will not long remain. Whether the Houſe of Commons, as at preſent conſtituted, is likely to encreaſe or diminiſh the debt, which gives birth to theſe proceedings, is obvious.

obvious. Here I will not take theory, but Mr. Young's favourite "Practice," and according to practice, our debt will rapidly increase, and our Freedom as rapidly vanish. Spain, was once the most powerful, because the most free nation in Europe: Her Cortes resembled our Parliament, but were, perhaps, much more pure. Corruption, indolence, pride, and oppression*, stole into her government, from whence they were imbibed by her Nobles, and her People: Her Freedom, of course, gradually disappeared, until its bare remembrance was lost; and behold now, how wretched are her inhabitants; how insignificant as a nation!

Besides, the ready acquiescence to Taxes, and to the arbitrary Laws found necessary to exact them; there are other circumstances, not less urgent in favour of Parliamentary Reform. Why were not the violators of the Constitution in the case of the Middlesex Election punished? Why was Lord Mansfield permitted to imprison Bingley two years against the Law? Why were Ministers allowed to continue the American War without the shadow of ability, or a hope of success, during several years, after the nation disapproved of it? Or what is more recent, why was not an inquiry granted into the conduct of Mr. Rose, in the Westminster Elec-

* The most detestable means of her oppression, was, the Inquisition, which has been long proverbially execrated by every honest Briton; yet, Mr. Young says, were he a Spanish Minister, he would not abolish it! Probably, he wishes to introduce it into England, and to place it under the direction of Mr. Reeves, than whom not a more fit Director could be found.

tion? Why have the chief agitators of the Manchester, Mount-ſtreet, and Birmingham Riots eſcaped juſtice? To theſe queries, Mr. Young, will, perhaps, anſwer, "Why! Becauſe, all "thoſe meaſures were only oiling the machinery "of Government, to make it go ſmoothly; "they were only ſome of the oil of Influence, "which is Corruption, in the eyes of Re-"formers."

It is not neceſſary to enumerate the penſioning of Magiſtrates, building of Barracks, and a thouſand other ſimilar inſtances, in order to convince every unprejudiced mind, towards what centre the whole tranſactions of Parliament gravitate; nor might it be ſafe to animadvert on them freely. Let thoſe, who deſire a more perfect illuſtration, read the late Hiſtory of this Country, and particularly of the preſent Miniſters, where they may collect a ſufficient number to fill a volume. Shew me one inſtance, during the boaſted adminiſtration of the laſt ten years, in which the Houſe of Commons has ſupported the intereſts of the People, and of juſtice, in oppoſition to the wiſhes of the Crown? If it can be ſhewn, that, upon one or two marked occaſions, it has done this, then, I may think, its miſconduct rather the effect of error, than of criminal acquieſcence: But if this cannot be ſhewn, then I muſt either conclude, our preſent Governors to be the wiſeſt that ever exiſted in the world, ſince they have not erred once in ten years, or that Parliament is ſo ſervile as never to thwart them. In the caſe of the late Ruſſian Armament, the Houſe of Commons, having no ſympathy of ſenti-

ment

ment with the nation, voted, according to the wishes of the ministers, first for, and then against, a measure. What was the consequence of this? They were proved to have acted contrary, and the Minister afterwards to have acted in conformity, to the will of the people. By this means all the public esteem was transferred to Mr. Pitt, which would have fallen to the Representatives of the people, if they had done their duty. Our Premier, in this way, has artfully gained all his popularity; for, while he affects to despise the will of the people, he, rather than hazard his situation, obeys it on all dangerous occasions. And, as in the Russian Armament, he robbed the House of Commons, so in the present War, he robbed the Crown of the public affection; for, when the calamities it brought on were daily rendering it more unpopular, his friends industriously circulated a report, that it was then continued quite against his inclination, but that higher powers (meaning the King and his friends) would have it so. By this means, his popularity was at once preserved, both among those who wished to terminate, and those who wished to continue the War. It has hitherto been the practice, that when any Act of Grace was to be done, the King, by being made the instrument in performing it, should reap all the advantage arising from the national gratitude: Mr. Pitt, however, has reversed this custom; and when any odious measure is to take place, the Crown is made not only the agent, but the parent of it, while his friends exculpate him, by shruggs, and hints of regret, at the necessity of submitting. Thus we

 find

find him at once robbing both the King and Commons of the public esteem and gratitude, and throwing all that is unfortunate or obnoxious to their charge: He puts himself where the Monarch formerly stood; becomes the dispenser of every thing that is gracious, and by this artful unconstitutional conduct, concentrates in his person all that is to be admired and beloved, either in the executive or legislative power, and filches a popularity, not more unnatural, than formidable and alarming.

Notwithstanding the contumely with which the will of the people, calmly expressed in an assembly of Delegates, is treated by the Anti-Reformers, yet they often justify their own conduct on that very will which they affect to condemn: If it is said, a Parliamentary Reform is necessary, in order to ascertain the will of the people in a peaceable constitutional manner, they answer, Parliament ought not to be guided by the will of the people, and therefore a Reform is needless: But throw the blame of the American War on Parliament, and they shift their ground, they change sides, and boast that it was popular. They justify themselves in commencing the American War, on the will of the people, and yet they deny that the will of the people should be their guide! It is necessary this should be decided; Either let the will of the people, or the will of Parliament, since they are to be distinct things, be the rule of action. If the will of Parliament is to be the rule, then the blame of the American War attaches to them alone, and justifies a Reform, in order to prevent another such evil: If the will

will of the people is to be the rule, then, as the Houſe of Commons voted directly againſt it, in the caſe of the Ruſſian Armament, that Armament juſtifies a Reform alſo.

But it will not be improper to enquire a little into the nature of the Will of the People. Upon examination, it will be found to be of two very diſtinct kinds, the one originating with themſelves, their own pure offspring, the other, a courtly baſtard. A clear inſtance of the latter may be found in the fate of Mr. Fox's Eaſt India Bill, which paſſed the Houſe of Commons without a murmur among the people, and was even approved, till the ſecret adviſers of the Crown raiſed an alarm about charters, and ſucceeded, in ſtimulating the public, to expreſs the ſtrongeſt diſapprobation of the meaſure. The popularity of the American War was alſo hatched in the Cabinet. The national indignation was inſidiouſly rouſed, by holding up the refuſal of the Americans to pay taxes, like ourſelves, while the true cauſe of the quarrel, the queſtion of Repreſentation, was kept in the back ground, or, if ſtarted, was anſwered, by the abuſes in our own;—by inſtancing Mancheſter, Birmingham, &c.—by the deformity of the Britiſh Houſe of Commons, was the American War juſtified, and therefore, had a Reform taken place twenty years ago, one chief ſophiſtical pretext of that unhappy War, had not exiſted. It is likewiſe a courtly popularity, which has ſanctioned the preſent War. Proclamations, camps, and addreſſes, were not regarded with indifference; Mr. Penſioner Reeves, from the Court, ſounded the trumpet of alarm, and

was

was echoed by the whole kingdom; thus a popularity, originating in the Cabinet, was given to the War, which I call a courtly baſtard popularity. But how was the American War ſtopped, or a War with Ruſſia prevented? Not by an expreſſion of the public will, created in, and directed by the Cabinet, but by an expreſſion of the public will, emanating purely from the people themſelves, and in direct oppoſition to the wiſhes of the Cabinet. On theſe occaſions, the people could not be duped; and I think the will of the people, that ſanctioned in its commencement, and the will of the people that brought to a concluſion, the American War, were as different in their nature as in their object. Miniſters will always be attempting to create theſe baſtard courtly wills, for their own ſelfiſh purpoſes, to the injury of the nation; it is the duty of the Houſe of Commons to detect and expoſe them, and to guard the people from being duped into ruin; but, inſtead of this, we find the Houſe of Commons generally the chief inſtrument in promoting the deluſion: in the Ruſſian Armament they were notorioouſly ſo. And therefore, to make them more careful of the intereſts of the people: to unmaſk, rather than cover the courtly deſigns, a Reform has become neceſſary.

Theſe two different wills of the people were to be traced in the ſentiments and conduct of the Alarmiſts and Anti-Reformers laſt winter. They exulted in the univerſal loyalty of the country, in the general affection of the people for the Conſtitution, and in their concurrence in the meaſures of government; they exulted

in

in the *courtly* will of the people. But when the queſtion of Reform was ſtarted they deprecated the will of the people as the mother of every calamity. If the War was conſidered, they vaunted that the will of the people was in its favour;—if Reform was conſidered, they reprobated the will of the people as the moſt miſchievous of all guides. Was it ever boaſted, or given as an argument in ſupport, of a meaſure, that the will ot the people was againſt it?—No.—Is not the reverſe almoſt always the caſe?—Yes. Is not this proof of the neceſſity of knowing the will of the people, and conſequently of Reform? Did not thoſe who boaſted the general approbation of the War, and the meaſures of government, and thereby applaud the Will of the people, in fact confeſs the neceſſity of Reform?—Nay, a more important confeſſion is to be found in the deſcription the Houſe of Commons gives of itſelf. In impeachments, ſuch as that now carrying on againſt Mr. Haſtings, they proſecute in the name of ALL the Commons of Great Britain. Thus they themſelves own, they ought to be elected by univerſal ſuffrage; for to act in the name of *all*, without conſulting, or even of being capable of knowing the will of the *Majority*, appears to be inconſiſtent with common ſenſe. And of this Mr. Young ſeems aware, when he aſſerts, (p. 90,) that the Houſe of Commons *are not* the Repreſentatives of the People, and ought not to be ſo called. Yet, it was for this very ſame aſſertion, that the Sheffield and Nottingham petitions for Reform were rejected laſt ſeſſion of Parliament, and even

deemed

deemed libellous! Is it not, therefore, extraordinary, that Mr. Reeves should recommend a book, containing the same assertions, which the House of Commons deemed a libel, when contained in a petition? And is it not still more extraordinary, that the very men, who bellowed so much about the dignity of the House being insulted by those petitions, should reward Mr. Young with a place, for writing that, which, in St. Stephen's Chapel, they affected to condemn!

The addresses, associations, and general approbation of them, I consider to be direct confessions, of the necessity of Reform, because they are confessions of the utility of knowing the will of the people. The House of Commons was instituted for collecting and expressing that will, and ought still to do it; a House of Commons purely elected, being the only Constitutinal mouth-piece of the people. For the government, therefore, to seek the sense of the country, in addresses and associations, and to pretend to be guided by the public will, when collected in that partial irregular manner, is, I think, highly unconstitutional, and a most dangerous innovation, tending to supersede the use of the House of Commons altogether. Nor, are our affiliated societies, less eager to embark in all such measures, than government are to encourage them. Acting in conformity to the spirit which first animated them, they still imitate the French; for, as the Convention decreed, on the 22d of November 1793, that no priest should receive his pension without producing a certificate of his having paid contributions of civism; so they have set on foot civil contributions for flannel

waistcoats

waiſtcoats, in all the public offices, to which thoſe clerks, who did not ſubſcribe, may ſee reaſon to believe, that they will be conſidered as *ſuſpected perſons*, and may even loſe their places. The Archduke Charles has alſo publiſhed a proclamation, ſoliciting patriotic gifts, and voluntary contributions, from all well diſpoſed perſons, in the Netherlands, for the ſupport of the War. Thus we find, not only the Engliſh affiliated ſocieties, but the German Government, imitating the French mode of raiſing the ſupplies, and it may ſoon be as dangerous for a man in Britain, as for a prieſt in France, to be without a certificate of his having made contributions of civiſm.

But, in conſidering how far our affiliated ſocieties, aſſociated for the purpoſe of protecting the Conſtitution, are themſelves deſtroying it, we ſhall find, that addreſſes are not only contrary to the ſpirit of the Conſtitution, as they preſume to ſpeak the voice of the people, which can neither legally, nor fairly be done, unleſs in the Houſe of Commons; but that thoſe ſocieties, in attempting to raiſe the ſupplies, have taken the actual, and moſt important part of the buſineſs of the Houſe of Commons into their own hands, and if they ſucceed in their deſign, will render Parliaments totally uſeleſs.

The civic contributions for flannel waiſtcoats, were firſt begun in Edinburgh, afterwards in Windſor, and then the project was taken up in London, by a perſon notoriouſly in the pay * of Government, and in the confidence

 of

* Beſides having a ſhare in the property of the newſpaper, called the Sun, it is confidently ſaid, he is allowed 600l. per annum

of perſons *, high in office, with whom he daily communicates. A public meeting was next called, at the Crown and Anchor Tavern, where one of Mr. Reeves's committee, Mr. Devaynes, was appointed perpetual Preſident, and they reſolved themſelves into a ſociety for levying contributions of flannel waiſtcoats, and money for purchaſing them. The Common Council of the City of London, following their example, not only voted ſupplies as a body, but nominated each of their members, tax gatherers,—collectors of voluntary contributions in their reſpective ſections; and Mr. Serjeant Watſon, in St. Andrew's, Holborn, opens his budget, with a poll-tax of five ſhillings per head! It may, indeed, be ſaid, that theſe proceedings, though not ſtrictly conſtitutional, are of ſo little importance, that they do not deſerve the notice of Government; that the ſums or clothes collected are ſo trifling, compared with the neceſſities of the ſtate, that they never can ſuperſede the buſineſs of Parliament in granting the ſupplies: But we ſhall find, that it is not the fault of theſe ſocieties, if their proceedings are not carried to the moſt dangerous lengths: for, although they began with flannel waiſtcoats, we find ſucceſs has induced them to paſs to the providing of mitts, drawers, caps, ſhirts, Welch-wigs, ſtockings, ſhoes, trowſers, boots, ſheets, great coats, gowns, petticoats, blan-

annum for conducting that paper, and the True Briton, the latter of which is as confidenly ſaid, to be the property of perſons in office.

* Mr. Long, under Secretary to the Treaſury, and Mr. Burgeſs, under Secretary to the foreign department.

kets,

kets, &c. &c. From clothing the army, they have begun to victual them. A ſchoolmaſter, in the True Briton, recommends ſplit-peas, as good for their health, and, therefore, fit to be provided by the affiliated ſocieties. From the army, they have proceeded to clothe the navy, and at laſt, tired of going ſlowly on from one ſtep to another, they expreſs their wiſh of raiſing the whole expences of the State, and thereby not only ſuperſeding the uſe of Parliaments, but of financial Miniſters; not only of taking the buſineſs of the Houſe of Commons into their hands, but of taking the buſineſs of the Chancellor of the Exchequer alſo! Mr. Chairman Bligh, and his affiliated ſociety, in Chelſea *, declare their opinion to be, "that in "conſequence of the public ſpirit diſplayed in "ſubſcribing for extra clothing to the army, "*and confirmed of the value of our excellent* "*Conſtitution*, they ſuggeſt that the whole "expences of the War might be defrayed in "the ſame manner; and, that in proſecuting "the War, they earneſtly wiſh that the Mini-"ſter, whoſe office it is to find ways and "means for raiſing the ſupplies, could be re-"lieved from the political neceſſity of impoſing "taxes on the people." Thus they would relieve the Miniſter, and the Houſe of Commons, from raiſing taxes, to take the buſineſs into their own hands! A propoſition more hoſtile to the Conſtitution, and government of this coun-

* See the Advertiſement, containing the Reſolutions of this ſociety, ſigned J. Bligh, dated from the King's Arms, Five Fields, Chelſea, and publiſhed in the Sun, on Saturday, Nov. 30. 1793.

 try,

try, than the imputed offences for which Messrs. Muir and Palmer, are sentenced to be transported. Yet, the editor of the Sun, in a note to a correspondent, about the same time, remarks, not that such a plan is contrary to the laws of the land, but that he is afraid it would not be *sufficiently* productive!

The History of this Country will justify me in asserting, that these proceedings are highly unconstitutional. Benevolences, or voluntary contributions, which at first were free, were afterwards made compulsory, and were carried to such an extent, that the act passed in the first of Richard the IIId. "Damning and annulling "for ever that mode of raising money," affirms, that these benevolences had been the ruin of many families, by obliging them to sell off their household goods, and reducing them to beggary, &c. The attempt to raise forced benevolences, in a great degree, brought Charles the Ist. to the scaffold, and so sensible was his successor, Charles the IId. of this, and the danger of at all raising money in that manner, that, in the second year after his restoration, and in the zenith of his popularity, he did not presume to do what a hired agent of Government, an editor of a newspaper, now takes upon him to put in practice; for we find, that in 1661, an act was passed "to impower the King to receive "from his subjects a *free* and *voluntary contri-* "*bution*, for his present occasions *," and the words of the act itself, not only expressly declare, that it shall not be drawn into example

* See Rapin's History of England, vol. 2, p. 626.

for

for the future, but that *no aids of that nature*, can be iſſued or *levied*, but by conſent of Parliament *.

Now, the greateſt want of Charles the IId. was money to eſtabliſh a ſtanding army, and as the preſent " free and voluntary contributions" are alſo for the army, the object to which the ſums raiſed are applied, is, in a certain degree, the ſame: At any rate, King Charles the IId's occaſions for money could only be the general occaſions of the Government, ſuch as maintaining the army and navy, &c. and, therefore, the purpoſes for which the free and voluntary contributions were ſubſcribed to him, and the purpoſes for which thoſe are now ſubſcribed to Mr. Devaynes, are generally the ſame. The act, ſays, that no aids of *that nature*, ſhall be levied without the conſent of Parliament, and as I conceive, that a " *Free and voluntary preſent*," whether paid into the hands of an Alderman, Common Councilman, a member of Mr. Reeves's committee, or an editor of a newſpaper,—or whether paid into the hands of agents, officially named by the King, as was done by Charles the IId. while it is paid generally for the uſe of Government, to be preciſely the ſame; as I conceive, all of that kind, to be ſtill " Free and voluntary preſents," collected from the people for the *ſame purpoſe*,

* The Title of the Bill is, *An Act for a free and voluntary Preſent to his Majeſty*.

" And be it hereby declared, that no commiſſion or " aids of this nature can be iſſued out, or levied, but by con- " ſent of Parliament; and, that this act, and the ſupply " hereby granted, ſhall not be drawn into example for the " time to come." (See the Statutes at large.)

and

and as the act says, that no aids of the *nature* of a "free and voluntary present," shall be raised without the consent of Parliament, I think, I am perfectly justified in affirming, the manner of now raising them, is *illegal*. It cannot be denied, that they are precisely of the *same nature* with those granted to Charles the IId. and there are the words of an act of the legislature, stating, that they cannot be levied but by the consent of Parliament. The present collectors of these aids can produce no authority for their conduct; and if the House of Commons were as tenacious of its privileges on this subject, as it has shewn itself on the subject of petitions for Reform, the measures it would pursue with respect to these collectors of voluntary contributions, are obvious.

It is not only by the words of an act of Parliament, that we ascertain these voluntary contributions to be unconstitutional, but a principal member of administration, the President of his Majesty's Council, and a great lawyer, the Earl of Camden, gave it as his opinion, in the House of Lords, during the American War, that they were highly so: Mr. Dunning, and many other eminent characters, not only agreed with his Lordship, but strongly reprobated such a mode of raising money for the public use. At that time, it was the fashion to subscribe for raising regiments and building ships *, and when our present affiliated societies

* The Earl of Londsdale engaged to build a seventy-four gun ship, at his own expence, but his sincere attachment to the Constitution, which he saw must have been violated, had he fulfilled his promise, made him decline so unconstitutional a measure.

sub-

ſubſcribe for the ſame purpoſes, which probably they ſoon will, they only then will have to pay the civil liſt, which their loyalty will induce them readily to do, and then bribery and corruption, at elections, may be prevented by never calling Parliament together, as there will be no occaſion for its meeting.

I ſhall not dwell on the reproach which theſe contributions throw on government, whoſe more immediate duty it is to provide, not only neceſſary, but comfortable clothing to the army, than to give immenſe ſubſidies to Italian and German Princes, or to laviſh rewards on the Alarmiſts; and who cannot excuſe themſelves by ſaying, either the Parliament, or public, would not conſent to pay the money: nor ſhall I dwell on the ſtill greater impropriety, to give it no worſe a name, of the members of adminiſtration, giving encouragement, through their agent, the editor, to ſo unconſtitutional a meaſure. Its introduction is of recent date, and, I think, it ought inſtantly to be ſtopped, becauſe, among other inconveniences ariſing from it, a very important one is, that three times the quantity of particular articles is provided, to that which is wanted, while, of other articles, not a third is ſubſcribed. This is evident at preſent. Of flannel waiſtcoats, a ſufficient number have already been contributed to give every ſoldier half a dozen, while the number of ſhoes would not afford them half a pair a-piece. Thus the public money is waſted, and the Conſtitution deſtroyed, by thoſe who profeſſedly aſſociate to defend it. Parliament is the moſt proper monitor

of

of government; and a House of Commons, freely and frequently chosen, by a majority of the people, is the only constitutional channel, through which, to levy money, for the public use; because, in such a House of Commons, the voice of the people would be truly and calmly heard. On the contrary, addresses and associations, either for expressing their opinion on public affairs, or raising supplies for the State, are particularly dangerous, as the government pretends to be guided by the sentiments conveyed in them, though they admit of hearing only one side of the question, and may often be adopted to give an appearance of popularity to very unpopular measures, thereby deceiving the King, breeding disaffection in the people, and leading the one or other, or perhaps both, to ruin. Addresses and associations, therefore, should be discouraged, as delusive, and a Reformed House of Commons be substituted in their stead, where the will of the nation might be fairly and peaceably ascertained.

These are, I think, sufficient reasons to shew the necessity of reforming the Representation in this country. If we enquire how far it can be constitutionally done, we shall find, that the ancient spirit, and principles, and "*practice*," of the Constitution recognized *all men of consideration in the State*, as having a right to be present in the King's Councils. At the conquest, indeed, and for some time afterwards, men of landed property were the only persons of consideration in the kingdom; and accordingly we find, in the reign of Henry the IIId, in the first House of Commons of which we have

have any account of thofe who compofed it, that it confifted *only* of four Knights from each county, who of courfe reprefented *landed* proprietors alone. The principles and " practice" of the Conftitution, however, being, that *all men of confideration*, who, confequently would be called on for pecuniary aid, fhould be prefent in the King's Councils, and trade beginning to fhew itfelf, Citizens and Burgeffes were fummoned from fuch towns as were growing into importance. And herein confifted the great excellence of the Englifh Conftitution: it adapted itfelf to all fituations, it opened its arms to all men of property as perfons more particularly interefted in the government of the country, and therefore entitled to a fhare in the Legiflative Affembly. But what an extraordinary deviation from the principle and practice do we now find? The men of the leaft confideration, a few of the pooreft beggars in the kingdom, create the majority of our Legiflators; while the men of moft confideration, of moft utility to the State, the merchants and manufacturers, are generally excluded. Conftruct the Houfe of Commons, according to the ancient principles and practice of the Conftitution, as manifefted by the admiffion of Citizens and Burgeffes to the National Councils; give every man, and none but men of property, a vote for Members of Parliament, and I am fatisfied.

Mr. Young (p. 223.) gives the authority of Dr. Brady, to fhew, that in ancient times, *liberi homines*, or free men, were only thofe who held in *capite*; and, throughout his whole book, he maintains, that landed proprietors were the only reemen, and that they all had a right to vote for Repreſentatives ; that the other inhabitants were of no more account in the kingdom than the cows, ſheep, and hogs, they drove; the artizans, manufacturers, labourers, &c. were all ſlaves and villains, and the privilege of ſending Repreſentatives, was a gracious donation from the King,—not a right of thoſe to whom it was given ; and in ſupport of this he proves, that ſeveral Monarchs called Members to Parliament from obſcure places. I have already ſhewn, that it was their right, according to the ſpirit and practice of the Conſtitution, which admitted all perſons of conſideration to ſend Repreſentatives ; and, it no more eſtabliſhes the right of the Crown to beſtow the privilege where it pleaſed, becauſe it did ſo, than any other improper act eſtabliſhes a right to do ſo. The ſelection of the towns as they grew into importance, being entruſted to the Crown, was, like many other duties, abuſed by Kings, who, apprehenſive of being in a minority in the Commons, ſummoned members from ſuch places as they, or their creatures could command ; a deſire to ſecure, or bring into office, ſome abject favourite miniſter, probably gave moſt of our rotten boroughs a right to ſend Repreſentatives. Some of our former Sovereigns, unconſtitutionally, made Members of Parliament from ſimilar motives, with thoſe which induced his preſent Majeſty, conſtitutionally, to make ſo many Peers, in 1784:—to ſecure Mr. Pitt in power.

The aſſertion, reſpecting tenants in *capite*, when properly examined, is more deſtructive to Mr. Young's object, than any other poſition in his

his book: For, admitting what he ſays to be true, which, I believe it pretty nearly is, that none were freemen, but proprietors of land holding in *capite*, i. e. freeholders; and that all freeholders, or freemen, had a right to vote in the election of Members of Parliament, it follows, that it is either a mockery to call the Engliſh a "*free* people," "a *free nation*," as he does (vide the note, p. 205) or an injuſtice, to withhold from them that right. He affirms, that formerly our mechanics, labourers, and manufactures, &c. were all ſlaves and villains,—that they were of no more importance than cows and hogs;—admitted. But if they were ſlaves, were they free? The queſtion muſt excite a ſmile.—They were ſlaves;—and if we are ſlaves alſo, then we have no right, upon the ancient principles of the Conſtitution, as laid down by Mr. Young, to petition for Reform.—But where is the man, who dare come forward, and openly tell us, we are ſlaves? What would be his fate?—What would be the indignation of every honeſt Engliſhman? Reeves and Young have indirectly told us this, but they have not had the audacity to ſpeak roundly out. The fact is, that the preſent freedom of England was gradually extorted, ſword in hand, from feudal ſovereigns, deriving their rights from the ſword of a conqueror; nobly extorted. But had not the ſlaves and villains the greateſt ſhare in extorting it? And ſhall they who cemented it with their blood, be deprived of all its benefits? While we are attempting to make freemen of the blacks in the Weſt-Indies, ſhall we meanly ſuf-

fer

fer, to be proved slaves ourselves? If it is true, as Mr. Young asserts, that in former times, none were freemen but freeholders, and that all freeholders, or tenants in capite, were invested with the elective franchise, then it follows, that all freemen had a right to vote: If six hundred years ago the majority were slaves, are we not now all called freemen? Is not the Negro, who, sixty years ago, was a slave in this country, called a freeman? And if every freeman had formerly a right to vote for Representatives in Parliament, they who are now deprived of it, are, in that respect, still slaves and villains. But our ancestors struggled for, and bequeathed us freedom, though not perfect freedom: The elective franchise was the principal article that escaped them, and they overlooked it, because, it was not then of so much importance, nor was it so much abused as at present; they left to us the honour of atchieving it. Have we not equal virtue and perseverance? Shall we not imitate their example? I am much surprised that Mr. Young, in describing the Constitution, did not discover and recommend a mode of constructing the House of Commons, which would be highly satisfactory to Government, which strongly resembles *his* theory of the ancient Parliaments, and is not quite unknown in the modern. As he asserts, that formerly none but tenants in capite, who held lands immediately of the Crown, had a right to sit in Parliament, or vote at elections, it might have occurred to him, that the ancient principles of the Constitution would be revived, if, instead of the right of election, and sitting in the House of Commons,

mons, being confined to thoſe who held *lands* of the Crown, it were given to thoſe who held *places*. Upon this plan of Reform, moſt of the Crown and Anchor committee, and even Mr. Young himſelf, would be entitled to a ſeat in Parliament.

"Hiſtorians are agreed as to the Parliament "of 1265, ſummoned by an uſurper, being the "origin of the Houſe of Commons," (p. 75.) But (p. 216) Mr. Young, contradicts this; he there quotes Sir Henry Spelman, and others, to ſhew, that in an hundred Parliaments *before* that period, the *boroughs* never were repreſented; implying thereby, that there *were* Knights of the Shire, though no Citizens and Burgeſſes, which is exactly what I agree to, and ſupports what I have ſaid of the ſpirit and practice of the Conſtitution, which called to the National Council only men of conſideration in the State. It is true, that prior to 1265, and even then, cities and boroughs were not repreſented, becauſe their inhabitants were of little or no importance; the landed proprietors were the only men of importance in the kingdom, and therefore, the Houſe of Commons was compoſed wholly of their Repreſentatives. But as the cities and boroughs became of *conſideration*, they alſo ſent deputies. Nor is it juſt to conclude, (vide p. 217) becauſe, during the 200 years after the Norman conqueſt, the Houſe of Commons was ſo inſignificant as not to be mentioned by hiſtorians, that therefore, it never was aſſembled: It would be equally juſt to conclude, becauſe we have no account of the meeting of every county court, and other inſtitu-

tion

tion of leſs importance, that therefore they did not at certain times aſſemble; or, becauſe there is no hiſtory of the inhabitants in America, previous to its diſcovery by Columbus, that therefore, previous to that diſcovery, there were no inhabitants in that part of the world. And, even ſuppoſe the Houſe of Commons were never aſſembled, during the 200 years alluded to, that does not prove it to have been unknown to the Conſtitution, more than aboliſhing the Trial by Jury, in certain caſes, proves the Trial by Jury to be unknown to the Conſtitution. The exiſtence of Repreſentatives of ſome deſcription, may be traced in every page of our hiſtory, and is coeval with all law and government in England. What, although they were occaſionally laid aſide, their rights invaded, or their conſtruction varied, as ſuited the ambitious views of the Kings or Barons, that does not prove they had no right to aſſemble? On the contrary, wherever we find the ſlighteſt traces of the Houſe of Commons, or wherever we find the moſt compleat deſcription and certainty of its exiſtence and power, there is no mention of its being a *new* inſtitution, which is ſtrong proof that it was an *old* one; for is it poſſible, that ſo important a member of the Conſtitution could be created and introduced without ſome notice being taken of its novelty?

Another inſtance, not only of how far a Reform can be conſtitutionally made in the Repreſentation, but alſo of its neceſſity, is the complete change in its ſpirit and ſentiment. The Conſtitution, formerly, ſuppoſed a continual jealouſy of the Crown, and fellow feeling with

the

the people, to exiſt in the Houſe of Commons; but now, and eſpecially by Mr. Pitt, it has been made to repoſe a continual confidence in the Crown, and has ſhewn, particularly on the Ruſſian Armament, that it has no fellow feeling with the people whatever. This dangerous reverſal muſt ariſe from the reverſal of the mode of rewarding the members, which is, alſo, a great and pernicious change: for, that Mr. Young's ſalutary Corruption, did not formerly exiſt, is plain, ſince the privilege of returning members, now ſo valuable, was then rather a burthen than a benefit; was then of ſo little importance, that many boroughs petitioned to be eaſed of it. To beget a jealouſy of the Crown, and reſtore the ancient nationality of ſentiment, in the Houſe of Commons, is, therefore, not only conſtitutional, but the moſt wiſe and neceſſary meaſure, for preſerving the Freedom and Proſperity of the People.

How far it is conſtitutional to ſhorten the duration of Parliaments, does not require much inveſtigation, becauſe the facts relating to the queſtion are of recent date, and clearly underſtood. Originally, Parliaments were only called for a particular purpoſe, and often ſat only a few days: Sometimes there were two, but generally one new Parliament, in a year. In the ſeventeenth century, the uſage varied, and was moſt groſsly abuſed by the long Parliament, at laſt diſſolved by Cromwell. Yet, the vile precedent was approved. and imitated by the Kings who followed, and William the IIId. made it a great favour to agree to the Triennial Bill. The Septennial Bill is juſtified by Mr. Young, who ſays

"The

" The Members of the House of Commons, when elected, and in combination with the other branches of the legislature, assume and possess, and give themselves such powers and privileges, as rendered the septennial act just as constitutional as the biennial." That act, however, was by those who made it, justified only upon the exigency of the times, and ought to have heen repealed when that exigency was past; but, without considering its legality, I shall remark, that, if Mr. Young's pernicious doctrine were true, there would not be the least security for the Liberties of the Nation: the three branches of the Legislature, in combination, might assume a power to repeal the Habeas Corpus Act, abolish the Trial by Jury, and the Liberty of the Press; give to the King's Proclamations the force of Law, as was done in the reign of Henry the VIIIth. and vesting the whole executive and legislative authority in the Crown, dissolve themselves for ever, and annihilate at once the Constitution and Freedom of Britain: This, according to Mr. Young, they might *constitutionally* do, by *assuming* powers and privileges; and, indeed, he seems desirous that they should do it, when he sets up as precedent, the example of Richard the IId. who dictated to the sheriffs, the names of those persons whom they should return to Parliament, and levied money without the consent of Parliament: Richard's fate, as well as Charles the First's, is well known. Were Mr. Young prime Minister, and his advice followed, he would probably occasion events, which no good man can wish to think of.

On

On the ſubject of the TIME for making a Reform, I can ſay nothing now. "To minds "unwilling to do right, all times are equally "inconvenient and improper. To him who "diſlikes the voyage, all the winds of Heaven "are unpropitious: He looks for nothing but "pretences to avoid it*." "This, indeed, "is a never failing argument, equally in times "of proſperity and adverſity; in times of War "and Peace. If our ſituation happens to be "proſperous, it is then aſked, whether we can "be more than happy, or more than free? In "the ſeaſon of adverſity, on the other hand, all "Reform or Innovation is deprecated, from "the pretended riſk of increaſing the evil and "preſſure of our ſituation. From all this, it "would appear, that the time for Reform "never yet has come; and never can come†." "When, indeed, the arbitrary monarchy of "France, was battering down by the exertions "of a great people, and nothing was ſeen but "virtuous exertion and exultation, it might be "admitted, that in ſuch a conjuncture, men "might run before the mark, and confound "principles together, which had no connection. "Such was the alledged, but not proved ſtate "of England, when Mr. Grey gave notice "laſt year of his motion. The objection had "then, therefore, at leaſt, a *plauſible*, though "not a juſt foundation. But, good God! how "different, on the admiſſion of the objectors "to the times, was the preſent moment?" the

* Vide Mr. Francis's ſpeech, May 7th.

† Vide Mr. Grey's ſpeech, May 6th.

N English

English " Starting back with horror at the " crimes and calamities of France, and seemingly forgetting all distresses in an enthusiasm " for their own Government! Surely common sense pronounced that to be the hour " for reformation, more especially when it was " left to themselves (the House of Commons) " to originate and to fashion it. So far from " being urged on by the people to go too far, " they trod like men that feared the ground " would break under them, and could hardly " be brought up to the point which their understandings dictated. Let them seize, therefore, this happy and providential crisis, to do " with popularity and safety, what to save their " country must be done at last*." But, instead of embracing this favourable opportunity, every means is employed by Government to defeat the cause of Reform, and calumniate its advocates; and the present mode of constructing the House of Commons, will, probably, be continued until some dreadful convulsion happens, which may threaten the annihilation of the Constitution itself.

In considering what Reform should be made, I shall neither recommend nor reject any particular plan, being perfectly of opinion with Mr. Grey, that, to constitute the House of Commons by universal suffrage, or any other mode, which would make it more independent than at present, would be a most salutary improvement. Mr. Young says, the Society of the Friends of the People, approve personal Repre-

* Mr. Erskine's speech, May 6th.

sentation;

ſentation; but I cannot diſcover, except in his interpretations, that they ever have either approved or condemned it, or any other rule of Reform. Inſtead, therefore, of enquiring what their plan may be, will it not be more in point to examine that propoſed by the moſt violent leader of the moſt violent ſociety in Britain?—For ſuch, I believe, Mr. Horne Tooke, and the conſtitutional ſociety, are deemed by Mr. Young, and thoſe who think with him.

Mr. Horne Tooke, in his letter to Lord Aſhburton, when he, and Mr. Pitt, Sir James Sanderſon, Mr. Froſt, and the Duke of Richmond, were joint Reformers, ſo far from approving univerſal ſuffrage, recommends a plan of Reform, perfectly agreeing with the ideas of thoſe gentlemen, who ſay, the Houſe of Commons is a Repreſentation of Property for he makes it the governing power in electing the Repreſentatives of the people. He maintains, that although all men may have a right to a ſhare, yet they have not all a right to an *equal* ſhare in this choice; for, ſays he, "There is "a very great difference between an *equal* "*right* to a ſhare, and a right to an *equal* "*ſhare*. An eſtate may deviſed, by will, among "many perſons, in different proportions; to "one five pounds, to another five hun-"dred, &c. each perſon will have an equal "right to his ſhare, but not a right to an equal "ſhare."

"This principle," (continues Mr. Tooke, alluding to univerſal ſuffrage) "is further at-"tempted to be enforced by an aſſertion, that "*the all of one man is as dear to him, as the*

" *all of another man is to that other.* But " this maxim will not hold by any means; for " a small is not, for very good reasons, so dear " as a great all. A small all may be lost, and " very easily regained; it may very often, and " with great wisdom, be risked for the chance " of a greater; it may be so small, as to " be little or not at all worth defending or " caring for. But a large all can never be re- " covered; it has been massing and accumu- " lating, perhaps, from father to son, for many " generations; or it has been the product " of a long life of industry and talents; " or the consequence of some circumstance " which will never return. Justice and " policy require, that benefit and burthen, " that the share of power, and the share of " contribution to that power, should be as " nearly proportioned as possible." Thus far Mr. Tooke speaks against the *equality of right* to a share in the Representation: He then speaks of the impolicy of making the elective franchise *universal*. " Freedom and security " ought surely to be equal and universal," (says he) " but the members of a society may be *free* " and *secure*, without having a share in the " Government. *The happiness and freedom,* " *and security of the whole, may even be ad-* " *vanced by the* EXCLUSION *of* SOME, *not from* " *freedom and security, but from a share in* " *the Government.*" Mr. Tooke then enu- merates the classes which ought to be excluded, and which certainly are the majority, as they comprise " the extremely miserable," " ex-

" tremely

" tremely dependent," " extremely ignorant," and " extremely ſelfiſh."

His plan of conſtructing the Houſe of Commons is, that the kingdom ſhould be divided into 513 diſtricts, each of which ſhould ſend a member: that none ſhould vote who were not aſſeſſed in two pounds to the pariſh rates, or land tax; that Parliaments ſhould be annual; that every elector at the time of giving his vote, ſhould pay two guineas, to be appropriated to the uſe of the nation; and, that where the numbe of electors fell ſhort of 4000, thoſe might vote over again, in proportion as they were aſſeſſed, and repeat their vote as often as was neceſſary to compleat the number of 4000, ſtill paying two guineas for each vote By this plan, a landholder, paying a large land-tax, might probably, have the privilege of giving one hundred votes, upon paying two hundred guineas. What plan would give the predominating influence in the choice of Repreſentatives, more compleatly into the hands of men of property than this? According to it, property would be *truly* repreſented, becauſe none but men of *ſome* property are aſſeſſed to the amount of two pounds to the pariſh rates, or land-tax: And even if univerſal ſuffrage were eſtabliſhed, yet the circumſtance of paying annually two guineas, for the privilege of voting, would effectually exclude the majority, who are poor, and would ſtill give the ruling influence in elections to men of property.

Such is the Reform propoſed by Mr. Horne Tooke, a leader, if not *the* leader, of a ſociety which Mr. Young deſcribes to be much more violent

violent than the Friends of the People ; and, if that ſociety are called more dangerous than the latter, and yet it appears, the object of their leader is ſo moderate, it is ſurely unneceſſary to vindicate the Friends of the People from the charge of entertaining miſchievous views, ſince Mr. Young admits them to be more moderate than the conſtitutional ſociety. I here think it neceſſary to remark, that the epithet, violent, applied to the conſtitutional ſociety, is merely Mr. Young's, not mine.

Compare Mr. Tooke's plan of Reform with that propoſed by a principal conductor of the preſent War, and conſequently a partizan and favourite of Mr. Young, I mean the Duke of Richmond. His Grace contended for perſonal Repreſentation in its *fulleſt extent*, and his coadjutors * were Mr. Pitt, Lord Kenyon, and the leaders of the preſent Adminiſtration ; yet it is ſtrange, that the Duke and his friends, who firſt recommended perſonal Repreſentation, and who truly have founded the ſocieties in favour of that meaſure, and the petitions which lately prayed for it, eſcape the cenſure of thoſe who aſcribe every miſchief to their doctrine ; and it is ſtill more ſtrange that ſuch as Mr. Tooke, who are *decidedly againſt* perſonal Repreſentation, ſhould be loaded with obloquy !

From what I have ſtated, therefore, it appears, that Mr. Tooke's plan agrees with the ancient ſpirit and practice of the Conſtitution,

* I do not mean to ſay, that Mr. Pitt, Lord Kenyon, &c. contended for univerſal ſuffrage, but as they acted cordially with thoſe who did they are equally guilty, according to Mr. Young's reaſoning.

which

which recognized only *men of consideration in the State* as having a right to a share in the great National Council; and that the Duke of Richmond's plan agrees perfectly with Mr. Young's original Theory of the Constitution, which gave every freeman a right to vote, and consequently, now, must make the elective franchise universal, since there are no slaves, but all are freemen in Britain.

For my own part, I think, the true object of a Reform is, not to give every man his natural right of a vote, but to make the House of Commons independent of the executive power, or of a small number of wealthy men, and to make it act upon an identity of interest with the people. The manner in which this would be best accomplished, would, in my opinion, be the rule of a Reform. Mr. Fox said truly, that the object of a Reform of Parliament ought to be the collection of the greatest number, not simply of wills, but of *independent* wills: and Montesquieu was of the same opinion; for, in speaking of the British Constitution, he says, it is necessary in a free Government that every man should have a suffrage who can be supposed to have *a will of his own*. I therefore agree with Mr. Tooke, that the happiness of the whole may be advanced by the exclusion of some, not from happiness, but from the elective franchise, because, a great manufacturer or landholder, or any other person, who employed, or could control, the extremely miserable, extremely dependent, or extremely ignorant, might influence them to vote as he pleased, and thereby acquire an undue power in elections,

elections, and invade the independence of the Legiſlature; for I conceive, that, univerſal ſuffrage, would render the miſerable and ſelfiſh electors liable to be corrupted; the ignorant liable to be miſled, and the dependent liable to be commanded. Theſe claſſes would generally, if not always, form the majority at elections, and conſequently, thoſe candidates who poſſeſſed wealth, eloquence, or control, might procure themſelves to be returned, although their conduct in Parliament had previouſly been injurious to the national welfare, and even diſpleaſing to the independent national judgment.

It is aſked, by Mr. Young, as the journeymen mechanicks, manufacturers, and labourers, never voted at elections, what right have they to petition for Reform; and they themſelves may join in ſaying, if, according to Mr. Tooke's plan, we are not to vote, why, indeed, ſhould we petition for Reform? To this, I anſwer, it is as much their intereſt to make exertions in favour of Reform, as it is the intereſt of thoſe who would be veſted with the elective franchiſe, which is, in itſelf, of no value to thoſe who poſſeſs it, but like the delegation, ought to be entruſted to thoſe who would exerciſe it with the moſt wiſdom and independence; and as wiſdom and independence prevail more certainly in the middling ranks, than in the whole maſs of the people, the elective franchiſe, ſhould, in my opinion, be confined to them; and I repeat, that it is as much the intereſt of thoſe who would not, as of thoſe who would have votes, that a Reform ſhould take place, and even that the elective fran-

chiſe

chiſe ſhould be ſo confined, becauſe the benefits that would flow from a Repreſentative body ſo conſtructed, would be general, and the poor, as well as the rich, would equally partake of them.

If, indeed, men were to be guided wholly by natural right, and fully to inſiſt upon the maxim, that no man is bound by laws to which he has not given conſent, it would come to this, that all men in the kingdom muſt aſſemble perſonally to form the Legiſlative Aſſembly; and this was pretty nearly the caſe in ancient times. But the ſyſtem of delegation was adopted, not only for the ſake of convenience, but becauſe, the wiſeſt and moſt independent men, in whom the whole maſs could confide, were appointed to make laws, and by the ſmallneſs of their number, were enabled to act with deliberation and ſound judgment. If, therefore, the ancient great National Council was thus narrowed, for the ſake of convenience, wiſdom, and independence, why ſhould not the conſtruction of the modern National Council be alſo, either narrowed or extended, to thoſe limits which are moſt likely to inſure convenience, wiſdom, independence, and impartiality? If the right is ſurrendered, in one inſtance, to procure certain objects, why ſhould it not be ſurrendered in another, if by that other ſurrender thoſe objects are more firmly ſecured?

This will be further illuſtrated by the Trial by Jury. The privilege of ſerving on Juries, which certainly is of a more clear and immediate value, than a vote for a Repreſentative, is not univerſal, but is confined to houſeholders and landholders, yet it is as much the natural right of every man as the elective franchise. And what is the reason we never heard of petitions and associations for extending to all men the privilege of serving on Juries? Because all men are satisfied, that by the principle, it is sufficiently distributed, (however, it may be secretly abused in practice,) to render Juries indedendent and impartial; and because, the poor labourer, or mechanic, although he knows he can never serve on a Jury, while he is neither a housekeeper nor a landholder, is, nevertheless, convinced that justice is as amply secured by those who do serve, as if the privilege were universal, and therefore, he does not associate or petition to extend it; yet he is as much interested in preserving it to householders and landholders, as if he himself were a householder or landholder; and if the elective franchise were as generally distributed, as the privilege of serving on Juries, we should neither have associations of the rich or the poor, for reforming Parliament.

But while I agree in opinion with Mr. Tooke, that the middling class of society, should elect the Members of Parliament, I am far from agreeing with him in the mode of election. There should be no such condition as that of paying two guineas at the time of voting, nor should any man be permitted to vote more than once.

From what I have now said, I think, a Reform is necessary; that the elective franchise should either be given *exclusively* to men of consideration, or universally to *all men*, (for,

to

to me, it is immaterial, whether it is poſſeſſed by all, or a part, if the Repreſentative Body is independent;) that the preſent time is peculiarly favourable for making a Reform; that Parliaments ought to be annual, and that the Repreſentatives ought to be liberally paid by their Conſtituents for their attendance. The means of preventing riots and corruption at elections, and making many other inferior regulations, are ſimple and obvious.

Nor are we to dread innovation, for, while he deprecates the deſtruction of "extravagant "Courts, ſelfiſh Miniſters, and corrupt Majo-"rities." Mr. Young ſays, that "to declare "againſt any meaſure, becauſe, an innovation "is a conduct worthy of children. It is not "for or againſt innovation, but what the na-"ture of the innovation ſhall be." Admitting then, the removal of corruption by Reform, to be an innovation, is it not a more laudable one than that which Mr. Young adviſes, the eſtabliſhment of a national militia of property? He cautions againſt taking away from the machine of Government, a rotten wheel, which all men, not excepting himſelf, have directly or indirectly condemned, and yet deſires the addition of a new one, which no man of eminence, has either approved or thought of. But he may be aſſured, his advice will not be followed by Government. The Crown will never part with the control over the military. During the American War, it found the conſequences of putting arms into the hands of the people in Ireland, and although, men of property proſtrate themſelves before the Throne at

 preſent,

present, yet it is obvious, they will not always continue in the same humour, because, their property marks them out as the prey of taxation, and when their ridiculous fears are over, they will regard Government with a jealous eye; and if armed and disciplined, might probably make both Reforms and Revolutions; might destroy selfish Ministers, and root out Corruption. Men of property are not only more intelligent, but more interested in the government of this country, than men of no property, and therefore are more likely to interfere in its conduct, and thwart its favourite measures. It is not from an opinion of the wisdom of our rulers, that the rich at present support them, but from a dread insidiously excited, that their property is in danger from the designs of those who oppose the Government. When this unfounded dread is past, they will be equally displeased with "extravagant Courts, selfish Ministers, and corrupt Majorities," for invading their property as they now are, with the Friends to Liberty, from a mistaken notion that they meditate its destruction. The same motive, which now makes them afraid to innovate, (the preservation of property) will, hereafter, make them clamorous for political œconomy,—for Reform. Government knows this well, and therefore, it will depend for support on the "Slaves and villains," on the "Beggars without a shilling," rather than on the opulent, who soon might be disposed to make elections for Members of Parliament, and dictate to Government, "at the point of the bayonet." If then, the House of Commons, is at all a good institution,

institution, and an evil does exist in it, are we not to ascribe the birth of that evil to the deviation from its principles, professions, and original practice? And how shall we expel the evil but by bringing it nearer to these?— This is Reform; and the moment we deviate from it, a dread of innovation becomes justifiable, lest it may be carried too far. But no such dread can reasonably be entertained while improvement is confined to the original practice, the principles, and present professions of the House of Commons, because a limit is marked out, beyond which it is impossible for Parliamentary *Reform* to go.

Mr. Young says (p. 81), that the people never had the power of changing the Constitution without being in its perpetual exercise. This is like his other absurdities; for it is plain the people *always* have the *Power*, though not always the *right*; and the "Practice" shews the fallacy of what he would inculcate, that if they began Reform they would always be altering. "People are not so easily got out of their "old forms as some are apt to suggest. They "are hardly to be prevailed with to amend "the acknowledged faults in the frame of Go-"vernment they have been accustomed to. "And if there be any original defects, or ad-"ventitious ones introduced by time or cor-"ruption, it is not an easy thing to get them "changed, even when all the world sees there "is an opportunity for it *." The history of all countries, particularly of this, shews, that

* Locke's Essay on Government.

the

the people are never eager to change their form of Government. A memorable and recent instance of this is on record. At the conclusion of the American War, the whole blame of which was thrown on the Corruption of the House of Commons, and when as many approved of Reform as at this time dread it, so fearful were the people of forcing Government, or so little inclined to interfere, that there were not so many signatures affixed to the petitions, praying Parliamentary Reform, as there were last spring. If the people are naturally fickle, why did they not come forward on that occasion? The fact is quite the contrary to what Mr. Young affirms, and just as Mr. Locke states it. History shews us, that Governors have generally, if not always, altered Governments for the worse, and that the people have always altered them for the better. I except the case of France, the experiment having neither had time nor opportunity to be made there; and indeed Mr. Young acknowledges, that the important transactions in that unhappy country have been effected, not by the people, but by the *terror* produced by a very *small minority*.

I have declined pointing out any of the abuses in the present mode of conducting elections, or shewing the absurd manner in which the elective franchise is distributed, because these subjects, and several others, are so ably treated in the Petition and Reports of the Friends of the People; nor do I think it necessary to reply to all Mr. Young's ridiculous animadversions on those publications. He says (p 84.),

"You

" You ſtate the Parliamentary Influence of the " Earl of Lonſdale, Lords Eliott, Edgecumbe, " &c. you ſtate a fact; but (p. 81.) with " this ſyſtem of influence, which ſeems Cor- " ruption to the eye of ignorance, the liberties " the people have been conſtantly improving; " —we are happy under the Government of " Influence, how then can it be bad?"—He might juſt as well ſay, " You ſtate the crimes of Barrington, Hubbard, and other highway-men; you ſtate a fact;—but with their ſyſtem of livelihood, which ſeems robbery in the eye of ignorance, the liberties of the people have been conſtantly improving. We are happy, though contributions are made on Hounſlow-Heath, how then can they be bad?" Corruption, as I have already ſaid, is a bad part of a good ſyſtem, and ought to be removed. And, though I by no means blame, or allude to the Noblemen above-mentioned, yet, I have no doubt, that tranſactions take place relative to Parliamentary Influence, which I, being an ignorant perſon, deem Corruption, that not only deſerve, but if publicly proved, would, for the ſake of decency, be as rigorouſly puniſhed as any offence committed on Hounſlow-Heath*.

* I will not, however, be too poſitive in this remark, for I was preſent when a very rich man of the name of Smith was, on the teſtimony of ſeveral others, committed for groſs perjury, by a Committee which was trying a conteſted election for Exeter in 1791, before which he had been examined as a witneſs. I ſoon afterwards ſaw, by the Newgate Calender, that he was impriſoned by virtue of the Speaker's warrant, to take his trial at the Old-Bailey for perjury. But by ſome means, which I could never learn, perhaps by Mr. Young's ſalutary influence, he was ſpeedily brought before the Houſe, reprimanded, and diſcharged; nor, although it was then hinted, that he was yet to be puniſhed, has any puniſhment been inflicted!!!

And

And we might, with equal justice ascribe, our happiness to the robberies committed there, as to the influence, which, according to Mr. Young, the ignorant think Corruption in the House of Commons.

But this boasted happiness is, I fear, much over-coloured. Those who can buy a three-and-sixpenny pamphlet indeed, the shopkeepers and merchants of the City of London, the members of country corporations, and all who possess the means of living easily, may well say, they are happy; but they should not take upon them to answer for the whole nation*. Do these men comprise the whole people? No. Not a tenth, perhaps not a fiftieth part of the people. Yet, as they are more intelligent, conspicuous, busy, and noisy, in the world, they certainly make a great appearance. My unfashionable idea of *the people*, however, comprises the Swinish Multitude, as well as the men of some property.

I shall not enter into an abstract definition of happiness. If it is presumed, that acquiescence in a state is a proof of its happiness, then the Turks and Tartars, and the West-India slaves, are happy, and it would be impolitic to improve their condition or reform the Constitu-

* A Farmer-General in Languedoc, who received as much money from the old French as Mr. Reeves now does from the English Government, was told many years ago, when Reform might have been made without being followed by any mischievous consequences, how necessary it was to retrench and amend the mode of carrying on the Government; to which, like our pensioners, he answered, *Mais pourquoi changer? Nous sommes si bien.*—But why change? We are so well.

tions

tions under which they live. And it will be found, that what is deemed happineſs in Britain is mere ſubmiſſion, ariſing, not from an enjoyment of the comforts of life, but from the ignorance of the lower claſs of people; an ignorance, which Mr. Young recommends to be perpetuated and increaſed; and, indeed, it is a ſure way of beſtowing what ſome men mean by happineſs; for how can a man regret the want of that to which he has never been accuſtomed? Had the inhabitants of this country been always confined to ſuch happineſs, they might now have been no better off than they were under William the Conqueror, or than the preſent wretched natives of Morocco. The diffuſion of knowledge has been a chief cauſe of the ſuperior degree of happineſs enjoyed by the Britiſh ſubjects; but this happineſs cannot be interpreted to be acquieſcence, or a blind and ignorant content, becauſe then the wild ſavages of America are happier than the moſt wealthy claſſes in Britain. It muſt be interpreted, proſperity, or a ſuperior degree of enjoyment in the neceſſaries and comforts of life, and in the civilized intercourſe of ſociety. By this rule, therefore, we muſt judge of it; for otherwiſe, we ſhall find the moſt wretched beings content in the midſt of want, and the moſt wealthy and proſperous diſcontented in the midſt of plenty.

If, then, we decide on the happineſs of the people at large in Britain, not by what may chance to make them acquieſcent, but by what rationally ought to make them content, we ſhall find their happineſs to conſiſt chiefly in the

assertions of those who really possess that, and in the ignorance of those who do not. That which *ought* to give content, and consequently constitutes happiness, is, I conceive, a plenty of good food and clothing, of all the necessaries of life, to such a degree, as would make every man and his family comfortable. How far that is the case I will leave any man to judge, who can impartially, and with some intelligence on the subject, compare all classes in his neighbourhood. He must not confine himself to the Royal-Exchange, to Grosvenor-Square, or Mr. Young's parlour; but let him examine the large towns, the manufacturers, mechanics, and country labourers, and he will find an immense majority of the people, who are not so well provided with the necessaries of life, as the paupers in a work-house. Even in London, the most wealthy spot in the empire, I will venture to affirm, that a great majority are not comfortably provided with the common necessaries of life; and that if those, who are comfortably provided, are compared with those who are actually starving, I believe, the latter will outnumber the former. So much for the general happiness enjoyed by the people in this country. Mr. Young, when feasting on venison and claret, with the Committee of Pensioners, in the Crown and Anchor Tavern, might well exclaim, "Are not we a happy people?"—But were he to go into the regions of Spitalfields, where he might seat himself among many thousands who want a morsel of bread to put in their mouths, and say the same thing, he would provoke the indignation of every sensible man, and

even

even Mr. Reeves, I hope, would blush at his impudence *.

But,

* It is rather singular, that formerly the most pompous eulogiums were always made on our government, and happiness, by those who were violating the principles not only of freedom, but of common justice. The following extract from Henry's History of Britain, p. 183 and 4, vol. vi. quarto edition, is one strong instance of this: "The King," (Henry VIII. in 1543) "had borrowed great sums from a "prodigious multitude of his subjects, of all ranks, for the "repayment of which, he had given bonds and other legal "securities. The Parliament, very generously, made the "King a present of all the money he had borrowed from his "subjects, and declared his bonds and securities to be of no "value. The King thanked his two houses in the politest "terms, for their generosity, and graciously accepted their "valuable present, while his creditors were left to condole "with one another, and, put up with their losses, as well "as they could. *The preamble to this iniquitous statute, is one "of the most extravagant pieces of flattery that ever was com-"posed.* In it they gave a *mournful description* of the *con-"fusion*, *poverty*, *distress*, and *misery*, of ALL OTHER NA-"TIONS, and drew a very *flattering picture* of the *riches*, "*peace*, and *prosperity*, of England, *during his Grace's "reign.*"——Judge Jeffries, in the memorable trial of Lady Lisle, spoke thus to the jury. "Besides, gentlemen, we cannot be "sufficiently thankful to our God, for the mercies we enjoyed "under that blessed King (Charles the IId.) for, we are to "consider, that we lived in all the affluence of peace and "plenty; *our Lives, Liberties, and Properties, inviolably were "secured*; *every man sat safe under the shadow of his own "vine, and ate the fruit of his own labour.* And while our "neighbours suffered the calamities of War, we were sur-"rounded with all the blessings of Peace, and slept securely "under the government of a gracious and merciful King." ——The Lord Justice Clerk, on the late trial of Mr. Muir, spoke in substance precisely the same. The only material difference arose from his natural *aversion* to inebriety, which induced him to convert Judge Jeffries' intoxicating vine into a sober fig-tree. He said, "It requires no proof to "shew, that the British Constitution is the best that ever "was since the creation of the world, and it is not pos-

sible

But, admitting the eulogiums on our happiness to be just, will not their truth be the greatest aggravation of the conduct of those who pronounce them, and yet plunge us from this elevated felicity into all the miseries of the most wanton calamitous War that ever afflicted Europe? In the same proportion as they extol our happiness, do they increase their own criminality, by depriving us of it: And it is in vain to say, that the War was necessary, or, that it was provoked by the French, for though a majority of people insist on these two points, yet a candid examination of facts, will shew, that they have no other foundation than the prejudices of those who believe them.

I have already shewn, that hostilities were resolved on by Austria, long before they were meditated by France *, who did all in her power to

" sible to make it better: *for is not every man secure? Does " not every man reap the fruits of his own industry, and sit " safely under his own fig-tree?*"

* The following extract is unquestionable proof of the wicked designs of the German Princes. It clearly establishes what is maintained in the early part of this Pamphlet, viz. that the continental Despots were the aggressors in the present War. It gives reason to suspect, that the King of France, designed by his flight, to put himself at the head of the invaders, as it shews, that long before his attempt to escape, he knew of the plot, yet concealed it; and it compleatly refutes the assertion in a late Pamphlet entitled, " Re- " flections on the propriety of an immediate Peace," said to be written by Mr. Vansittart, that the Convention at Pilnitz, was only formed in consequence of the imprisonment of Louis, and that when he was set at liberty, it ceased to exist, because, it shews, that the plot against France, was formed when the King enjoyed more indulgence than at any other period during the Revolution, and when the new Constitution of France, wore the most suspicious aspect. M. Bigot de

to prevent them. And although Mr. Young asserts, that "this country had no right to interfere in the affairs of France, previous to the 10th of August, and that till then our Government was rather friendly than otherwise," yet it will easily be shewn, that he is quite mistaken, unless he means such friendship as the Duke of Brunswick's, and that the War might, and ought to have been avoided, as the French were even more desirous of keeping peace with Britain, than they had been to prevent a rupture with Austria.

Our Government, indeed, observed a strict neutrality previous to the 10th of August, but

de Sainte Croix, who was Minister of Foreign Affairs, to Louis the XVIth. at the time that Monarch was dethroned, and who is now an emigrant in London, has, since his arrival here, published a History of the Conspiracy of the 10th of August, in which he says, p. 152, "Dès le *Printems* de "1791, le Roi empêchoit l'execution d'un plan secret arrêté "a Mantoue pour attaquer, deux mois après la France, dont "les armées etoient alors incomplettes, et les frontiéres sans "défense."

"In the spring of 1791, the King prevented the execution "of a secret plan, determined on at Mantua, for attacking "France, two months afterwards, the armies of which "were then incomplete, and the frontiers defenceless."

This gentleman's authority is of the highest nature. He now avows himself always to have been a determined Royalist. With a laudable love of his King, however, he thought he could most sincerely serve him by disguising his sentiments, and remaining about his person, which he did as long as it was safe to do so. He was a particular confident of Louis the XVIth. and he now abuses the Constitution of 1789. But what is stronger proof of his being a Royalist, and a confident of his late King, is, that he is admitted to St. James's, and caressed by our Government; and, even the well known Peltier, in his Dernier Tableau de Paris, calls him "le veritable homme du Roi."

not

not from any good will towards France. It was the dread of the resentment of the British people, and the belief, that the Duke of Brunswick would effect his purpose without our assistance, that prevented Administration from openly joining the concert of Princes in their first operations. Sufficient proof of this was on record before the 10th of August, and subsequent events have set the fact beyond all dispute. The hostile disposition of the Court of St. James's, towards the French Constitution, was believed all over Europe, and never even questioned in England. The French knew and avowed it; but they relied on the love of Liberty inherent in Englishmen, for defeating the designs of Government against their Freedom: And for a while, this notion of a difference of sentiment, between the King's Ministers and the people, seemed to be justly founded.

Mr. Burke, denounced the French Revolution previous to the abolition of titles, and before so much blood had been shed as lately was spilt in Bristol, about the payment of a halfpenny. He has continued his furious Anathemas, and long before the 10th of August, was feasted at the cabinet dinners of our Ministers, and caressed by that Monarch, whom he had declared the Almighty to have hurled from his Throne, whose houshold expences he had curtailed, and whose displeasure was well known, in consequence, to have been incurred. What then was the cause of Mr. Burke becoming so great a favourite, excepting his abuse of the French Revolution? Was this a symptom of our

Government

Government being rather friendly than otherwise?

In the summer of 1791, when our Government knew that the German Princes were planning a War against France, did not a newspaper, notoriously in the pay of certain persons, high in office, teem with the most artful falsehoods and gross calumnies, for the purpose of deterring the admirers of the French Revolution from celebrating that event on the 14th of July, or of producing a riot which might disgrace the meeting? Did not a mob assemble round the Crown and Anchor Tavern, in London, which, thanks to their own discretion and good intentions, rather than to those who attempted to dupe them into violence, dispersed without doing any mischief? Did not a similar mob assemble in Birmingham, which committed the most horrid excesses for the honour of Church and King? Was not that mob instigated by persons, who supposed they were pleasing and serving the Government, and do they not yet remain unpunished? But from these events, can any thing be discovered in the conduct of our cabinet, that shewed it to be "rather friendly to the French Revolution than otherwise?" A politician, would have formed his opinion of the sentiments of our Government from the contents of such a newspaper, because, it would not dare to take a side on a question of such magnitude and continuance, *against* the will of its patrons; and, through its channel, Administration might inculcate such doctrines as it might be impolitic to avow. In such a newspaper, they speak in the dark; they assert

what

what they pleaſe, without being reſponſible, or known, or even perhaps, ſuſpected. The public look for the printer's name at the bottom, to ſee who is the author of the contents, when, probably, it would be more juſt to look to the vicinity of Whitehall.

Mr. Pitt himſelf, in the debate on Mr. Grey's notice of his motion for a Parliamentary Reform, three months before the 10th of Auguſt, called the French Conſtitution, ſuch, as if formed in the morning, could not exiſt till noon. He alſo reprobated the wild French theories, which, he ſaid, were ſubverſive of all order and government; and although he did not preach War againſt France, yet he countenanced thoſe who did, and condemned as dangerous every principle of the Revolution: Nor did any member of Adminiſtration ever hint that they diſapproved of Mr. Burke's war-whoop.

Was the conduct of our Miniſters in declining to negociate between France and Auſtria, in favour of Peace, when ſolicited to that effect by the former, no proof that they wiſhed to ſee a War? Was the balance of power in danger, by the Empreſs of Ruſſia's retaining poſſeſſion of Oczakow, and in no danger by the combined armies gaining poſſeſſion of Paris, for, ſuch was then the expectation? Could we go to War about a ſingle remote town, and yet refuſe to negociate, when the exiſtence of a great neighbouring nation was in queſtion? "But "we had no right to interfere, unleſs called "upon by all the parties *."—No! Then we

* Vide Lord Grenville's note to Monſ. Chauevlin.

have

have no right to interfere in behalf of Poland, unleſs called upon by the Empreſs of Ruſſia; then, we had no right to interfere about Oczakow, in behalf of the Turks, becauſe, the ſame gracious Dame did not call upon us; and we have no right now to interfere in behalf of the French Royaliſts, becauſe, the Republicans do not call upon us! We had a right;—it was our duty. We might have preſerved a limited Monarchy in France, averted the dreadful calamities of the preſent War, and ſaved an amiable unfortunate King from the ſcaffold.

Another pointed inſtance of the ſecret hoſtility of our Government, towards the new Conſtitution of France, is to be found in the correſpondence which paſſed between Lord Grenville and Monſ. Chauevlin, in May, 1792. The latter, invariably ſtiles Louis the XVIth. "King "of the French," which was the title decreed by the National Aſſembly, and the former as invariably ſtiles him, "His moſt Chriſ-"tian Majeſty," which was the title during the Deſpotiſm. Thus, the Britiſh Government, three months before the 10th of Auguſt, fully manifeſted its unwillingneſs to acknowledge the new Conſtitution: It was manifeſted in the ſame manner, as was afterwards openly declared, on refuſing to acknowledge the Republic, in diſtinctions of names and forms; and betrayed a ſympathy, at leaſt, if not an actual connection, with the Duke of Brunſwick. If to this, we add the uncontradicted paſſage in the Declaration of the French Princes, on the 10th of September, 1791, wherein the King of France, is "aſſured that *every* power in Eu-

" rope," (among which, Britain muſt be included) " is favourable to the enterpriſe of the " Duke of Brunſwick," and the very warm reception, both at Court and by Miniſters, of that public plunderer, Calonne, it would be the height of folly to queſtion the regret of our Cabinet, at the fall of the old French Government, and the ardent deſire for its reſtoration.

In addition to theſe proofs, which exiſted previous to the 10th of Auguſt, of the unfriendly diſpoſition of the Britiſh Court to the French Revolution, others have occurred ſince that period, which illuſtrate and confirm my opinion of the ſecret hoſtility of our Miniſters, and fully contradict Mr. Young's aſſertion, that, " till then, our Government was rather friendly " than otherwiſe."

Mr. Pitt, declared, in the Houſe of Commons laſt winter, " That as a right hon. Gen" tleman, (Mr. Fox) had rejoiced at the re" treat of the Duke of Brunſwick, ſo he, on " his part, would ſay, he conſidered it as the " greateſt misfortune that could have befallen " mankind." Lord Auckland, in his Memorial to the States General, dated Jan. 25th. thus expreſſes himſelf, when ſpeaking of France, " It is not *quite four years* ſince certain *miſ" creants*, aſſuming the name of Philoſophers, " have preſumed to think themſelves capable " of eſtabliſhing a new ſyſtem of civil ſociety." Lord Hood, in his firſt proclamation to the people of Toulon, not only has imitated Lord Auckland, in alluding to " the miſery which " for *four* years has afflicted France," but de" clared, " that it is for the *re-eſtabliſhment*

" *of*

" *of the French Monarchy*, that Britain has " armed." But, indeed, the late Proclamation of his Majesty, sets the fact beyond dispute, that we are fighting to give a Government to France, and is therefore, strong presumptive proof of the hostile disposition of our Court, previous to the 10th of August, and, combined with other circumstances, fairly justifies us in concluding, that it was only the fear of discontent at home *, and the confidence that our exertions were unnecessary, which prevented us from being more early engaged in the War.

Much proof cannot be required of the unfriendly disposition of our Court after the 10th of August. Withdrawing our Ambassador, and refraining to send another, was an unequivocal demonstration of displeasure, and a sure presage of hostility. The scandalous and incessant abuse of Mons: Chauevlin, in a newspaper, (the Sun) conducted by persons connected with, and at the devotion of Administration, was surely some ground for supposing there were those who wished to drive him from this country, and thereby precipitate a War. The French, on the other hand, strongly evinced their desire to keep Peace with this country, by continuing Mons. Chauevlin at our Court, after the British Ambassador was withdrawn from Paris: This was an instance of humiliation, which, even amidst all their successes, exultation, and pride,

* Mr. Burke, a few days before the declaration of War, said, in the House of Commons, that he only pardoned the Ministers for their slowness in beginning the War, on account of the necessity of waiting till the public temper was inflamed to a sufficient pitch to second them effectually. For nearly four years he had been waiting for that fortunate period, which had at last arrived.

 they

they submitted to, in hopes of maintaining tranquillity: And among many others, equally unquestionable, may be enumerated, the refusal of giving permission to Dumourier, to enter Holland, who, in a council at Liege, on the 5th of December, affirmed, that he could easily march to Amsterdam, and destroy the Dutch Government, if he received orders for that purpose. The Executive Council, however, would not give him any such orders, for fear of provoking a rupture with Britain; a conduct, which they, no doubt, soon repented, as they saw by the stoppage of corn, the alien bill, and the speeches of Ministers in Parliament, how unfounded was their expectation of continuing Peace: They saw, that the antipathy of the British Government to their Revolution, which had been manifested from the beginning, and had gradually increased and displayed itself, was at last, going to break out into open War. The King's death gave a plausible pretext for dismissing Chauevlin, and by provoking the indignation of Englishmen, prepared their feelings to plunge into a War of vengeance; for such it certainly was on the part of the British people, even in its outset.

With regard to the professed grounds of commencing the War; the decree of fraternity, the opening the Scheldt, and the aggrandizement of France, they have all been so amply discussed, that it would be superfluous in me to animadvert on them; and, as was often said in Parliament, there can be little doubt that they might have been amicably settled, if a pacific disposition had been manifested by our

Ministers,

Ministers, and if they had entered into a proper negociation. They indeed, pretended, that the French had given in their ultimatum, but our Ministers have shewn, that when it suited their purpose, they could consider ultimatums only as preliminaries, for, in the late dispute with Spain, they appeared as anxious to avoid, as, with France, they since appeared, eager to precipitate a rupture.

Such were the pretexts for commencing the War: Its * real grounds, the subsequent conduct of Ministers, has fully illustrated; they have shewn that Mr. Young was right in saying, its object was to destroy a combination of Reformers. Thus, then, according to the late Earl of Chatham and Sir George Saville, the American War was begun in order to gratify the Corruption of the House of Commons, and according to Mr. Young, the present War is to preserve its rotten Constitution. Indeed, Mr. Young's opinion is confirmed by every circumstance; for, was not the late alarm directed wholly against Reform? Was not the proclamation, in May 1792, produced in consequence of the society of the Friends of the People being instituted for the purpose of procuring a Reform? What could be the object of that proclamation, if it was not to excite an alarm against Reform? Did it not immediately divide the kingdom into Reformers and Anti-Reformers? Was it not the avowed determination of

* Mr. Bowles, one of the Crown and Anchor committee, in his "Real Grounds," published last winter, says, it is merely on our part a War of *Defence*, and that no country has a right to interfere in the internal concerns of another.

Govern-

Government to reſiſt Reform, and the dread, that in the conflict, the Conſtitution would be deſtroyed, that firſt founded the alarm? It was from the ſpeeches of thoſe in power, from proclamations, camps, and addreſſes, that the kingdom firſt began to think itſelf in danger. In the ſame manner as the popularity of the American War was planned in, and directed by the ſecret Cabinet, was the late alarm planned and directed by the tools of Government. Alarms have always been found uſeful to thoſe who profit by "extravagant Courts, ſelfiſh Miniſters, and corrupt Majorities." The alarm excited by the riots in 1780, deſtroyed all hopes of a Reform at that time; and the alarm at the concluſion of 1792, has again defeated, for the preſent, the ſame cauſe. Thus we find, that alarms will always be hatched, when Parliamentary Reform is likely to ſucceed, and yet, that the want of that Reform brought on the American War, the moſt ruinous this country ever ſaw, and has involved us in another, the conſequences of which cannot be calculated, although they threaten to be much more dreadful.

After a period was put to negociation, excepting ſome underhand intercourſe, which, it would appear, Miniſters entered into merely to give a colour to an affected deſire of Peace; after the diſmiſſal of Chauevlin, what was to expected?—War.—His diſmiſſal was an unequivocal mark of hoſtility on our part, for ſo ſuch a ſtep has always been conſidered by nations in ſimilar circumſtances. The office, then, of commencing the War was thrown upon the French, who, it was not to be ſuppoſed, amidſt their ſucceſs, would

would betray a dastardly fear, by declining it: It was not to be expected that they would then shrink from a rupture with a country, which shewed it would begin War as soon as it could with advantage, and which had cut off all chance of the continuance of Peace, by driving away the Ambassador. Yet Mr. Dundas had the assurance to declare, in the House of Commons, that the War, on our part, was simply defensive! A declaration, which he could only have been encouraged to make by the ready belief then given to whatever was said in support of Government. He might as justly have declared, that the seizure of Poland was simply defensive on the part of Russia and Prussia; and indeed, those powers made that their pretext; they said, they divided Poland in order to defend themselves against Jacobinism!

War, however, being commenced, it is not so important at present to investigate its original pretexts, as to enquire what are now its real objects, how long it is likely to continue, and what will probably be its termination and consequences. Upon the first of these points, there are as various opinions as there are about religion: Some are for fighting to restore the ancient Monarchy, and exterminate the present popular principles; others, desire the restoration of the Constitution, founded in 1789; a third party, support the War in hopes of gaining territory; a fourth, wish the throat of every Frenchman may be cut; and a fifth, support it, because—they hate the French. Mr. Young, though not singular, differs somewhat from all of these; he supports the War, in hopes of de-

stroying

ſtroying a combination of Reformers, and procuring Peace for the next fifty years.

To thoſe who would continue the War, in hopes of reſtoring the ancient Monarchy, which certainly cannot be done, without deſtroying the preſent popular principles, I ſhall obſerve, that a War againſt opinions never was ſucceſsful. Peruſe the hiſtories of the Wars againſt religious Opinions, againſt religious Reformers, againſt the Principles of Freedom in Holland, againſt the Principles of Freedom in America! Were any of theſe ſucceſsful, were any of the ſame kind ever ſucceſsful? No. In the third campaign, the cauſe of the Americans, ſeemed to be quite hopeleſs, twenty times more ſo than that of France now is, yet it ultimately triumphed. Are not the French the moſt powerful Nation in Europe? Have they not formerly, when leſs intereſted in the cauſe, contended againſt and repelled all Europe? Are they not now animated even to madneſs with hatred againſt Kings and Nobility? Does not every ſucceſs of the Combined Armies encreaſe the unanimity, and conſequently the ſtrength of France? If enthuſiaſm in La Vendee has ſo long reſiſted that power, which ſo lately threatened the conqueſt, and ſince, has ſucceſsfully withſtood all Europe; if in one department it has coped with the competitor of Germany, Italy, Britain, Spain, Holland, &c. what may it not be expected to do in eighty departments? We are led, indeed, to believe, that bribery will produce revolts, and divide the French; but this is the very ſame expectation which was held out during the American conteſt, and then much

more

more ſucceſsfully practiſed than hitherto has been done in France. The ſame men are purſuing the ſame policy. But Hawkeſbury, Dundas, Howe, Auckland, and Loughborough, may have no more reaſon for exultation than they had in 1780: Bribery may, indeed, do much miſchief, and it is natural for thoſe who believe it perſuaſive, to try its effects on others. But " extravagant Courts, ſelfiſh Miniſters, " and corrupt Majorities," are not " inti- " mately interwoven" with French Freedom, and therefore cannot be expected to produce proſperity and happineſs in that nation. They do not fight for the glory of a Court, or the folly or ambition of a Miniſter; every man thinks he fights for himſelf. Even the Touloneſe, while ſurrendering their town, declared their firm attachment to the Conſtitution founded in 1789; and the reſtoration of that Conſtitution is certainly the furtheſt ſtretch from Republicaniſm to which the French people will conſent to go. It therefore follows, that either the allies muſt relinquiſh their original views, or animate the French nation, as one man, to maintain the conteſt againſt them. And here I will appeal to Mr. Young's favourite " Practice" and " Events," and deſire to know, if a War againſt a people, againſt ſo powerful a people as the French, has ever been ſucceſsful?

To thoſe who wiſh the reſtoration of a limited monarchy, of the Conſtitution founded in 1789, it cannot be neceſſary to ſay much to convince them of the hopeleſſneſs of their object. They are, indeed, the only reaſonable claſs, and it is therefore lamentable, that they ſhould have the leaſt proſpect of ſucceſs. It was that Conſtitution which Mr. Burke reviled, which Mr. Pitt condemned, and which, as I have already ſhewn, never was ſincerely approved by our Government. It is that Conſtitution which Lords Auckland and Hood attempted to hold up to deteſtation, when they mentioned the miſcreants, who, for *four* years, brought miſery on France. But what is more, it was againſt that Conſtitution, before it was even finiſhed, that the German Deſpots made War, and to acknowledge it, would be to acknowledge they had failed in their deſign, that they were defeated. If further proof is wanted, that the Conſtitution of 1789, and the preſent Government of France, are equally odious to the continental Deſpots, look into the priſon of La Fayette, who attempted to fix that Conſtitution, and to ſave and ſupport the King:—Roberſpierre or Hebert, if, in their power, could not be treated with more cruelty.—Nay, it is even vain to expect, that the allies deſign the reſtoration of the *genuine*, the *ancient French Government*! The States General was a part of the ancient Government, and it was the States General that brought about the Revolution, and framed the Conſtitution founded in 1789, and accepted by the King in 1791. The Convention at Pilnitz was formed againſt the States General, after it had given itſelf another name, indeed; and Lords Auckland and Hood have called them miſcreants, who have brought miſery on France. It was the States General which began the Revolution,

and,

and, according to the allies, began all the present mischief. It cannot, therefore, be the restoration of the *ancient* Constitution which is intended, it can only be a crippled Despotism.

To those who consider the objects of the War, to be the acquisition of territory, it may be observed, that all which we shall probably conquer and retain, will, by no means, compensate for the expences incurred by the continuance of hostilities; and even acquisition of territory, may be of no solid advantage, if we are to believe the speeches and writings of the supporters of Government, who have inferred, from the national prosperity of the last ten years, that the loss of America has been rather a benefit than an injury to Britain. To persons who consider conquest as the object of the present struggle, I will not remark, on the infamy of making War for plunder, because, with them, and the tyrants of the continent, such a remark would be treated as a jest.

Those persons who would continue the War, merely because they hate the French, and hope to cut their throats, I consign over to the Crown and Anchor committee, hoping there are sufficient humanity and religion, in that worthy body, to make them blush at their brutality, and tremble at their breach of the laws of God.

Mr. Young, is for continuing the War, to destroy a combination of Reformers, and give us fifty years Peace! This shews the depth of his penetration. I appeal to all the "Experi- "ments," "Practice," and "Events," that he can produce, whether all Wars have not, instead of destroying, created Reformers. As

R 2 the

the people feel the weight of burthens, they begin to think of lightening them, and consequently, the first thing they turn their thoughts to, is Reform. Was not this particularly the case of the American War? What produced such a combination of Reformers in 1780, if it was not the expences of that contest, and the mismanagement of the public purse? The same effects, will result in time, from the present War. Every new tax will make Reformers of the class which is fixed on to pay it: And even Mr. Young himself, may again think a Reform desirable, if the necessities of the State should oblige Government to discontinue his salary, and encrease the land-tax.

If he could give any proof in support of his assertion, that the present War will produce fifty years Peace, then indeed, however unjust it might be, there would be some policy in continuing it. But what reason have we to expect a Peace of fifty years? Whatever may be the fate of France, does the History of Britain or of Europe justify such an expectation? At the beginning of 1792, Mr. Pitt, assured us, of fifteen years peace; at the beginning of 1793, we found ourselves plunged into a most expensive and alarming War! Is Mr. Young a better prophet than Mr. Pitt? A little more than a year before the commencement of the present War, Mr. Pitt was desirous of involving us in hostilities with Russia, on account of her aggrandizement, and is not the same cause of quarrel likely to exist, in an encreased degree, whenever our dispute with France shall conclude? Nay, as all the powers in Europe are only smothering their old rooted animoſities, in order to join in a common cauſe, will they not quarrel in caſe of a failure in their preſent project, by blaming each other with the fault; or in caſe of ſucceſs, will they not quarrel about the ſpoil? If Auſtria does not gain ſomething conſiderable, either in France or elſewhere, can it be ſuppoſed ſhe will allow Ruſſia and Pruſſia quietly to retain what they have taken of Poland? In which ever point of view we look at the preſent attempt upon France, either of failure or ſucceſs, the reſult is more likely to leave the ſeeds of future Wars, than the proſpect of any former ſtruggle in Europe. The Empreſs of Ruſſia is perfectly well aware of this, therefore, ſhe allows the other powers to waſte themſelves, and reſerves her ſtrength till the day of reckoning ſhall arrive *.

But it would be endleſs to expoſe the folly and injuſtice of the general motives for continuing the preſent War: It is of moſt real importance to know, what Adminiſtration deſign by it: And here, if we are to be guided by their

* This cunning Princeſs had ſucceeded in perſuading the late King of Sweden, to take an active part in the preſent cruſade, and it is tolerably well known, that her deſign was to have ſeized his dominions, when he had ſo far exhauſted himſelf, as to be incapable of reſiſtance. This is the reaſon why Sweden and Denmark, now obſerve a ſtrict neutrality, and keep a watchful eye over her. The King of Pruſſia has been drawn into the ſame ſnare that was laid for the late King of Sweden, but it is generally believed, that the purſe of another power, as well as the aſſurances of the Empreſs, was, in the *very firſt inſtance*, employed to prevail on him. The conſciouſneſs of his own danger from the Empreſs, now makes him ſo unwilling to waſte his troops againſt France.

declarations,

declarations, it is but honeſt to confeſs total ignorance, for it would ſeem they do not know themſelves. But it is not from the unintelligible hypocritical memorials of Miniſters, that the deſigns of a Government are to be diſcovered, ſo much as from the general tenor of their conduct.

The Engliſh Court profeſſedly began the War, in conſequence of the decree of fraternity, the attempt to open the Scheldt, and the aggrandizement of France. When ſatisfaction on all theſe points was obtained, and France was ſo far humbled, that ſhe would have agreed to any reaſonable terms of accommodation, Mr. Fox, in the month of June, moved an Addreſs in favour of Peace, as the avowed cauſes of War no longer exiſted. To this, Mr. Pitt objected, on the ground, that, although certain points might be the occaſion of a War, yet in its conduct and events, there was no ſaying what objects might ariſe, which it might be prudent to obtain; that, therefore, though the original grounds of the War no longer exiſted, yet his Majeſty's Miniſters thought it would be proper to continue hoſtilities, in order to procure indemnity for the paſt, and ſecurity for the future. As to theſe two words *indemnity* and *ſecurity*, while it remains undefined, what indemnity and ſecurity are deſired, as is the caſe at preſent, they have no meaning at all, becauſe, they may be made to mean every thing, or any thing, or nothing: They may be interpreted juſt as the Miniſter pleaſes: He may deem a *promiſe* to pay a certain ſum, as was the caſe in the late diſpute with Spain, a ſufficient indemnity, and an aſſurance of faith, though no more

more to be depended on than the faith of the Empreſs and King of Pruſſia, ſufficient ſecurity: Or he may deem nothing leſs than the complete conqueſt of France, to be ſufficient indemnity and ſecurity. To fight for theſe two objects, unleſs they are preciſely defined, is to fight on the moſt blind ſpeculation.

Fighting for new objects, that may ariſe in the conduct and events of a War, is nearly the ſame thing, as fighting for undefined indemnity and ſecurity; and in ſpeaking of the one, the other may always be underſtood to be implied. They are both equally the Miniſter's ſpeculations; for how can the people know when the Miniſter will think he has obtained ſufficient indemnity and ſecurity, or when he may think it proper to deſiſt from attempting new objects, that may ariſe in the conduct and events of a War? The preſent War was profeſſedly begun for certain ſpecified objects, but in its conduct and events, thoſe original objects being obtained, we are next to continue hoſtilities for undefined indemnity and ſecurity, and then we are to eſtabliſh Monarchy in France!—The conduct and events of the War may yet give riſe to new objects, and our wiſe Miniſters may think they have not indemnity and ſecurity, unleſs they not only eſtabliſh ſuch a government in France as may pleaſe them, but alſo ſeize ſome of her territory.—The conduct and events of the War may again give riſe to new objects, and indemnity and ſecurity may be thought to require, that we ſhould deſtroy the government we had juſt given to France, as the King of Pruſſia did that which he recently

guaranteed

guaranteed to Poland, and we may agree to divide the whole French territory among the allies.—Still, in the same manner, new objects arising, may carry us further, and it may be thought necessary, for indemnity and security, to obey the exhortations of some of our divines, and to exterminate the whole French people. —Nay, if success attends us, why should we stop short with France? New objects may arise in the conduct and events of War, which may, according to Mr. Pitt's reasoning, justify its continuance, in hopes of the conquest of the whole world!

But, although from their declarations, we cannot precisely ascertain what are the objects of Ministers in the present War, we must conjecture from their conduct, that they are much beyond what it is thought prudent to avow. Why was our intention of giving a monarchical form of government to France concealed, till the surrender of Toulon? Had any new circumstances occurred in France, which made it more necessary to interfere in her internal concerns, in August, when Lord Hood took possession of that town, than in February, when the War was begun?—No. But in February, the people were not ripe for approving such a project, therefore, it was concealed from them: Nor are they now ripe for approving, what in the conduct and events of this War it may be thought proper to attempt. The ultimate objects must be brought forward by degrees, otherwise they might, perhaps, startle the nation.

Since

Since not only the British Government, but the allies in general, appear, by their inconsistent conduct, to conceal the true objects of the War; since, by taking Valenciennes for the Emperor, Toulon for Louis the XVIIth, and summoning Dunkirk to surrender to the King of Britain *, there appears to be something of selfishness, under all the plausible disinterested professions of giving happiness to France, how are we to solve this mystery? How are we to be guided in searching for the truth? Are we not to judge both of men and governments, rather by their actions, than their professions? If, under pretence of improving an estate, an attorney had taken possession, and by dint of law had wrung it from the legal proprietor; if the same attorney were to offer himself to another man, who knew of this transaction, and to say to him, "your estate is much deranged; your "grounds are neglected, and your tenants idle, "dissipated, and wicked; put your estate into "my hands for a short time, I will make it "productive and beautiful, and your tenants "industrious, virtuous, and happy:—it will, "indeed, cost me many thousands of pounds,— "perhaps half my fortune; but I am resolved "to do all for your benefit, though I owe you "no gratitude, and expect no return."—If a man who was known to have acted so treacherously in one instance were to attempt to

* The Prince of Saxe Cobourg's proclamations, in April last, in the first of which he engaged to restore the Constitution of 1789, and in the second, recalled that promise, should also here be recollected.

repeat

repeat his villany, would he be believed or trusted ?—Would he not rather be kicked out of the house of him to whom he made the offer ?—If, then, it is from the actions of the man that we form our notions of his character and designs, rather than from professions which we know him most scandalously to have belied, why shall we not form our opinion of the character and designs of a Government in the same manner ?—Have not Prussia and Russia robbed Poland, under the pretence of giving her a good Government, and making her happy ?—And are they not now holding out the same pretences to France, in hopes of getting possession, and plundering, in the same manner, that nation ?—Has a single power in Europe remonstrated against the robbery of Poland, as it was their duty, and more particularly the duty of Britain, which affected to be alarmed at the cession of Oczakow ?—Is not silence, in this case, consent ? How then are we to guess at the objects of the present War against France, but by looking at what has been done in Poland, since the same powers are combined against the one, which actually robbed, or tacitly consented to the robbery of the other ?—which consented to the dismemberment of Poland, which had neither interfered in the internal concerns of other powers, nor infringed treaties, nor violated the rights of nations, nor aggrandized herself by conquest ; whose new Constitution was approved by Mr. Burke, and the other gentlemen in this country, who were the most implacable enemies of French principles, and even sanctioned by

its

its neighbour, the King of Pruſſia, who afterwards made it the pretext for his robbery.

Such is the prelude to what, in common ſenſe, we muſt conclude, is deſigned to be acted in France. If bribery can produce treachery and civil commotion, which, ſeconded by external force,—if, in ſhort, by any means,—for the laws of nations and humanity are laughed at,—the allies can conquer France, they will treat it as they have done Poland, and diſmember it in ſuch a manner that it never may again liſt its head among nations. They will give it ſome puppet for a monarch, and, under pretence of awing Jacobiniſm, will keep up a large ſtanding army, for which France will be obliged to pay. This done, the balance of power, for which we have ſquandered ſo many millions, will be compleatly annihilated; and if Ruſſia, Auſtria, and Pruſſia can agree about the diviſion of the ſpoil, they may divide all Europe among themſelves *. They may make a ſecond partition of France, as they lately have done of Poland;—they may do juſt as they pleaſe all over the continent of Chriſtian Europe, for there will be no power able to oppoſe them.—And even Britain will not long be ſuffered to retain her independence, when the navies of France, Spain, Holland, Sweden, and Ruſſia, can be turned againſt her;—nay, they will probably make her the moſt exemplary inſtance of their vengeance, becauſe ſhe has been the nurſe of thoſe principles, againſt which, in France, they are now making War.

* For a moſt excellent view of this ſubject, ſee the Letters of the Calm Obſerver.

Such, I believe, are the real objects of the present War; and, if the allies are successful, they will, in due time, be unfolded; but whether defeat or triumph follows their arms, the ultimate consequences must be equally pernicious to Britain. For, if their true objects are gained by the conquest of France, Holland and Britain will immediately be at their mercy, and we have seen in Poland what their mercy is: If, on the other hand, the allies fail, we shall be obliged to sit down in disgrace a few years hence; and the large additional burthens may provoke a disappointed and aggrieved people not only to make Reforms, but dangerous innovations. In Lord Cornwallis's late peace, the preserving of Seringapatam was justified on the policy of supporting the balance of power in India; but how much more strongly does the same reasoning apply to the preservation of France? Shall our *gratitude* to Austria and Prussia induce us to ruin ourselves?—A gratitude, which is by no means due to them, as it was not for Holland but for themselves they fought. The wisest policy for Britain, therefore, is to follow the example of the Empress of Russia, and rather strengthen than waste herself, now she has gained all she desired when entering into the contest. To suppose that Prussia, Austria, and Russia design, by this War, to give happiness to France, is so truly ridiculous, that it does not deserve a serious comment;—read their own recent histories.

The duration of the War, or the events that may take place during its continuance, it is vain to calculate. It was positively asserted

of

of the American War, at its commencement, that it would be finiſhed in one campaign; and laſt February, we were taught to expect the ſame thing of the rupture now exiſting. Wars of a nature like the preſent, though even of leſs importance, have, however, laſted to a period, which might excite ridicule if the ſame duration were predicted of the ſtruggle now making in France. Wars in former times have been continued in that nation forty years. —The War by which Holland was enabled at laſt to throw off the Spaniſh yoke laſted ſixty years, although Spain was then the moſt formidable and Holland the moſt inſignificant country in Europe. Mr. Young by predicting, that the preſent war will bring us fifty years peace, and that every year's War will bring ten years peace in its train, calculates its continuance at five years. On this point, he is much more honeſt than thoſe who have written on the ſame ſide; for they have, and always will, aſſure us, that another campaign will ſettle it; and they will hold this language, even after the experience of twenty years, ſhall have twenty times confuted them. It is impoſſible to calculate the duration of the War; but, while the allies make the ſubjection of France their object, it muſt wear the appearance of a long, bloody, cruel, expenſive, ruinous conteſt. It is not that the Duke of York takes Valenciennes, or Lord Hood, Toulon, or Lord Howe, Breſt and Bourdeaux, or the Prince of Saxe Cobourg, Rouen, Lyons, and Paris: The greateſt part of France, may be conquered by treachery and force; but will it long remain ſo? Can all the powers

powers in Europe keep a ſtanding army, liable to imbibe the principles of Liberty, ſufficient to awe France into perpetual ſubjection? Will not the inhuman conduct of Pruſſians and Auſtrians, which has already ſhewn itſelf in Alſace and Lorraine, provoke frequent and formidable inſurrections? The example of this country ſhews, that where the principles of Liberty are ſown, force will rather nouriſh than deſtroy them, and as the principles of Liberty are firmly implanted in the breaſts of the French people, they never can be rooted out. Temporary calamity may diſguſt them at their Governors, but they never have been, nor never will be diſguſted at their principles. France may, indeed, be apparently overcome, and Peace eſtabliſhed; but a people, filled with high notions of Freedom, never will long ſubmit to Deſpotic ſway: Frequent Wars will occur, until at laſt, the conquerors will be exhauſted, and Liberty will triumph. Mr. Young infers, becauſe the Engliſh Republican Spirit in the laſt century ended in Deſpotiſm, that therefore, the Republican Spirit in France will end in Deſpotiſm alſo:—Deſpotiſm, may poſſibly, ſucceed the preſent Republic, and reign for a while as it did in England; but did not the ſame principles which brought Charles the Iſt. to the block, alſo expel James the IId. and bring about the Revolution of 1688? And will not the doctrines now ſown in France, ultimately ſettle ſome form of Government, whether Monarchical or Republican, founded on the principles of Liberty? But it is extremely improbable, that a great and powerful

nation

nation of Enthusiasts will be overcome, even by treachery and force. Their strength must not be calculated by a narrow Court Policy; nor, because Hessians, Hanoverians, and Sardinians, will not fight without money, in what is deemed a common cause, must it be concluded, that Frenchmen are equally mercenary: There is a National Treasury, more powerful than all the tax offices in Britain, in the breasts of Frenchmen:—a love of Liberty. The American paper was lower than even that of France has been, yet America triumphed; and though their Government has excited our contempt and horror, yet it cannot be denied that the French troops have lately displayed energy, enterprize, and bravery, scarcely equalled, certainly never surpassed in the world. Whatever fond hopes may be formed of the next campaign, I fear they will prove illusive, for our future success is not to be calculated by the events of last summer. Another Dumourier, may not be found, to destroy the principal army, and leave the northern frontier unprotected: On the contrary, we have seen the ruinous effects of his treachery repaired, and the tide again turned against us: Nor will his treatment encourage further treachery, or the treatment of the Toulonese, encourage Royalism. It may even be seen in the slighting treatment of the Ex-Princes of France, that the Allies do not design to restore them to their former fortunes, but that they intend something both against them, and the Nation at large, which, it is feared, those noblemen will not agree to, and therefore, instead of being held up as conspicuous leaders in what is professed

to

to be principally their own cauſe, they are kept in the back ground, and treated with coldneſs.

The ſubjugation and partition of France, together with the eſtabliſhment of an impotent Deſpotiſm, being therefore, the evident objects * of the continental Triumvirate, it may be uſeful to enquire whether Great-Britain will aſſiſt them to the full extent of their views; how ſhe can ſtop ſhort of them, and make Peace; whether, in any ſtage of the War our Government will be diſpoſed, of itſelf, to put a period to hoſtilities; whether, it will not be obliged to do ſo by the remonſtrances of the people; in what manner it can make Peace, and what may be the conſequences of being compelled to make it by the public.

The firſt of theſe enquiries need be but ſhort; it is but to read the Treaty with the King of Sardinia, wherein, it is agreed, to pay him 200,000l. per annum, during the *whole courſe of the War*, and the other Treaties with Ruſſia and Pruſſia, through which we guarantee the dominions of all the belligerent powers againſt the arms of France. By theſe Treaties, we perceive, that as long as the French poſſeſs a ſingle

* It has been ſaid, that the ceſſion of the ſtrong holds on the northern frontier of France, would ſatisfy the Allies, and I have little doubt, that they really would do ſo, for the preſent. It would indeed, be a ſmall ceſſion of territory, but, it would in fact, be a ceſſion of much more danger to this country, than, not only the ceſſion of Oczakow, but of all Turkey in Europe. If the Allies poſſeſſed that bulwark, they might not only confine the French, while they plundered Holland, Denmark, and Sweden, and as they have done Poland, but the whole of France would be laid open to their maurauding incurſions.

inch

inch of ground belonging to Auſtria, Sardinia, or any of the allies; or, as long as the King of Sardinia thinks proper to carry on the War, we are bound to carry it on alſo, which is ſimply, that while any of the allies continues hoſtilities, we are bound by Treaty to join them, and without a breach of faith, cannot ſtop ſhort, and deſert their cauſe. If to theſe Treaties, we add the conduct of our Ambaſſadors in Denmark, Sweden, Tuſcany, and Genoa, we may very reaſonably conclude, that the Britiſh Cabinet is not only embarked to the full extent of the views of the Princes on the Continent, but is one of the moſt zealous, and even furious of the allies; for our Government ſeems eager to ſurpaſs in violence all that has been done by other powers. Peace, therefore, originating in the Britiſh Cabinet, muſt be at a very great diſtance.

The next queſtion is, will the people patiently ſubmit to a long continuance of the diſtreſſes which are always brought on by War, and invariably encreaſed by its protraction? Will they quietly ſee their blood ſhed, and their enormous debts doubled, in a vain attempt to give a King to France, and to aggrandize, by the plunder of her territories, the ambitious Deſpots of the continent? The Hiſtory of the American War, ſhews, that national diſtreſs will certainly open the eyes of the people to the folly of Government; and the growing diſſatisfaction at the preſent War, ſhews, that a campaign or two more, will make it as unpopular as ever that of America was. It will daily become more manifeſt, that we can derive no benefit equal to the riſk we run, and the actual loſs we muſt ſuſtain by the continuance of hoſtilities. I therefore think the people will, at ſome period, not very diſtant, perhaps, put an end to this War, as they did to that with America, by petitions and addreſſes. If then, in one, two, or three years, the people *demand* a peace, *it muſt be granted*. But how is it to be made ?— By doing that which Government has ſo much reprobated, by negociating with, and acknowledging the French Republic. It has indeed, been ſaid, that Britain may withdraw her forces, and by ſome underhand means, procure a ſeceſſion of hoſtilities, which, until a regular Government is ſettled, will be equal to a formal Peace: But when the French find the maſs of the Engliſh people reſolved on a termination of hoſtilities, will they not inſiſt upon an avowed negociation with, and an acknowledgment of the Republic ? When they find the Court of St. James's, unable longer to carry on the War, will not they inſiſt upon their own terms ? And will not a humiliating compliance, as was the caſe with America, be the conſequence ? It is with this War, as it is with Parliamentary Reform: At preſent, Peace and Reform, might be made with the greateſt advantage, in the ſame manner as a Peace with America, long after the commencement of that unfortunate conteſt, might have been made on beneficial terms. But obſtinacy has of late been the characteriſtic of our Government. After the firſt campaign with America, ſhe might have been reconciled to us; after the firſt campaign with France, we have it in our power amply to

obtain

obtain reparation for all which gave us offence. It is ridiculous to talk of the inhumanity of negociating with the present rulers of France, when we recollect, that we in 1777, negociated with, and made *dear Allies*, of the wild savages in America, and instigated them to make War upon the United States, which they did in the most horrible manner: it is ridiculous to talk of our dignity being insulted by negociating with the rulers of France, when the ignominious treatment of the Representative of our King, by the Ottoman Porte, is recollected*: it is ridiculous to say, we can have no security for the continuance of Peace, as the rulers of France may daily be supplanted, for, no Government in Europe, observes Peace longer than it is its interest to do so, and without expatiating on the late want of faith in Russia, Prussia, &c. with regard to Poland, I will venture to affirm, what is certainly true, that every party which has governed France, during the last four years, and every party likely to succeed to the Government, would, has been, and will be desirous, and even proud of keeping Peace with Britain. But of late, our Court has commonly persisted

* Before our Ambassador is introduced to the Grand Seignor, he is obliged to eat some food, which is given him in the Palace, and to put on a cloak, worth about 30l presented to him at the same time. When he comes into the sublime Presence, he is held by the arms by two officers, who will not permit him to bow of his own accord, but who, laying their hands on his head, *force* him to bow. They then say to their Sovereign, "Here is a poor man We found him "hungry, and we fed him; we found him naked, and we "cloatned him."—Where is the *dignity* of the King's Representative on this occasion?

T 2 to

to the laſt extremity; till the popular tide has riſen to ſuch a height that it was forced to unconditional ſubmiſſion. And, I fear, the preſent conteſt will be proſecuted, till Peace muſt be made on *any* terms, and then Mr. Burke, may do what he ridiculed in Lord North's Adminiſtration, towards the concluſion of the American War, and ſay to the French, "Now do have "a King * !"

The evident determination of the Government to proſecute the War, is not ſo dejecting a circumſtance, as the too general encouragement given, not only to panegyrics on the corruptions and defects of our Conſtitution, but to the moſt falſe accuſations, and the moſt ſhameful calumny againſt thoſe who deſire the reſtoration of tranquility. To petition for Peace, is deemed ſedition; to contend in Parliament for Peace, is deemed treaſon, for what elſe can we conclude, from the abuſe thrown on the Glaſgow petition, and the inſinuations of Mr. Powis †, reſpecting Mr. Fox. The many wicked aſperſions thrown on the character and conduct of the latter of thoſe gentlemen, may, however, be juſtly conſtrued into eulogiums on his public

* This, indeed, has already been ſaid in Mr. Pitt's late extraordinary Maniſeſto.

† This gentleman, in the Houſe of Commons, after beſtowing many eulogiums on Mr. Fox, ſaid, though he was perfectly convinced of the Right Hon. Gentleman's integrity, yet his conduct in that Houſe, was exactly ſuch as an advocate of the French Convention would purſue. This, out of doors, was turned into a downright aſſertion as a fact; and Mr. F. was even repreſented in the print ſhops, as the advocate of the French, with a brief and a fee in his hand.

virtue; for, if ever there was a man, who conſcious of acting with rectitude, maintained the true intereſts of his country with firmneſs, conſiſtency, and moderation, againſt all that could deject and terrify, he is the man: If ever private intereſt and public fame; if ever the ſweets of ſocial life, and the proſpects of ſtate elevation, were ſacrificed to the national welfare, and to the liberties and happineſs of mankind, they were ſacrificed by Mr. Fox, laſt winter. He ſtood forward, almoſt alone, and with gigantic power, arreſted the Government in its wanton intoxicated career. Sedition and inſurrection had been declared to exiſt, the Attorney-General's table was ſaid to be loaded with hundreds of indictments, and thouſands were recorded as diſaffected perſons, upon the authority of anonymous letters*, and the veracity of common informers. The ſuſpenſion of the Habeas Corpus Act was announced in the Houſe of Commons, and had it taken place, it is probable, that every man who preſumed to enquire into the propriety of the meaſures of Government, who praiſed Liberty in England, or who dared look cheerful when events occurred favourable to it in other countries, would have been dragged to a dungeon. But Mr. Fox, ſtood forward with truth and energy. The Government was awed:—It pauſed:—and, finding the proofs of inſurrection and ſedition vague and trifling, it refrained from meaſures, which, the deluſion of the people might then, indeed, have

* This was done by Mr. Reeves. See Mr. Law's letter on his ſeceſſion, from the Crown and Anchor Committee.

applauded,

applauded, but which their ſober reaſon, at an after period, muſt have condemned and execrated. He undauntedly ſtruggled to avert the calamities of War; he did not ſucceed: But he ſucceeded in what was of much more immediate importance perhaps, in ſhielding the remaining Liberties of the Engliſh people.

His enemies have alledged motives for his conduct, not only baſe, but incredible. The Tory Jacobins, have accuſed him of being the hired advocate of France; the Revolutionary Jacobins, with being ſpurred on only by a ſelfiſh ambition, and the moderate, honeſt alarmiſts, though agreeing with neither of theſe, were not inclined to attribute virtuous motives to a man, who not only differed from them in political ſentiment, but whoſe character they found equally beſpattered by the extremes of both parties.

The accuſation of the Tory Jacobins, is evidently ſo unfounded, that it is unneceſſary to waſte time in refuting it. The ruling Powers of France have changed ſo often, that ſuch a thing, had it exiſted, muſt long ago have been diſcovered. Nay, one of the charges againſt the Briſſot party, made by the party of the Mountain, is, that they too precipitately involved France in a War with Britain; and even the ſupporters of the War at home, affirm, it was unprovoked on our part, and that the French were anxious to commence it. Briſſot's, was the ruling party laſt winter, and if it was true, that they were eager for hoſtilities, is it probable, they would bribe any man to prevent them?

them? Nor could the detraction of the ruling men * in the Convention, at the moment the rupture was made, be construed, as a proof, that Mr. Fox was connected with them. But, last winter, passion had so blinded the most alarmed of the alarmists, that the most palpably unfounded assertion, if agreeing with their wishes, received the most implicit credit: For, "there are seasons of believing, as well as dis-"believing: And, believing was then so much "in season, that improbabilities, or incon-"sistencies, were little considered. Nor was "it safe so much as to make reflections on "them. That was called, the *blasting of the* "*plot*, and disparaging the King's evidence †."

The conduct of many parliamentary men gives some colour of truth to the charge of the Revolutionary Jacobins. It is an incontrovertible fact, that opposition to Government, has too often arisen only in the hope of gratifying a personal ambition; but it is also a fact, still more incontrovertible, and a fair examination of circumstances, will clearly shew, that Mr. Fox, last winter, could not be actuated by any motives of that nature; but, that on the contrary, his conduct was the very last which would have been pursued, either by an avaricious, or by an ambitious man: For, if his prime object had been a place, or a pension, there never was a more favourable opportunity

* See Kersaint's Report, wherein Mr. Fox, is much more calumniated, than Mr. Pitt.

† See Bishop Burnet's account of the Alarmists, at the time of the pretended Popish Plot, in his History of his own Times. Vol. I. P. 448.

for

for gaining it. To oppoſe Government was then generally deteſtable, almoſt dangerous: to deſert principles and parties, and coaleſce with Adminiſtration, was deemed by the country, the height of public virtue. It was honourable in the extreme, for Whigs and Tories to embrace and co-operate: Conſiſtency of conduct became a crime, and apoſtacy the pureſt patriotiſm. The people conſidered it Mr. Fox's duty to join the Court party; his acceptance of an official ſituation, and thereby gratifying avarice, and even ambition would have received the warm applauſe and gratitude of his countrymen, as a ſacrifice of party views and perſonal antipathies, to what they believed the national welfare.

Such were the temptations to induce Mr. Fox to follow his own private intereſt, and indulge his ambition. If, on the other hand, we view the reaſons he had to *deter* him from ſupporting Peace and Reform, we ſhall find them not only inconſiſtent with avarice and ambition; not only that he was to forego all hopes of ſharing the honours and emoluments of office; not only that he was to incur the reſentment and odium of the nation, and be branded as the leader of ſedition, on the one ſide, and accuſed of puſilanimity and inſincerity, by thoſe, among whom he was claſſed, on the other; but his deareſt friends, and moſt valuable connections, were to deſert and revile him with a malignity, and injuſtice, which his oldeſt enemies never could arrive at. Of about two hundred coadjutors in the Houſe of Commons, ſcarce fifty adhered

adhered to him;—of about one hundred in the House of Peers, there remained not more than six!—Instead of being courted and adored, to be shunned and calumniated, by an host of men of the greatest fortunes and talents in the kingdom, was surely no encouragement either to avarice, or ambition. To have all classes, to have Tories and Whigs, to have those who are called Jacobins, and those who were called Friends, join in the outcry against him; to lose both popularity and court favour, and even the the enjoyments of private society; to encounter at once, the frowns of the throne, and the indignation of the people, required courage, independence and abilities rarely to be met with. The undaunted, disinterested exertions of Mr. Fox last winter, in favour of Freedom, expiate all his former errors. Indeed, a recollection of circumstances gives reason to hope he never will again be betrayed into such errors as those which some years ago rendered him most unpopular. For if we may believe report, the most odious of those measures were prompted and executed by persons who have since betrayed and deserted him. The coalition in 1783 was projected by a noble deserter, now at the head of the law department, and the negociation was carried on, and the measure enforced by him and his train of alarmists. The East-India bill, which begot the *charter alarmists*, and at once pushed Mr. Fox from power and popularity, was the production of Mr. Burke, whose measures Mr. Fox found it always more easy to support in public, than oppose in private. To the dogmatick opinions of that gentleman, therefore, the miſtakes of Mr. Fox are greatly, if not wholly, to be attributed, and ſo well aware is Mr. Pitt, of Mr. Burke's unruly temper, that it is not probable, he ever will conſent to his admiſſion into the cabinet. If to the coalition and the India bill, is added, the ſupport Mr. Fox gave to certain great perſonages, who have alſo deſerted him, then, all that has made him unpopular, may be ſummoned up. It is his perſonal attachments that have injured his public character, and we now find thoſe for whom he has made ſo important a ſacrifice, eagerly aggravating the approbrium which originated in a reſpect for their opinions, and a zeal for their ſervice. But their conduct may prove fortunate for his reputation. Unincumbered by their baneful influence, and following the dictates of his own reaſon, his integrity and wiſdom, muſt ultimately be acknowledged; and though he may ever remain unrewarded with either place or popularity, the purity of his views, and the prudence of his councils, may yet ſave this infatuated country.

It would be endleſs to enumerate the libels that have been, and daily are, publiſhed againſt him. Mr. Young's book contains one of the moſt fallacious and wicked; and it may ſerve as an epitome of the others. In the debate on Parliamentary Reform, on the 7th of laſt May, Mr. Fox ſaid, " *If* the King and the Houſe " of Lords were unneceſſary and uſeleſs branches " of the Conſtitution, let them be diſmiſſed " and aboliſhed; for the people were not made

" for

" for them, but they for the people *. If, on " the contrary, the King and the House of " Lords were felt and believed by the people, " *as he was confident they were*, to be not " only useful, but *essential parts* of the Con- " stitution, a House of Commons, freely chosen " by, and speaking the sentiments of the " people, would cherish and protect both " within the bounds which the Constitution " had assigned them †." Mr. Young artfully drops the hypothesis, and throughout several pages, accuses Mr. Fox with recommending the dismissal of the King, and abolition of the House of Lords!—He omits the context, wherein Mr. Fox says, he is confident the people *feel* and *believe* the King and the House of Lords to be *useful* and *essential* parts of the Constitution, and that a House of Commons, freely chosen, and speaking the sentiments of the people, would *cherish and protect them*. Could there be a greater tribute of respect and approbation of those two branches of the Constitution than was paid by Mr. Fox, in declaring the people love and will protect them?—Could there be a more gross misrepresentation and flagitious calumny than the assertion of Mr. Young?

* Mr. Young, in a note on this passage, says, the Nobility and the King made the people, and that therefore the people were made for them! Upon his own mode of arguing it may, however, be proved, that the King was made for the people; for did not the people make the Brunswick the Royal Family of this country? Mr. Young, I suppose, would have the English people made *for* the King, as the Hessians are made for the Prince of Hesse:—to be sold.

† See Debrett's Debates.

Despising the thousands of atrocious libels, and regardless of his own interest, still we see Mr. Fox, unsubdued by menace or allurement, persevering with intrepidity and moderation, in support of the Peace, Liberties, and Happiness of his country. But whatever consolation may be found in his conduct, the general view of public affairs is full of dejection and alarm. On the continent, the laws and rights of nations are trampled on with impunity, without remonstrance, and an extensive dangerous system of robbery is established. The balance of power is lost,—almost forgotten; and whether a Republic is attempted in France, or a limited Monarchy, like our own, in Poland, the fact of desiring Liberty, *in any degree*, is so offensive to the Combination of Despots, that they instantly take arms against it;—they deem a wish for Freedom sufficient to justify all sorts of massacre, devastation, and plunder. There appears to be no medium;—no hope of compromise can at present be entertained. An universal War is kindled, which threatens the complete annihilation of Liberty on the one side, or the total destruction of all established Governments on the other; for such appear to be the views of the two parties, accordingly as the scale of success inclines in their favour. A permanent and equitable Peace, therefore, can only be expected, after a long, equal contest, shall have destroyed the means of further warfare; after both parties, in point of conquest, shall find themselves just where they began, but mutually weakened by bloodshed and expence; after they ſhall have exhauſted themſelves into tranquility.

At home the proſpect is not leſs full of dejection and alarm than on the continent. In Ireland, a moſt extraordinary bill has paſſed, to prevent the people from expreſſing their wiſhes: —In Scotland, the moſt *unprecedented* puniſhments have been inflicted on thoſe who have adviſed a peaceable and conſtitutional Reform of Parliament. Theſe new and alarming experiments have been ſucceſsfully made in the extremities of the Empire, and it would appear that force is preparing, in order to inſure their reception, in the interior. Barracks are erecting in every part of England, where a ſtanding army is to be kept, inſulated from the people; and if that is found inſufficient for the purpoſes of Government, foreign Mercenaries may, by treaty, be landed* to overawe and ſecure ſubmiſſion. Our Conſtitution ſo much boaſted for its bleſſings, and its excellence, is libelled with impunity, as corrupt and ugly, by thoſe who ſupport the Government, and the libellers are rewarded with places and penſions for ſaying, that "extravagant Courts, ſelfiſh Miniſters, "and corrupt Majorities," are intimately interwoven with the practical freedom of Britain, and *are good*, while thoſe who affirm they do exiſt and *are bad*, are puniſhed with the pillory,

* The 7th article of the late Heſſian Treaty ſets forth, that "If it ſhould happen, they" (the Landgrave's Troops) "ſhall be employed in Great Britain or Ireland, as ſoon "as the notification, in ſuch caſe, ſhall be made to the "Serene Landgrave, they ſhall be put on the ſame footing, "in every reſpect, as the national Britiſh Troops."

not

not for ſaying they are bad, but for ſaying they do exiſt. To call the Conſtitution *pure* * has become a crime ;—to call it *corrupt* recommends to miniſterial favour. Mr. Young ſays " its ſpirit and principles admit of torturing " at pleaſure" (p. 199) and I fear it is at preſent juſt what the Government chooſes to make it, —juſt what the people will bear. The Freedom of the Preſs is deſtroyed by aſſociators † for its defence ; the ſacredneſs of the pulpit is brutally attacked by pretended combatants for religion ‡; all confidence in public men has received a mortal blow by thoſe who have called moſt loudly for confidence §, and the profeſſed champions of the Conſtitution are the moſt buſy in " knocking it down." Petitions are treated with contempt ; petitioners ſtigmatized as traitors, and the vague charge of ſedition, has put a ſeal on mens lips. We are to be brought back to darkneſs and barbariſm ||

* See Mr. Young's remarks on the petition of the Friends of the People

† Mr. Reeves, while he charges publicans to beware of taking in what he calls ſeditious newſpapers, &c. ſays, he wiſhes to ſupport the true Liberty of the Preſs !

‡ See the account of the treatment of the Rev. V. Knox by the Militia Officers who have taken up arms againſt the *Atheiſts* of France.

§ By the apoſtate in the cauſe of Parliamentary Reform.—Mr. Pitt.

|| Mr. Young not only recommends the abolition of Sunday Schools, and the Liberty of the Preſs, but ſays, the poor ſhould not be taught to read, leſt they ſhould read ſuch dangerous books as Mr. Paine's !—I wonder he did not alſo recommend the cutting out of men's tongues, leſt they ſhould ſpeak ſeditious words. Without tongues they would be eaqually, perhaps more ſerviceable as ſlaves; as hewers of wood and drawers of water.

as

as the only ſtate in which we can be happy, for knowledge in the poor, is found dangerous to the State, and ignorance and intolerance its beſt ſecurity. There are but two meaſures neceſſary to accompliſh all this: Firſt, eſtabliſh a ſtanding force, ſufficient to intimidate or puniſh the refractory;—Secondly, ſuppreſs the Freedom of Speech, and of the Preſs.

But all exhortations in favour of Freedom, are ſo generally conſidered, at preſent, as wild and deluſive theories, that it may not be improper to call in the aſſiſtance of Mr. Young's "Experiment," "Practice," and "Events," to ſhew what have been the conſequences of times ſimilar to the preſent. I ſhall leave the reader to judge from the following extracts from the ſecond vol. of Rapin's Hiſtory of England, how far the concluſion of the reign of Charles the IId. reſembled the preſent time. But I beg the compariſon may be underſtood as relating to the nation at large, and not as applying to his Majeſty. With ſome changes of words, but none of meaning, I think, the national temper in 1684, and in 1793, will be found to be ſtrongly alike.

"From this time, the King, during the reſt "of his life, governed not only without a Par- "liament, but with an abſolute power. When "he ſaw himſelf out of the reach of the Par- "liament, he entirely threw away the maſk of "diſſimulation, and ſhewed, that the Popiſh "Plot, the proſecution whereof he had lately "recommended ſo earneſtly to the Parliament, "appeared to him but a mere chimera, or at "leaſt, he did not think it near ſo dangerous as "he

" he would have had it believed. It is necessary
" to unfold the causes of so surprising a Revo-
" lution. By the artifices of the Court, and
" the natural inclination of many Englishmen,
" the kingdom was divided into Whigs and
" Tories. This division was so carefully fo-
" mented by the Court, and the Popish party;
" that at last it became very great. To render
" the two parties irreconcileable, it was insinu-
" ated to the Episcopalians, of whom the ma-
" jority were Tories, that both Church and
" Monarchy were in danger, and that the scene
" of *forty-one* * was going to be revived. That
" the Presbyterians †, under colour of providing
" for the preservation of Liberty, really in-
" tended the destruction of the Church, and
" the introduction of Presbyterianism ‡, in or-
" der to which, they were pursuing the same
" course they had taken in 1640, and the fol-
" lowing years, by undermining the founda-
" tions of Monarchy, for the more easy subver-
" sion of the Church. These insinuations had
" the greater effect, as what had once hap-
" pened, and whereof, the memory was still
" fresh, might happen again. The Episcopa-
" lians, terrified with the prospect of falling
" into the same state, from which they had
" been miraculously delivered, considered the

* "The scene of forty-one," the Commonwealth, terrified the nation then, in the same manner as the scene in France now does.

† For Presbyterians may now always be understood Reformers.

‡ And introduction of Republicanism.

" introduction

" introduction of Popery *, with which they " were alarmed, as a distant and uncertain evil, " and the establishment of Presbyterianism †, " as certain and present. It is even very pro- " bable, that many whose passions were violent, " looked upon Popery as the less evil. In this " belief, they threw themselves, as it were, " desperately into the Court Party (p. 723.)

" Addresses became so much in vogue, that " the smallest Corporations feared the resent- " ment of the Court, if they neglected to ad- " dress. The King received them all very gra- " ciously, and distinguished those who brought " them with particular marks of his favour. " The Lord Mayor, Recorder, and some others " of the City of London, waiting on him at " Windsor, with one of a very contrary nature, " were denied admittance, and ordered to at- " tend the Council, at Hampton-Court, where " they received a reprimand from the Lord " Chancellor. It was pretended that these loyal " addresses, as they were called, expressed the " sentiments of the people in general, though " they came but from one of the parties. But " what may make it presumed that the King " did not much depend upon the people, not- " withstanding these numerous Addresses, " which weekly filled the Gazettes, is, that " he never after dared to call a Parliament‡. " If these Addresses had expressed the general " sense of the people, what could have hin- " dered the King from calling a Parliament,

* For Popery may always be understood absolute power.

† Republicanism.

‡ For calling a Parliament, it may here be understood, calling a *reformed* Parliament.

" which, to judge by these Addresses, must have " been devoted to him.

" The King was not satisfied with discou- " raging those who would have presented dis- " agreeable Addresses to him, but also silenced " and imprisoned the news-writers, which were " not of his party, while others had liberty to " publish daily invectives against the Whigs and " the late Parliament (p. 724.)

" Every man, who was not of the Court " Party, and a furious Tory, was called a Pres- " byterian †. The Clergy, particularly distin- " guished themselves, by shewing their attach- " ment to the principles and maxims of the " Court. The pulpits resounded with the doc- " trine of passive obedience and non-resistance. " The Clergy, seemed to make it their business " to surrender to the King, all the Liberties " and Privileges of the subject. According to " the principles they preached, no Eastern " Monarch was more absolute than the King of " England. This doctrine was supported in " the Courts of Justice, by all the Judges and " Lawyers, to the utmost of their power. All " this was followed with numberless Petitions " and Addresses. Any man's thinking of asso- " ciating the subjects against the King, was suf- " ficient, according to the current principles, " to charge the whole Whig Party as guilty of " the greatest crime imaginable. Thus, the " violent Tories, who then prevailed in the " Corporations, were not satisfied with perse- " cuting the Presbyterians, but also made the " King an arbitrary and absolute Monarch, as

† A Republican.

" if

" if there had been no other expedient to ſave
" the Church of England from the attempts of
" the Preſbyterians.

" Though ſupported by the Court and the
" Magiſtrates, the Tory Party had the advan-
" tage, the Whigs were not diſcouraged, in
" the expectation of cauſing ſome turns, by in-
" forming the people in pamphlets of their dan-
" ger. This did but exaſperate the patrons of
" paſſive obedience. They took occaſion from
" thence to carry the doctrine ſo high, *that*
" *when in the reign of James the IId, reſtric-*
" *tions became neceſſary, they knew not how*
" *to make them*, and many even perſiſted in
" ſupporting this doctrine, rather than own
" they had been in the wrong, to carry it to
" ſuch a height (p. 725.) In ſhort, a kind of
" infatuation ſeized the kingdom, and one
" Party, inſtead of coming to a temper, vio-
" lently embraced whatever was moſt contrary
" the other" (p. 726.)

The King having thus far ſucceeded, thought another alarm neceſſary, in order to terrify the people into a more full compliance with his deſign, and accordingly, the Rye-Houſe Plot was ſet on foot, by which, " the whole kingdom
" being ſtruck with terror, the King believed
" he ought to improve it to the eſtabliſhment
" of his abſolute power, ſo as to have nothing
" to fear from any future oppoſition. This was
" by depriving all the Corporations, and conſe-
" quently all his ſubjects, of their privileges. It
" was not proper to uſe abſolute power, but to
" proceed in a manner more politic and more
" dangerous to the people, by engaging them

" to make a voluntary ſurrender * of their char-
" ters, in order to receive ſuch new ones as the
" King ſhould pleaſe to grant. For this purpoſe,
" Courtiers and Emiſſaries were ſent to the
" more conſiderable Corporations to inſpire
" them with terror, and intimate to them, that
" ſcarce one could eſcape, ſhould the King ex-
" erciſe ſtrict juſtice. This chiefly concerned
" the Whigs and Non-Conformiſts, for the
" Tories were generally very readily blinded to
" obey the pleaſure of the Court. Jeffries, par-
" ticularly diſtinguiſhed himſelf in his northern
" circuit, at the ſummer aſſizes. He forgot
" nothing capable of terriſying the people, aſ-
" ſuring them, that a ſurrender of their charters
" was the only way to avert the miſchiefs which
" hung over their heads. Other Judges and
" Emiſſaries did the ſame, and at laſt, the larger
" Corporations being thus gained, the leſſer
" neceſſarily followed. So a ſudden and great
" change was ſeen in England, namely, the
" Engliſh nation, without Rights or Privileges,
" but ſuch as the King would vouchſafe to grant
" her; and what is more ſtrange, the Engliſh
" themſelves ſurrendered to Charles the IId.
" thoſe very Rights and Privileges, which they
" had defended with ſo much paſſion, or rather
" fury, againſt the attempts of Charles the Iſt.

" To make the people in ſome meaſure fully
" ſenſible of their new ſlavery, the King affected
" to muſter his forces, which, from one regi-
" ment of foot, and one troop of horſe guards,

* Mr Young adviſes the people of England, to ſurrender almoſt every Liberty they poſſeſs.

" (raiſed

" (raiſed by himſelf, with the murmurs of " many of his ſubjects) were encreaſed to four " thouſand, compleatly trained and effective " men. It might then be ſeen, that the Mem- " bers of Parliament *, who oppoſed the raiſing, " or at leaſt the eſtabliſhment of theſe guards, " were not altogether in the wrong. But the " zeal of the Tory Party was now arrived to " ſuch a height, that they looked on every " thing which contributed to render the King " abſolute, as a ſure means to ruin the Whigs, " and conſequently as a triumph for them. " They prepoſterouſly imagined that the Court " only aimed at the deſtruction of that odious " Party, and was ſolely labouring for the " Tories" (p. 734.)

Such were the effects of the pretended plots, and the unfounded alarms in the reign of Charles the IId. They ſo ſucceſsfully induced the people to ſurrender their Liberties, that James the IId. was encouraged afterwards to attempt the eſtabliſhment of Deſpotiſm. A Revolution then became abſolutely neceſſary; and, thanks to the puſillanimity of that Prince, it was made without bloodſhed.

The baſe inſidious tools of Corruption are endeavouring to delude the nation into the ſame predicament in which it was in 1684. They have ſought for that which men moſt value, and they find it to be " PROPERTY." In order, therefore, to deter him from overthrowing the pernicious ſyſtem in which they fatten,

* Here let Mr. M. A. Taylor's oppoſition to the eſtabliſhment of Barracks be remembered.

they cry, "Reform will rob you of your Pro-"perty!"—But theſe are the deluſive, treacherous cries of the hyæna, and will betray ultimately into certain ruin. A Parliamentary Reform has been approved, at various periods, by a majority of men, both in Parliament and out of it, and even thoſe who never ſupported the meaſure, have, notwithſtanding, indirectly condemned the preſent conſtruction of the Houſe of Commons, or approved the principles on which a Reform is demanded*. When times of affliction and uneaſineſs occur, therefore, our defective Repreſentation will be deemed, and too juſtly, I fear, the cauſe of them. A Reform will then be made, not with caution, and a dread of going too far, as would be the caſe at preſent, but with indignation and vengeance. Moderate men will not be liſtened to. The moſt wild theoriſts will be entruſted with the work, and inſtead of a peaceful, ſalu-

* The king, in his ſpeeches to Parliament, after the American War, when Reform was ſo much agitated, expreſſed his deſire to ſupport the different branches of the Conſtitution, in their *due balance*:—to ſupport the *true ſpirit* of the Conſtitution, and to uſe his authority for the good of the people, for which purpoſe alone it was given to him. Theſe ſentiments, according to Mr. Young, are dangerous to the Government. And even Mr. Burke, about the period alluded to, ſaid, the King had gone ſo far as to recommend Reform from the Throne.

In addition to the above, Mr. Burke has called our Repreſentation the "ſlough of ſlavery:" Mr. Powis, in 1784, boaſted of aſſembling a little ſenate of independant Members round him, by which he implied, the majority were not independent. And the Dukes of Portland and Devonſhire, with many more Peers, ſigned a proteſt in 1777, againſt an increaſe of the civil liſt, becauſe it was reported, the money was employed in *corrupting* Parliament.

tary

tary Reform, we ſhall, probably, be involved in all the calamities which at preſent torture France.

Mr. Burke, not when he gloried in the eſtabliſhment of a *Republic* in America, but long after he began to reprobate the eſtabliſhment of a *limited Monarchy* in France, ſaid *, " Great diſcontents frequently ariſe in the beſt " conſtituted Governments, from cauſes which " no human wiſdom can foreſee, and no human power can prevent. They occur at " uncertain periods, but at periods, which " are not commonly far aſunder. Governments of all kinds are adminiſtered only by " men; and great miſtakes, tending to inflame " theſe diſcontents, may concur. The indeciſion of thoſe who happen to rule at the " critical time, their ſupine neglect, or their " precipitate and ill-judged attention, may aggravate the public misfortunes. In ſuch a " ſtate of things, the principles now only " ſown, will ſhoot out, and vegetate in full " luxuriance. In ſuch circumſtances, the " minds of the people become ſore and ulcerated. They are put out of humour with " all public men, and all public parties; they " are fatigued with their diſſentions; they are " irritated at their coalitions; they are made " eaſily to believe (what much pains are taken " to make them believe) that all Oppoſitions " are factious, and all Courtiers baſe and ſervile. " From their diſguſt at men, they are ſoon led " to quarrel with their frame of Government,

* See his appeal from the old to the new Whigs.

" which

"which they presume gives nourishment to "the vices, real or supposed, of those who "administer in it. Mistaking malignity for "sagacity, they are soon led to cast off all "hope from a good administration of affairs, "and come to think, that all Reformation "depends, not on a change of actors, but "upon an alteration in the machinery."

Before the minds of men are sore and ulcerated, and the principles now sown, shoot out into full luxuriance, let us, therefore, give each part its proper force, and amend and renovate the machinery of the State, while there is no danger that in doing so it will tumble to pieces. War is the parent of Discontent, and Discontent is the nurse of Revolution. A continuance of hostilities will produce the times which Mr. Burke describes, and then, as in France, it will be too late to Reform. Instead, therefore, of wasting our blood and treasure to make a King of France, and to give felicity to that nation, let us seize this favourable opportunity to repair and invigorate our own Constitution; for the only means of promoting and insuring prosperity and happiness to Britain are a speedy Peace, and an effectual Parliamentary Reform.

FINIS.

www.ingramcontent.com/pod-product-compliance
Lightning Source LLC
Chambersburg PA
CBHW021127270326
41929CB00009B/1078

* 9 7 8 3 7 4 3 4 0 8 2 7 2 *